STAGE DIRECTIONS

MICHAEL FRAYN

Stage Directions

Writing on Theatre 1970–2008

faber and faber

First published in 2008
by Faber and Faber Limited
3 Queen Square London WC1N 3AU

Typeset by Faber and Faber Ltd
Printed in England by Mackays of Chatham plc, Chatham, Kent

All of the pieces contained in this volume were first published individually by Methuen,
except for 'On the Roller-Coaster', which first appeared in the *Observer* in 1970, and
'No Show', which first appeared in the programme for the revival of *Donkeys' Years*
at the Crucible Theatre, Sheffield, in 1992.

The following are reproduced by permission of Methuen Drama,
A & C Black Publishers Limited, 38 Soho Square, London W1D 3HB:
Introduction to Plays 1 © Michael Frayn, 1985
Postscript to *Copenhagen* © Michael Frayn, 1998
Postscript to *Democracy* © Michael Frayn, 2003
General Introduction to *Chekhov: Collected Plays* © Michael Frayn, 1978,
1983, 1986, 1987, 1988
Introduction to *Wild Honey* © Michael Frayn, 1984

A CIP record for this book
is available from the British Library

ISBN 978-0-571-24055-5

2 4 6 8 10 9 7 5 3 1

Contents

Introduction

An introduction to an introduction, or to a collection of introductions, might seem to be like an overture to an overture, or an apology for an apology. Particularly since plays, which is what these introductions are introducing, surely shouldn't need introductions in the first place. They should be able to walk on to the stage and introduce themselves without any preliminary speeches of welcome from their author or anyone else. So a word of explanation, at any rate, as to why there are any introductions here at all.

All my early plays had to fend for themselves. When the first collection of them was published, though, I thought I would take the opportunity to say something about how I came, rather late in life, to be writing plays at all. And when, over the years, two more volumes appeared, I thought I might, with the benefit of hindsight, say something about an aspect of plays which is necessarily overlooked when they are first produced and published – how they were perceived and received by audiences and critics. A play is not in the end simply words on paper but a living experience, and its inmost nature is shaped by the (often changing) forms this experience takes.

In the case of three of my later plays (*Copenhagen, Democracy*, and *Afterlife*) I did provide accompanying essays when they were first published because they all involve real historical characters and real historical events. I still felt that they should stand on their own feet, and make their own impact (or fail to) without the need for any preliminaries. But then after the event I thought I should try to make clear for anyone who was interested what I'd invented and what was drawn from the historical record – and to give some account of what that record actually was. So I appended to each of them an explanation in the form of a postscript.

The distinction I am trying to make in these postscripts, I should say, is not exactly the traditional one between fact and fiction. Fact is what the historical record attempts to give expression to, and exactly what kind of separate existence facts have beyond that expression, and what kind of relationship the two have, is a matter of philosophical debate (and one that I have discussed at length elsewhere). Then again, even acknowledged fiction is attempting to come at the factual nature of the world, and of events, though in a somewhat different way. Fictions influence the ways in which we see facts, rather as the historical record does – and in some cases have an effect upon the historical record itself. They certainly did in the case of *Copenhagen*, and in the later additions that I've attached to the original postscript I've traced the way in which the production of the play brought to light new material that changes the record and casts a rather different light on the events from which the play took its rise.

Two of the earlier works, *Wild Honey* and *La Belle Vivette*, were in fact published with introductions. They are both adapted from works by other writers, and it seemed to me (perhaps inconsistently) that I should make as clear as I could beforehand what the original source material was like before I got my hands on it.

The same goes for the translations proper. All these are from the Russian, and all but two of them of Chekhov. I think my introduction to the Chekhov makes it obvious why I have devoted so much attention to his work. What I haven't explained, though, is how I got into translating him in the first place, which happened in the confused, sideways fashion in which one stumbles into so many of what turn out to be major undertakings in life.

The National Theatre asked me to translate some Goldoni. I explained that I couldn't really read Italian – even modern Italian, let alone the eighteenth-century Venetian dialect in which some of Goldoni's plays are written. The then dramaturge at the National, John Russell Brown, brushed this frivolous objection aside. Translating a play, he explained kindly, didn't involve reading the original. You simply looked at a selection of existing translations and rewrote them.

He sent me a stack of Goldoni in various English versions. Eager as I was to work for the National, I found the task impossible. I felt as if I were trying to see Goldoni through a series of variously warped, speckled, and dusty windows. I hesitantly suggested another possibility – that I try translating something from the original text, which I could perhaps manage if it happened to be in Russian. Professor Brown was rather taken with this novel idea, and I began with Tolstoy's *The Fruits of Enlightenment*. I see from my files that the original plan was for me also to do another Tolstoy play, *The Power of Darkness*, so as to make a contrasting pair, a comedy and a moral horror story. I can't find any record of what happened to the latter part of the plan. Perhaps it was quietly shelved after *The Fruits of Enlightenment* was produced, and it became apparent, in spite of an outstanding production by Christopher Morahan, and a fine cast headed by Sir Ralph Richardson, that the theatre was not really Tolstoy's forte.

The experience, though, led to my later collaboration with Christopher Morahan on two much more successful ventures, *Wild Honey* and a film, *Clockwise*. It also persuaded Peter Hall to entrust me with translating *The Cherry Orchard* for his own forthcoming production. So I started Chekhov at the wrong end, not only because it is his last play, but because it is the hardest to translate satisfactorily, just as it is the hardest to direct. It became for me nevertheless not only a totally absorbing new intellectual adventure but an overwhelming emotional experience – and I found myself launched on what, for a time at any rate, seemed almost a kind of alternative career. It was also a crash course in playwriting. Translating a play (in my view) requires you to marinate yourself in the original text. You have to understand how the play works – and you begin to discover surprising things. One of them, in the case of Chekhov, is how much story there is in those last four plays, how closely they are plotted.

So – a belated acknowledgment of my debt to Carlo Goldoni.

There is quite a lot of my life in this book. Not all of it, though. I began my professional career in the theatre very late. Most playwrights, I think, start young, when they are full of passion and certainty; and often, by the age of thirty-six, which I was when my first play was produced, have already got it out of their system, and sunk exhausted into obscurity, celebrity, or drink. What held me up was early failure, even before I'd got my foot on the first rung of the ladder. In my last year at Cambridge I wrote most of the Footlights May Week revue, and complicated things for myself by observing a rather austere aesthetic. No references to current affairs, or undergraduate life, or show business, or any of the other standbys of student shows and what was then called intimate revue. The humour was to be entirely abstract. I had got the idea from seeing a show in London called *Cranks*, created by the choreographer John Cranko. *Cranks* had made people laugh. My imitation of it did not. Every year, after its run in Cambridge, the May Week show transferred for a brief run in the West End (at the old Scala Theatre in Charlotte Street) – a precious opportunity for all of us with professional ambitions to get ourselves noticed. My show was the first that did not transfer.

So I turned against the theatre, and when I began to write columns in the *Guardian* and the *Observer* a few years later I devoted a fair number of them to mocking everything about it – the conventions upon which it depended, the fashionable plays of the day, and the embarrassed anticipation aroused in an audience that the actors would forget their lines or drop their props. The first seeds of *Noises Off*, I see with hindsight, were already there. And, like the atheist who comes to mock but stays to pray, I was gradually reeled in, first by writing a couple of television plays, and then by accepting an invitation to contribute to an evening of one-act plays about marriage. It's always difficult to resist a challenge, and I wrote a simple-minded piece about a young couple who make a nostalgic return visit to the hotel in Venice where they had spent their honeymoon – accompanied now, however, by their young baby, which of course changes everything. The show was to be produced in the West End by the well-known New York producer Alexander Cohen, who specialised in introducing reluctant audiences to difficult new material – he had mounted the first production of Pinter's *Homecoming* on Broadway. So I was astonished when the director rang in some embarrassment to say that Cohen had rejected my play because it was too filthy. Too *filthy*? My innocent little sketch? 'Alex,' explained the director, 'says he could never produce a play in which a baby's diaper is changed on stage.' So I wrote some more short plays and had an evening of my own (*The Two of Us*). It was catcalled and heckled by the gallery claque who used to attend first nights then, and all the reviews but one were terrible. However, it ran for six months (thanks mostly to the reputation of its stars, Richard Briers and Lynn Redgrave) – and this time I didn't retire to sulk in my tent, but defiantly wrote two more full-length plays. My defiance was not rewarded – they were both failures.

Even after this late start, there's still about half a lifetime covered here. Looking back over these pieces has revived a few painful memories, but many happy ones. Writing books is a solitary vice, and it is a pleasure sometimes to get out of the house and work with other people. The collaborative nature of the theatre arouses a good deal of scepticism among people outside the business. I am always being asked if I have any control over what happens to my plays. It's not a question of control, though. The text of a play is only one of the elements in a production. Directors and designers have to bring their own imaginations to bear, and the more I have worked with them the less I have understood how they do it. Actors, too, have to find ways of expressing the written characters through their own personalities and ways of being. They must bring their own living selves to the enterprise, just as the writer does. Theatre people are often mocked for their supposed vanity and egocentricity (and I realise I have contributed to this with *Noises Off*). But in my experience most actors are more mutually supportive than the people I know in other professions. The risks they take through their exposure on stage are so frightening that on the whole they tend to make common cause and help each other out, like soldiers in battle. The more I think about the courage an actor needs to go out on stage, particularly on a first night, in front of the unseen faces concealed behind those blinding lights, and throw himself on the uncertain resources of other people's sympathy and his own memory, the less I understand it, and the more I admire it.

So, to all the people I have worked with in the theatre over this last half-lifetime I dedicate this book.

COLLECTED PLAYS

Plays: 1

*Alphabetical Order, Donkeys' Years, Clouds,
Make and Break, Noises Off*

The first plays I ever wrote have not survived to be included in this collection. They date from the period when I was resident playwright at
a small theatre in the suburbs of London – a theatre so small that I was
also director, set-designer, and wardrobe mistress. In fact I was the
architect and builder. I was more – I was the creator of all the actors
and actresses employed there.

I must have been about eight or nine at the time, and it was an
insane venture, undertaken purely in imitation of an admired friend; I
did not in fact have any of the manual skills necessary to build or oper-
ate a puppet theatre. Still, it was quite a thorough introduction to the
business. I have not exercised such control over the production of my
plays since. Thank God.

But the odd thing is that I can't remember anything about the plays
themselves. I can remember reciting the dialogue in a variety of
humorous voices. I can remember the difficulty of reading my handwriting by the light of the paraffin lamp and the torch bulbs that illuminated the stage, while both hands were above my head holding the
actors up. I can remember some of the actors. They were not very
good; I have had better since. While my attention was occupied with
the text they would leave the floor and float an inch or two above it,
or buckle hopelessly at the knees and lean against the set, obviously
the worse for drink. They loved to make large gestures with their
arms; and once they had got their arms up it was difficult to persuade
them to get them down again. I can remember fixing cuffs of lead foil
to their wrists to restrain their exuberance. But what they said, what

3

they did, what they were trying to tell the world – that I can't remember. The text was a tedious minor adjunct to the staggerings and lurchings of the puppets, to the complex receding planes of the set, to the warm glow of the lights, to the rich blue of the curtains, to the splendour of the cardboard proscenium arch painted with gold enamel from Woolworths. I had ambitious plans, delayed only by lack of Arts Council funding, to extend the gold-painted cardboard until my entire bedroom had become an auditorium, with gold cardboard boxes, circle, upper circle, and gallery, all filled to capacity at every performance with my parents and sister. But it never crossed my mind to keep copies of the plays I was intending to present in this opulent establishment, so that they would be preserved for collection in the *Complete Works*, and critical analysis in a scholarly introduction. I assume that they were relevant to the lives of my audience. I imagine I was going to denounce the hypocrisy and oppression of family life; expose the violence of the society in which my sister was growing up; show up some crucial failure of feeling in my mother; help my father by explaining to him the banality of his thought and the meaninglessness of his work.

But I wonder. Because the same amnesia about text and content emerges again in the next stage of my career. Embittered by the failure of local or central government to finance me, and possibly also by the inability of my actors to stand unsupported by the furniture, I abandoned playwriting and turned to conjuring. Once again I cannot remember the didactic drive that must have underlain this. All that comes to mind is the apparatus – pillboxes and matchboxes with laboriously constructed false bottoms and secret compartments, little cylinders which you concealed in your fist while you stuffed a handkerchief into them, and which then shot away up your sleeve on a piece of elastic, or else caught on your cuff and didn't. Above all I remember the most elaborate piece of apparatus that I built myself – a complete conjuror's table, with a little black cloth which should have been velvet but was in fact blackout material (this must have been around 1943). The cloth concealed a shelf at the back where disappearing coins and billiard-balls could be lodged. The cabbalistic design on the cloth camouflaged a piston set into the table-top, on which gold watches borrowed from the audience could be placed while they were covered with a top hat and lowered into a concealed cylinder made out of an old toilet-roll. Or could have been, if anyone in the audience (which at matinees consisted exclusively of my sister) had possessed a gold watch, and I had possessed a top hat, and if the piston had not been wedged tight inside the cylinder. My carpentry had still not caught up with my ambitions, and this table had the same uncertainty on its feet as the puppets. It was balanced on a tripod made out of three unwanted brass stair rods. During a performance, as the palmed half-crowns slipped out of my perspiring hands, the table would show signs of losing its nerve. It would begin to give little uncertain lurches towards the wings, as if it were trying to run away, splaying out its legs like a newborn foal. One of the legs, curiously, would always get further than the others, and the table would develop a dangerous list. The concealed billiard balls would roll off the secret shelf and thud heavily down on to the floor. Unable to use my hands for fear of dropping more half-crowns or taking my thumbs off the missing spots on doctored playing-cards, I would try to hoist the table back with my elbow; whereupon the wandering leg would drop out of its socket altogether, with a characteristic hollow bongling sound, and the audience would have to come up on stage and replace it – by touch, since she had to keep her eyes closed in order not to see the secret shelf.

But what was the meaning of all this? How did it reflect the social structure of the early 1940s and the epic struggle of the Second World War? That I have forgotten.

If I failed to take better note of my artistic intentions at the time I blame it on my father. He encouraged the wrong tastes in us. He should have conducted us in family prayers and taken us to church, so that we acquired a sense of public ritual and of the corporate affirmation of belief. Instead he wrote comic sketches for production at Christmas, starring himself as a schoolmaster with a pair of Will Hay pince-nez. My sister and I played the pupils, his feeds, leaving my mother to soldier on alone as the audience. I do remember odd bits of these entertainments – an argument for making children learn things by heart – even if I have forgotten my own works. 'Where have you been?' – 'Ware.' – 'Yes, where?' – 'Ware! On the road to Cambridge!'

5

– 'Yes, but *where* on the road to Cambridge?' Etc. This is the language that fed my dramatic imagination in the years to come.

He also let us listen to the wireless – to *ITMA* and *Much Binding-in-the-Marsh*, to *Happidrome* and *Monday Night at Eight*. At specially solemn festivals he would take us to the local music-halls. The halls were dying by then, of course, and in any case the suburban establishments that we went to must have been pallid reflections of their inner-city counterparts. But to me they seemed even more glorious than the completed theatre in my bedroom would have been. I went on my own sometimes – after school, to the Kingston Empire just down the road. I remember girls with incredibly long legs riding on chromium-plated monocycles, and edging cautiously about the stage balanced on top of a huge ball faced with a thousand mirrors, that sent the beam of the follow-spot cascading out in a blinding silver spray right to the back of the pit, where I was sitting. I wish I could write a play that had even a suggestion of the perfect shininess of that chromium, or flashed even half as much light around the audience as those mirrors did. I was shocked by some of the comedians, I have to confess ('Is it wrong to stick pins in ladybirds?' – 'Of course it's wrong to stick pins in lady-birds!' – 'Then why do they sew buttons on flies?'). But once, at the Croydon Hippodrome, I almost died laughing – literally. It was a family occasion – I think my birthday – and we had a box as a special treat. I remember the sheer happiness of the evening. I embarrassed my family by standing up and playing an imaginary violin all the way through the overture. Then I laughed so much at a comic conjuror whose tricks all went sublimely, perfectly wrong that I almost fell out of the box into the orchestra pit beneath, and had to be hauled back by the seat of my trousers. I can't remember the name of this wonderful act – nor whether I had taken up conjuring myself by this time, and was laughing, as audiences ought to laugh, because of its relevance to my own problems.

My passion for gilt proscenium arches and chromium monocycles has faded a little since then. But what I remember best from all my subsequent years of theatregoing are the evenings when the sparkling mirrors flashed their light over me in *some* sense. You sit through all the solemnities and pieties, all the things that ought to stir you to pity or indignation and don't, and you never know what's going to catch you by the throat. Suddenly the old trick has happened yet again and you're sitting up, entirely alive – more than alive – outside yourself. Sometimes it has been sheer theatrical bravura that has kept me on the edge of my seat all evening – Michael Blakemore's production of *The Front Page* at the National, for instance, or the Terry Hands *Cyrano* at the RSC, in Anthony Burgess's amazing translation. But then so has the pure exhilaration of language – in Mamet, for example – and the blaze of plot and language combined, in Racine. So has sheer truthfulness, as in Mike Leigh's organically grown confections, or the David Storey plays, which demonstrated to me for the first time that the great world of work in which we all live could be represented on the stage. So has laughter. You smile your way through a dozen comedies with reasonable pleasure – and then suddenly the unreasonable has happened, and you're not just amused – you're legless. Total intoxication with no after-effects except laughing again at the memory; a benediction as pure and surprising as spring. If I had sat in a box at Alan Ayckbourn's *The Norman Conquests* or *Absurd Person Singular* I should certainly have fallen out of it, and as long as I remember anything at all I shall remember all the other evenings when the stage has dissolved into an aqueous bright confusion of laughter tears – *The Knights of the White Magnolia* at Hampstead and *Turning Over* at the Bush, the moment when the barometer falls off the wall in *Hay Fever*.

I'm still amazed by conjuring tricks, too; though the magic these days is not so likely to be accomplished by secret drawers and elastic. I'm thinking of those heart-stopping moments when the world is transformed in front of your eyes. Sometimes by surprise, as in the first scene of *The Philanthropist,* when the undergraduate executes the stage-effect he has just described in his essay; Christopher Hampton tells you in advance exactly what the trick is going to be and how it's going to be done, and you still sit unable to breathe for five minutes afterwards. Sometimes the transformation is emotional – as when Oxenby suddenly surrenders to the moment in *The Dresser*, and leaps for the thunder-sheet he has earlier refused to touch. Sometimes the whole earth shifts, as when Joe Egg, the uninhabited shell of a child in Peter Nichols's play, gets out of her wheelchair at the end of Act One, and runs forward playing a skipping game, so that all the bitter wrongs of the world are for one moment of hallucination righted.

These epiphanies are not isolated events, of course. The charge builds and builds before the lightning strikes; and the particles in which the electricity is stored are the audience. I sometimes feel that the skill of audiences is not always sufficiently noted. Some theatregoers arrive late, certainly, some of them comment on the performance aloud and wait for the laugh-lines to cough. But the surprising thing really is how few behave like this, and how many understand the conventions and are prepared to abide by them. To find two, or five, or ten good actors to perform a play is difficult; to find two hundred, or five hundred, or a thousand good people to watch it, night after night, is a miracle. So many people in one room who will sit quietly and listen for two hours – not calling out slogans, not breaking down under the strain of so much communal self-discipline! To be a member of a good audience is exhilarating. The sounds that it makes around you are as much a part of the show as the sounds from the stage: the sound of alert anticipation before the curtain rises – the sound of silence – the sound of implications being understood – the sound of generosity in laughter and response.

And once the electricity is in the air even some quite circumstantial event can trip the spark. I remember a moment at Greenwich, on the first night of a musical by Sherrin and Brahms called *Sing a Rude Song*. It was the story of Marie Lloyd, and it ended with Marie coming back at the end of her career, after all her troubles, and singing very simply the song that had first made her famous – 'The Boy I Love Is up in the Gallery'. It was a touching conclusion, but on the first night it became more than touching, because Barbara Windsor, who played Marie, was struggling with a cold, and on that last number her voice finally disappeared. She stood there, a young girl again, smiling up at her boy while she sang him her song – and not a sound came out. We all wept like children. How unfair. But how blessed. Like finding money in the street.

These corrupt tastes and doubtful beginnings are the background to the plays I started to write in middle age. I find it as difficult to locate any didactic intention in them as I do in my attempts at conjuring. I sometimes feel a little ashamed when sympathetic critics try to rescue me from my disgrace by identifying good and bad characters, or right and wrong causes. Some reviewers saw *Alphabetical Order*, for instance, as a polemic against the dangers of soulless efficiency, with Lucy, the untidy senior librarian, as heroine, and with Leslie, her tidy-minded assistant, as villain. *Make and Break* they read as an exposure of Garrard, the obsessive businessman, and as an attack upon the whole ethos of modern commerce. It seems ungrateful to disagree, and I suppose my own opinion lacks the objectivity of theirs. But I think *Alphabetical Order* is about the *interdependence* of order and disorder – about how any excess of the one makes you long for the other – about how the very possibility of the one implies the existence of the other. I think *Make and Break* is about how we all compulsively exploit the possibilities of the world around us – about how we eat it – how we *have* to eat it – how we transform it into food and clothes and housing and of course lay it waste in the process. Is Garrard more monstrous than the rest of us? If he seems so, isn't it because he lacks our saving hypocrisy – because he fails to dissemble the appetites that we all have, that we all *must* have if we are to survive? I can't help feeling, too, that if the play is seen as some kind of attack upon business, or industrialism, this is merely because it is assumed that no one would ever write about these subjects *without* moral condescension of one sort or another. I don't understand why this should be so; it seems to me unbecoming for writers and critics to condescend towards the people who feed and clothe them. It's true that some of the things industry produces are harmful or unnecessary. But Garrard makes walls and doors. Could anyone really think I am advocating a world without walls and doors? All I'm trying to show is what they cost.

So far as I can see, all of these plays are attempts to show something about the world, not to change it or to promote any particular idea of it. That's not to say there are no ideas in them. In fact what they are all about in one way or another (it seems to me) is the way in which we impose our ideas upon the world around us. In *Alphabetical Order* it is by classification, in *Make and Break* by consumption. In *Clouds* this imposition of ideas is at an even more fundamental level – in the very act of apprehending the world at all. Could anything be simpler –

could anything be more *passive* – than opening our eyes and letting the world enter? But what these people see as they travel about the unfamiliar and ambiguous land they are visiting depends upon what they think and feel; the complication in this rationalist scheme being that what they think and feel is affected by what they see. In *Donkeys' Years* middle-aged men find themselves confronted by the perceptions they formed of each other – and of themselves – when they were young, and by the styles of being they adopted then to give themselves shape in each other's eyes, and in their own. In the ensuing years they have all, consciously or unconsciously, slipped out of these shells, and when for one night they try to re-inhabit them the effect is as absurd as wearing outgrown clothes would be. The actors in *Noises Off* have fixed the world by learning roles and rehearsing their responses. The fear that haunts them is that the unlearned and unrehearsed – the great dark chaos behind the set, inside the heart and brain – will seep back on to the stage. The prepared words will vanish. The planned responses will be inappropriate. Their performance will break down, and they will be left in front of us naked and ashamed.

It might be objected that one single theme is somewhat sparse provision to sustain five separate and dissimilar plays. I can only say that it is a theme which has occupied philosophers for over two thousand years, and one which is likely to occupy them for at least two thousand more. In fact it is *the* theme of philosophy, the central puzzle at the heart of all our speculations upon epistemology and perception, upon free will and determinism, upon the value-systems of ethics and aesthetics, upon the nature of mathematics and God and language; it is the central puzzle of life. The dilemma is this: the world plainly exists independently of us – and yet it equally plainly exists only through our consciousness of it. We are circumstantial specks, insignificant local anomalies, amidst the vast structured fabric of the objective universe. And yet that universe has vastness only in relation to ourselves and the things around us – has structure only in so far as we give it expression in our perception and language – has objective form only in so far as we conceive it from our single standpoint in space and time. We are everything and nothing. We are responsible for everything, and responsible for nothing.

I should like to be able to say that I did not choose this theme. It is more fashionable these days for a writer to be chosen by his material, like an old-fashioned bride; it makes the material sound stronger and more imperious. The truth is that I don't know whether I chose it or not. Some of these characters walked into my head uninvited, and told me their story as soon as they sat down. But then I have to ask myself if they knew they could get a meal and a bed for the night by telling me the kind of story I wanted to hear. Others I dragged in off the street by force. They didn't want to talk. I had to pretend to them that I knew the whole story anyway, confront them with the confessions of their accomplices. Some of them I was forced to take down to the soundproof interrogation room and show the bloodstains on the walls. Was I uncovering the evidence, or was I creating it? Was the world telling me what it was like, or was I telling the world? The question is impossible to answer, even in theory – because of course it is just one form of the very dilemma that I am writing about. And that dilemma is a permanent feature of our universe; it is not one that can ever be resolved. It can only be expressed, and the drama has always been the natural medium for the exposition of irreconcilable forces.

Foolhardy of me, perhaps, to draw attention to all this. Because it may be objected that these five plays depict only isolated incidents on the great battlefield, and not the battle as a whole – that they are only slight and smudged sketches, and not the great set piece in oils that such a titanic struggle demands. This is true. But then they are not intended to portray the entire battle. They are what they are, they show what they show, and that is all there is to it, just as the great ball of mirrors at the Kingston Empire rolled and flashed, and the monocycle teetered and gleamed, and that was all there was to that. The manager might have explained privately after the show that the ball illustrated certain of the laws of optics, and that the ability of the girl with long legs to remain upright on the monocycle could teach a serious-minded boy like myself something about the laws of dynamics. But nothing he could have said would have made the chromium brighter or the glittering light represent anything but itself.

The greatest impact I ever had on an audience, in fact, the nearest I ever came to the ball of mirrors, was not with a play at all. It was with one of my early conjuring tricks – a pure event, without subtext or external reference of any kind. I was entertaining a capacity house one Christmas (my grandmother, uncle, and aunt were all present as well as the regular subscribers) with a technically advanced trick in which I put a glass of water beneath a black cloth, then flung it straight in the faces of the audience; whereupon, so the instructions in 100 *Tricks a Boy Can Do* asssured me, they would duck in terror, only to discover that the glass of water had dematerialised in the air. It went well. Distracting the audience's attention with suitable patter, I got the glass of water covertly out from under the black cloth (more blackout material), and safely down on to the secret platform behind the table. The table staggered nervously back under the weight, but held with the top at about twenty degrees from the horizontal. I carried the black cloth, draped round the cardboard disc that was secretly sewn into its lining, slowly towards the audience, careful not to spill a drop, and flicked it straight at them. And for once they were just as amazed as the book had said. In fact I discovered the force of the expression 'to bring the house down'. Because the cloth caught the Christmas decorations, and the whole lot came down on the heads of the audience in one instant multitudinous avalanche of paper-chains, streamers, cards, holly, and balloons. No one noticed that the glass of water had dematerialised – there was no one left to notice. The entire *audience* had dematerialised.

Now I come to think about it, though, I suppose this was my first unconscious attempt to resolve the great dilemma of man-in-world or world-in-man – by abolishing man. I see with hindsight, of course, that this impatient youthful radicalism resolves nothing. But the sounds the audience made as it went! In all the forty-odd years that have gone by since that Christmas, and all the plays I have written, I have never achieved a moment of quite such pure theatre.

(1985)

Plays: 2

Benefactors, Balmoral, Wild Honey

You can classify plays in any number of ways – as comedies or tragedies; as verse or prose, as high comedies, low comedies, black comedies, tragi-comedies; as art or entertainment. But however you do it they all fall into two even more fundamental categories – they are all hits or flops. The present collection contains one example of each, and one that was at different times both.

This way of looking at plays may seem crass, even corrupt. But a play as written is not a finished product. It's merely a prospectus, a scheme for a proposed event. That event, when it occurs, is a transaction between the play's makers and its audience, an offer accepted or rejected. The success that the play has, or fails to have, may be critical or commercial, or both, or neither; and it may change, of course, from production to production. Whatever form it takes, though, it's the nature of the response that characterises a play most distinctly, and colours everything about it.

What's so alarming, if you have to watch the evolution of a play from draft to draft, from production to production, even from night to night, is how fine the divide is that sends the waters this way or that way, to end up so far away in the frozen north or the sunlit south, and how difficult it often is to tell from one moment to the next which way things are going to go. Audiences have communal responses, and communal responses are unpredictable and violent because they are self-reinforcing. You begin to warm to what you're seeing; your warmth warms the people around you; their warmth warms you back; your corporate warmth warms the performers; you all warm to the performers' warmth. Or you chill, and the chill spreads around, then up to the stage and back. In all responses in the theatre there is an element of either love or hate. Love encourages and cherishes and overlooks faults; hate discourages and wishes for failure. Loved performers respond with love; performers who feel the audience's antagonism reply in kind. And as always, love and hate lie close together, ever ready to change places. The history of every drama, when you come to look at it, is a drama in itself, with the same tendency to sudden shifts of feeling and reversals of fortune.

First the unequivocal hit. *Benefactors* was a success in both London and New York, and all that comes immediately to mind now of its genesis is a steady upward path, difficult but continuously rewarding. If I think harder, though, it wasn't quite as simple as that. I recall a moment of panic at the first read-through, for example, when the whole complex structure that I thought I had created seemed to have shrivelled to dust at its first exposure to the air. And another at the first preview, which coincided with some unfortunate public event – a Tube strike or a freak storm, or just possibly both, I can't remember – as a result of which the theatre was almost empty. The events of the play, which had grown dense and absorbing in the close confines of the rehearsal room, seemed suddenly lost and tiny in all that space.

And I'm completely forgetting the play's appalling heredity. It was the offspring of an earlier play called *Up*, written some ten years earlier and never even produced. This in its turn was the rewritten son of my second play, *The Sandboy*, which was produced at the Greenwich Theatre in 1971. It opened during some kind of dispute in the newspaper industry, as a result of which only one review appeared the following morning, a shattering dismissal in *The Times* by Irving Wardle. I realise with hindsight that it was probably a fair enough assessment, and I've just braced myself to open my files and see precisely how fair. But it's not there. I've suppressed it, even from myself. The story of this particular play's life is one of trying to conceal and extirpate humble origins. The cheering and uplifting conclusion is that it can be done.

*

The thorough-going flop in this collection is *Balmoral*. Even this, though, in the course of its tangled and painful history, seemed for one wild moment to be heading towards a happy ending.

It was first produced, under its present title, at Guildford, in 1978, with a distinguished cast, and with Michael Codron waiting to take it into the West End; and it was terrible. I withdrew it and completely rewrote it. The new version was done in the following year at the Greenwich Theatre, under a new title: *Liberty Hall*. It was a wonderful production, one of the best I have ever had. George Cole played Skinner, the great Scottish comedian Rikki Fulton came south to play McNab, and the director was Alan Dossor, who is among other things a master of physical comedy. It's painful to recall one's failures in life, but there were things about that production that still come back to me and make me laugh. One of them was built into Poppy Mitchell's set – the visible track that the regular passage of McNab, on his thieving journeys over the years across the Balmoral breakfast-room, had worn in the tartan linoleum. Another was the great panic-stricken clearing up, when Godfrey Winn (Julian Fellowes), running to answer the door, skidded wildly in the pig-swill spread out over the floor by McNab for Skinner's inspection – and skidded not once but every night, each time as helplessly and unforeseeably as the first. Also the moment when Skinner, bowed and staggering under the great weight of the expired Walpole, sat down on the hot paraffin stove . . .

We had one single preview before we opened, and at once, on our very first time in front of an audience, we stepped into the realms of theatrical gold. I don't think my memory is playing me false when I recall that in Act One, at any rate, the audience became hysterical. The startled cast lost control. For minutes at a time the proceedings on stage became completely inaudible. When the evening ended I believed that I had done what I had been trying to do for so long – I had written a farce that worked.

The next night, as so often happens after a particularly good first preview, the show was down. In fact it was down to nothing, as flat as a flat tyre. Again I don't think my memory is overdramatising the occasion when I recall that the evening passed in absolute silence, with not a single laugh from beginning to end. This was the press night, and the reviews next morning were lacklustre. The glow we had seen at the preview had been fool's gold.

As the run went on we got quite a lot of our laughs back, though we never quite recovered that first wild glory. But any prospects of further life for the play had been killed by the press night. One of the practical lessons I learnt from this is that you might settle for very few previews, or none, but that in no circumstances must you compromise on a single one.

I subsequently rewrote the play yet again, and then again, and it's been produced once or twice since. But it's never had much success. I see now, with hindsight, that it couldn't possibly work, because it's based upon an entirely abstract notion, a pure counterfactual – a past that never happened, that never *could* happen. This is of course the subject of the play – the idea that things could be other than they are, the notion of imposing a fiction upon reality, of making the dead alive, of reading servitude as liberty – and of altering reality in the process. In the first place I think this was simply too oblique to grasp – people were heard coming out at the end saying to each other in bewilderment, 'But there *wasn't* a revolution in this country . . .' And in any case it's not a possible basis for farce. Farce, I now realise, has to be rooted in immediately believable reality. Desperation may eventually drive the characters to the most fantastic and improbable lengths, but the desperation has to be established first, and its source has to be the threat of an embarrassment so familiar that the audience's palms sweat in sympathy.

No, it's more complicated than that. Your palms *don't* in fact sweat in sympathy when you watch the ignoble terrors and stratagems of the characters in a farce. You refuse to let yourself identify with the characters, or feel their feelings. You reject absolutely the idea that it could be you up there, so idiotically embarrassed, so transparently mendacious. Their situation is too humiliating to be owned up to. They are somebody else, somebody who could never be you.

This is what gives farce its hysterical edge. Your refusal to recognise yourself has an element of violence in it. You know perfectly well that, just like your scapegoats up there, you *do* on occasion tell lies to avoid social embarrassment to yourself or others. You know that in your dreams you *are* discovered with your trousers round your ankles, performing acts which in waking life you take great if usually unconscious pains not to be discovered performing. You are attempting by your laughter to demonstrate, both to the rest of the audience and to yourself, that you do not lie, or fear public exposure. And in this you are lying once again, and risk being found out, and must laugh louder to show you are not lying. You are like the bully who conceals the despised characteristic in himself by persecuting it in others. You have to shut off your brain and behave like a madman.

Farce is a brutally difficult form. It is also of course a despised one. In laughing at it you have lost your moral dignity, and you don't like to admit it afterwards – you don't like to concede the power of the people who have reduced you to such behaviour.

So *Balmoral*, I now realise, was doomed from the first by a fundamental conceptual error. It was a *Titanic* searching for its iceberg.

In which case how could it have made people laugh that once . . . ?

Well, all theories of comedy and farce break down at some point, some sooner than others. This particular theory fails at the very first performance, which suggests that it may be even more inherently defective than the play itself.

The play that fell into both categories at different times was *Wild Honey*; it was a great hit in London, and a failure in New York.

Its history, like that of the other two plays, was long, but for most of it, as in the history of the Russian provinces where it's set, little happened. The National Theatre first sent me the Russian text, at Christopher Morahan's suggestion, in 1978. I had seen and enjoyed his television production of Dmitri Makaroff's Royal Court version, with Rex Harrison, back in the early sixties, but had never read the original before, and could remember nothing but the image of Platonov asleep with his hat over his face. Chekhov's text, I discovered, was 150 pages long – at least six hours' worth of material – untitled, and, in the version which the NT had found and photocopied, bristling with the hostile thickets of now near-obsolete hard signs that characterise the old orthography. The first chance I got to read it was while I was in bed with influenza. Slowly, through the veils of my fever and the limitless tangled undergrowth of Chekhov's first two acts, the most wonderful characters and scenes began to emerge. I at once longed to work on it, and sent the National Theatre my detailed proposals for adapting it, down to the title itself. I even included a twenty-page scene-by-scene synopsis of the original so that they would know exactly how much I intended to change – not realising, in my headlong rush of enthusiasm, that there was a translation of it by Ronald Hingley available in the Oxford Chekhov. The response from the National to all this was appropriately Russian: no response. Nothing. Not so much as a printed postcard of acknowledgement.

So that was Act One of this particular meta-drama. Act Two was constructed on a time-scale entirely suitable to the leisurely exposition of Chekhov's original; another four years elapsed before the play was actually commissioned.

When it was finally produced, in 1984, it followed a converse course to *Balmoral*. Performances started with a dress rehearsal so awful that I made plans to emigrate before press night, and then matured steadily through a week of previews. Ian McKellen told me later that it was only from the audience reaction during the previews that he had discovered the play was a comedy. The press night, by the time we got to it, was one of those occasions you dream of, when cast and audience together seem to catch fire, and produce a warmth and glow that linger for hours afterwards.

It had a very good run at the National. And then it failed in New York. Success and failure in the New York theatre are particularly immediate, dramatic, and total. First nights in London are fraught occasions because the critics are there to pass judgement; first nights in New York are even more fraught because they are not. Everyone is in a great state of dinner jackets and celebrity, but the critics have been and gone – they've seen the show at one of the previews, and their notices are already printing in the first editions that will hit the streets shortly after the final curtain. There is a traditional first-night party afterwards at Sardi's, halfway through which some mysterious messenger brings the traditional early copy of the *New York Times*. Its judgement is as absolute and final as God's. The verdict spreads through the room like a stain through water, imperceptibly and imme-

diately colouring everything rose-pink or ash-grey. If it's good someone gets up on a chair and reads it aloud. There are stories of people
launching excitedly into a public reading only to find halfway through
that it is in fact the order for execution. There are other stories of the
waiters removing all the bottles of wine from the tables as soon as the
word reaches the kitchens, and of the whole party melting wordlessly
away into the night. There is even one story about a cast who heard in
the interval what the review was going to be, and who didn't bother to
perform Act Two.

With *Wild Honey* I can't remember much about the performance
itself, except that someone introduced me to Jackie Onassis in the interval, and I failed either to recognise her or to catch her name. The party
afterwards, though, was a spectacularly sumptuous occasion, even by
New York standards, held not in Sardi's but in the oyster bar under
Grand Central Station. Somewhere around midnight the shadow of
Frank Rich's review in the *Times* passed across the room like the Angel
of Death. 'Rich is bad,' someone whispered to me. It had the ring of an
unanswerable moral principle, like 'Black is beautiful'. My disappointment was tempered by my curiosity to see what would happen. It was
my third play in New York, and after two successes I half-expected, as
at the end of one's third wish in a fairy story, to see not just the champagne disappear but the whole oyster bar with it, followed by Grand
Central Station and New York itself, and to find myself suddenly trans-
ported back to my humble woodcutter's shack in the outer suburbs of
London. But, exactly as in a play, even these expectations were
reversed, and we roystered, not to say oystered, on through the night
undeterred. Rich is bad, no doubt about it, but rich can also be rather
pleasant while it lasts. The play closed three weeks later; the principal
producer told me he had lost about a million dollars.

I suppose, looking back, that the glorious first night in London
marked the climax of my career in the theatre. *Benefactors* had opened
three months earlier at the Vaudeville, *Noises Off* was still running
across the road at the Savoy; for just over a year, until August 1985,
when *Wild Honey* closed, I had three plays on in London. Since then I
have done almost nothing in the theatre but straight translations, and
one new play, *Look Look*, too humiliatingly unsuccessful even to

reproduce here in the flops department. Someone told me recently, with many convincing examples, that few playwrights' careers last longer than fifteen years. My first play, *The Two of Us*, was produced in 1970, so maybe my grand climax was also my final curtain.

Including *Wild Honey* in a collection of my own plays may seem to imply unjustifiable claims about the extent of my contribution to it. I decided to put it here, though, rather than in my collection of Chekhov translations, simply to avoid any possible confusion between translation and adaptation. The introduction I wrote to the first single-play edition of the text, which is reproduced later in this volume (see below, p. 223), not only gives the fullest possible account of Chekhov's original, and of all the considerable mysteries and uncertainties that surround it, but also attempts to make clear what my adaptation involved.

Not clear enough, though, I realise with hindsight. When the play was produced some playgoers, even some reviewers, credited me with (or blamed me for) the more farcical elements. They supposed, in other words, that it began as more or less pure Chekhov and finished as more or less impure Frayn. The converse (sadly) is true. Most of the liberties I took were in getting the action of the play under way with reasonable despatch. It's true that I have emphasised the farce in what follows rather than the moralising and melodramatic elements which are also present in the original. But the farce is essentially Chekhov's own handiwork, and I have focussed the play around it because it seems to my (perhaps corrupt) taste to be by far the most successful, characteristic, and original element of the play that Chekhov wrote. I have reorganised and tightened the sequence of farcical encounters in Anna Petrovna's garden at the end of Act One, and around Platonov's house in the early part of Act Two. In general, though, the more farcical the play becomes the closer it is to the original. Most of the wonderful black farce towards the end – the great confrontations in the schoolroom between the drunken and demoralised Platonov and each of the women in turn with whom he is involved – is pure Chekhov. I wish I had written it, but I didn't. I merely trimmed it and fitted it all more tightly and securely together. And, of course, translated it. I shouldn't like to forgo the credit for that.

I don't know why anyone should be reluctant to recognise this aspect of Chekhov. He after all began his career as a professional humorist, and became a serious writer only by quite gradual evolution. The surprise is that he was writing scenes as funny and profound as these even before that career had started. This I find not just surprising but incomprehensible; and having seen them actually played in production I find it even less comprehensible now than when I first read them, shining like buried treasure among all the muddle of the original. In these scenes Platonov becomes in my view one of the great comic characters of the world's theatre, and this volume would be worth the price for them alone.

(1991)

Plays: 3

Here, Now You Know, La Belle Vivette

Most of the plays in this volume were written and produced in the rather bleak part of my career that followed after the failure of *Look Look* in 1990 had put an abrupt end to the successes of the eighties, and before the kiss of life was most improbably administered eight years later by the success of *Copenhagen*. None of them failed as resoundingly as the wretched *Look Look* (only one good review; closed in less than a month) but they seemed to confirm the general rule that the longest a playwright can hope to remain on the upward slope is twenty years before the melancholy downward trudge back to his native obscurity begins.

Here did actually raise the total of good notices from one to four when it was produced at the Donmar in 1993, which I suppose was encouraging; but the other notices ranged from regretful disappointment, through mocking parody, to downright vituperation. You can sometimes learn a lot from bad reviews, as you probably can from any other form of punishment (though the lesson is usually a rather oblique one), and as I nursed my wounds I began to see that I had managed to put a lot of people's backs up in the very first scene, which had perhaps blinded them to what followed. People had leapt to the conclusion that it was to be an evening about the impossibility of human communication, the failure of feeling, and the meaninglessness of life; whereas it seemed to me to be about the way we do actually construct a world and a life for ourselves. I began to yearn to have another go at it. So when a production in New York was proposed and the director, Jason Buzas, suggested quite a lot of restructuring, I was very ready to listen. Buzas put forward a number of shrewd ideas that I have incorporated here, and I am very grateful to him.

The production in New York failed to materialise, but the revised version of the play has now been performed in a number of European countries. *Here* there has so far done a lot better than *Here* here. This may suggest that the rewrites have had some beneficial effect, or else that critical standards are lower abroad; or perhaps merely that the title needs a bit of work on it as well.

Since I have spent my life writing novels as well as plays, one of the questions which people always ask is how I decide whether a new idea is one for a play or for a novel. The answer is that I don't. The matter decides itself. The idea that takes shape inside one's head has its form written upon it; that's what makes it an idea and not just a piece of wishful thinking. The one exception to this simple rule is *Now You Know,* which in its time has been both a novel and a play.

It first presented itself to me as a play, and it was as a play that I wrote it. I wrote many drafts of it, but they didn't work, and I set it aside. Then it came to me that what the story needed was to have access to the private thoughts of each of the characters, and to their unspoken thoughts about each other. So I wrote it as a novel, with the events seen through the eyes of each of the eight characters in turn. But, once the novel was published, I started thinking about these people again. And now that I had been inside each of their heads it seemed to me that it would be worth making another attempt to tell the story as a play, where one sees only as much of each person as he or she chooses to reveal – or fails to keep concealed. Which is of course how we are forced to see the people around us, all the time we are not writing novels about them.

La Belle Vivette is my one venture into opera. Dennis Marks, who was then Director of English National Opera, invited me to translate Offenbach's *La Belle Hélène*, and I accepted on condition that I could supply my own story and characters, for reasons I have explained in introduction to the text.

Writing lyrics turned out to be quite amazingly hard work – partic-

ularly since they had to be fitted to a pre-existing score. My guide and
taskmaster was James Holmes, who was to conduct the piece, a man
of legendary sweetness and boundless musicality. I was perpetually
astonished by his ability to sit down at the piano with a new lyric, and
accompany himself as he sang it at sight. I was perpetually cheered by
the unfailing enthusiasm with which he did it; and chastened as he
then gently explained that I had once again miscounted the beats in
the bar and misplaced the natural stress, that I had once again piled
inarticulable consonants upon unshapable vowels. I rewrote and
rewrote and rewrote; it was almost as difficult as farce. When we had
finished Jim sat down at a piano one Sunday afternoon in a rehearsal
room at the Coliseum and played and sang all three acts through solo
to Dennis, a feat so astonishing that it seemed to justify all my efforts
in itself.

Rehearsals began, in the ENO's shabby warren of rehearsal rooms
out near West Hampstead Underground station. I went in almost
every day, enchanted by the new world that I had wandered into. The
dais at the front of the rehearsal room was divided into two separate
kingdoms. The lefthand kingdom was ruled by Jim and the musical
staff. The righthand realm belonged to the director, Ian Judge, and the
production team. I don't know which half of the operation entranced
me more. In all my years in the theatre I'd never seen a director handle
such a large cast or shape such an endlessly fluid piece of action in
front of my eyes. I'd certainly never been involved in such a joyous
flood of music-making. I had expected opera-singers to be difficult and
temperamental; they turned out to be without exception charmingly
good-natured and straightforward. I had expected them to save their
voices during rehearsals by marking instead of singing out, but they all
sang out almost all the time, from first thing in the morning until last
thing at night.

In the event I don't think anyone heard many of the words I'd
laboured so long over. The hugeness of the Coliseum and its notorious
acoustics swallowed them up, in spite of the efforts devoted by Jim
and the cast to diction, and in spite of discreet miking. What words the
critics did manage to catch they mostly didn't like. The book, which
had seemed so threadbare to me, was apparently to them a precious

artistic heritage which had to be preserved from any attempt at restoration. We did nineteen performances, which is a respectable number in the opera-house, and the audiences seemed to enjoy it; but then we did have the incomparable Lesley Garrett singing Vivette at most of the performances.

ENO were going to revive it in their 1999 season. But by then Dennis Marks had left, and Nicholas Payne, his successor, evidently abandoned the project. Or so I assume. No word was spoken, not at any rate to me, or to Jim, or to Ian Judge; but then large organisations, in my experience, rarely trouble to communicate with contributors for whom they have no further use. Eventually Tanya McCallin, who was designing *Manon* for them, told me that she had been given bits of our set to cannibalise. Well, it's one way of informing the next-of-kin.

So my one excursion into opera (or at least operetta) remains an isolated detour, a strenuous holiday from plays and novels. An intensely enjoyable one, though. And one day I like to think that perhaps someone might revive it – maybe in the way in which it was originally presented by Offenbach himself, not as a grand production in a major opera-house, but as a musical in a boulevard theatre, with a small chorus who can dance as well as sing and a small pit orchestra.

(2000)

AND ALSO . . .

On the Roller-Coaster

A diary of my first venture into theatre, *The Two of Us*

May 1969

Michael Codron writes to say that he likes the three short plays I sent him. This is very agreeable of him – particularly since one of the plays is about a dreadful producer taking an appalling writer out to lunch, something that I didn't quite have the courage to tell Mr Codron when he took me out to lunch at the Café Royal last month.

In fact he says he feels an immediate bond of sympathy with the producer. 'He likes Wyngard – *loves* him!' I report to my wife, beginning to talk the same way as my writer, Askew, talks to Mrs Askew after one of his expansive lunches with Wyngard. It proves the authenticity of the dialogue anyway.

The plays are all two-handers: Mr and Mrs Askew, a farce, and a short play commissioned by another management for a symposium on marriage, then rejected on the grounds of obscenity (a dirty nappy appears in it, stark naked). I undertake to write a fourth to complete the evening, and the contract is signed. Now all we have to do is to find an actor, an actress, and a director, and we can start. July, Michael thinks.

May 1970

In fact a year goes by, with Michael phoning almost daily to report progress. Somebody's agent *loves* it: somebody else is passionately interested, but has taken the script off on location with him to Sumatra, and hasn't been heard of since. Richard Briers and Lynn

Redgrave are two of our earliest ideas, but are quickly eliminated because he isn't free in July and she is busy having a baby. *Everyone*, it soon becomes plain, is either contracted or pregnant.

No shortage of directors, however. We go through five directors in succession, with three near misses on the way. Some of them talk seriously about the theory of comedy; some about back projection and strobe lighting: some about which is the best hotel to stay in if we open in Brighton. Each in his turn disappears to direct a film, or *Gammer Gurton's Needle* at the Bangkok Festival.

By Christmas almost everyone in the country has read the script, and only one thing has been definitely established – the fact that no one likes Mr and Mrs Askew and their adventures. We reduce the show to three plays; we consider expanding the obscene play and having only two; we put Askew back and I hack him about, moving the end of the plot round to the beginning, taking out all the names of real actors and actresses, which have embarrassed everyone; rewriting its three scenes as one scene, as two scenes, as two and a half scenes.

The seasons pass, delivering Mr Briers from his various contracts, Miss Redgrave of a baby girl. The fifth director departs. The sixth reigns for a week. The fourth makes a brief reappearance, followed by reprises from the first and the seventh. The second suggests the eighth, Mark Cullingham. We have lunch with him, and shackle him to the leg of the table until he has signed the contract. We seem to be in business.

Mark and I set to work to weave all the various Askew texts into one final definitive edition. Lynn is astonished to find that the real names have gone; we put them back in. Michael discovers that we have removed Wyngard, the unspeakable producer; we put him back in. In the end the play is more or less as I originally wrote it, the only difference being that everyone's confidence in it has now been entirely restored. We all love it! Good old, lovable old Askew – I knew all he needed was a little work on him.

June

We rehearse in a drill-hall off Oxford Street, frowned at on all sides by portraits of former colonels of Queen Victoria's Rifles. Every day the sun beats down through the glass roof, turning the hall into a tropical house. The stage management improvise a kind of awning beneath the glass, giving the whole enterprise the air of a May Ball, or a coming-out dance.

The plan of the set is marked on the floor with sticky tape. Richard and Lynn move tentatively about, trying to remember eleven parts between them. They are woken by non-existent babies; they run in and out of invisible doors, tapping their feet to mark the moment of closing. 'Bang,' says Sue, the stage-manager, being a chair collapsing off, or a pile of plates falling on the floor. It's as if the plays have evaporated in front of my eyes! All that solid text – can it really have boiled away to something so thin and small? At the end of the first week the obscene play and the farce are the only ones that look at all possible.

'Sorry, Michael!' says Richard from time to time. 'But we got *some* of your lines in today, didn't we?' 'Poor Michael!' says Lynn. 'Oh dear oh dear oh dear!' says Richard, in his Gielgud voice. The personalities of all the comedy actors in the business, from Wilfrid Hyde White to Terry-Thomas, pass over him from moment to moment, like slides across a screen. 'Poor boy!' says Lynn in *her* Gielgud voice. 'Poor dear boy!' Cast and director mutate into Olivier, Scofield, Hordern, Coward and various other actors I haven't heard of. It's all much funnier than the dialogue I've set down for them. 'Oh dear oh dear oh dear!' I find myself saying in Richard's Gielgud voice, recounting the day's events to my wife. Worse than Askew.

By the end of the second week, halfway through the month's rehearsals, the filthy play and the farce have slipped back, and Mr and Mrs Askew have come through on the rails, moving us all to tears. We are scheduled to open in Cambridge, in a fortnight's time, for the traditional pre-London tour, and then to come into the West End. We shift our rehearsals into a real West End theatre – the Garrick, where Ned Sherrin's musical *Sing a Rude Song* is playing, and weave our tiny plots in and around the lofty Victorian ironwork of their set. More and more people begin to agglomerate round the two central figures – understudies, costume designer, wardrobe mistress, dressers, composer, lighting expert, publicity people. I begin to wish I'd written rather bigger, deeper plays for them all to stand on.

Michael Codron comes in to watch a run, a solitary castaway in the red plush sea of the stalls. We sit in absolute silence while Lynn and Richard gallop unnerved through the long night of the nappy and the agony of Askew. It's only when we get to the third play, where Lynn has to play a woman in her fifties, that the atmosphere changes. This, which Lynn has had a terrible struggle with, is now clearly the front-runner.

Michael is very firm afterwards; I feel as if I'm up before the head-master. The first half is terrible. What are we going to do about it? Can we change the running order? When can he see it again, entirely reworked, and made funny, and moving, and real, and audible? Tomorrow morning?

Mark staves him off until the end of the week. In the event he creeps in unannounced – and, by heaven, it *is* funny and moving, and real, and audible! Smiles, congratulations, relief all round. My faith in my old friend Askew is restored once again – until Mark's agent and mine come in next day, and their laughter dies away, and afterwards no one can think of anything to say except to discuss the wigs with great intensity. Up, down, up, down – it's like spending two months on a roller-coaster.

July, Cambridge

A flash flood has swept through the Arts Theatre the day before we move in; the air is full of the smell of sodden carpets. My memories of this otherwise delightful theatre are a little unsettling. It was here that I sat during my last year as an undergraduate, pressed back into the shadows of Box A, watching the first night of my Footlights May Week revue falling leadenly into the stalls like unrisen sponge-cake. The last time I was here, a few years ago, playing a tiny part on stage in a benefit night organised by David Frost, I knelt on an upturned tack.

The stage crew and the production people move like the waking dead among the half-built complexities of our revolving set; they have been up all night getting the previous show out, and ours in. The rest of us sit slumped in the pitch darkness of the stalls, hypnotised by the slow changing of lights and the rehanging of doors on stage. It's like a dream. Now it's dark and it's Sunday; now it's dark and it's

Monday, with eight o'clock bearing down upon us, towering over us.

Lynn, wearing a thin nightdress to rehearse the first play, stands in the dank coolness of the auditorium complaining that she is suffocatingly hot. Richard breaks off in the middle of the rehearsal and snaps, 'There are *dogs* in the theatre. Either they go or I do.'

'Don't worry!' says everyone to everyone else. 'Just think of tonight as a public dress rehearsal.' I walk from the theatre to the post office (it's light outside, I discover), and following the strict instructions of Peter Nichols, whom I have been consulting nervously on points of theatrical etiquette, send telegrams to the cast back in the theatre. It seems almost logical, on this strange apocalyptic day.

Well, we survive; one of the kindly audiences for which Cambridge seems to be noted laughs determinedly. Afterwards we are all relieved, exhausted, sentimental – and yet haunted, I think, by that shadow of disappointment which often follows climactic events. Why wasn't it even more climactic? All right, they laughed. But why didn't they laugh until they fell helpless on the floor, and had to be removed by ambulancemen?

Next morning, before the cast are up, Mark and I meet Michael and the general manager, David Sutton, in the lounge of the hotel to make a sober assessment of the evening. A qualified success, judges Michael. The farce went flat halfway through and needs extensive surgery. Worse, the audience really weren't interested in the Askews and their problems. Can I write an entirely new play to replace Askew in time to rehearse it and get it into the show before we are due to open in London at the end of the month?

I brood gloomily on these two problems as the week goes by. The show improves from night to night, becoming shaped by the audience's laughter, like a landscape eroded by watercourses. New streams of laughter appear; old ones dry up, or alter their course; the contours of the show become more definite. We tend the landscape; cutting, planting, clearing undergrowth. It becomes increasingly clear that Michael is right – the adventures of Askew, in spite of all the cast's efforts, are emerging as a great waterless plain.

The audiences remain good. But we get a bad review in the local paper, and a West End manager comes down to see the show and fails to make an offer. Michael comes out after the Wednesday-night performance saying, 'Cut, cut, cut, cut, cut!' and announcing that he will not take the show into London unless Askew is done away with. Oh dear oh dear oh dear.

And then we're on the up again. After Michael has gone back to London on Wednesday night I think I see a way of restructuring the middle of the farce. I walk up and down outside the hotel in the dark, working it out; lie awake all night thinking about it; sit in my room all next day writing the scene, inspired; make five copies of it, and rush them round to the theatre before the evening performance, feeling as if I were an undergraduate again with my weekly essay, or more jokes for the Footlights. Lynn and Richard read it through, and we all fall about with laughter, it's so funny. I go back to the hotel to get some sleep, exhausted but exhilarated, feeling I can do anything, even write a new play before the end of next week.

By Friday morning everyone has had second thoughts, and the scene is never performed.

Brighton

Listening to the blood-freezing silence of the first-night audience in Brighton, I realise it's not one new play we want – it's four. The whole show has become a dust-bowl!

'It's always like this on the Monday night in Brighton,' says Michael, as we sit until half-past twelve afterwards in a restaurant next to the theatre, almost as silent as the audience. He asks me how I felt about Askew tonight. I admit that I have grown to hate Askew and his wife, their home, their friends, their unborn children, yea, and their children's children. 'Tonight for the first time,' confesses Michael, after we have gazed at the tablecloth in silence for another twenty minutes or so, 'I even hated Wyngard.'

Back home in London next day I stare at my typewriter so hard, in my efforts to will a new forty-minute play out of it, that I discover for the first time how the tabulator works. This is a solid and undeniable gain, anyway. And late in the afternoon, perhaps encouraged by the prospect of getting itself typed with proper margins, the ghost of an idea does begin to emerge.

34

I start to draft it on the Wednesday morning, and on Sunday evening rush the finished product round to Michael. He likes it! He *loves* it! (No, no – no more Askew!) Everyone seems happy with it, and next day Michael takes us all out to the Ritz to celebrate. It's a brilliant summer's day; the windows are open on to the park. We all start to get nostalgic for the dear dead Askews. What a lovely couple they were! Michael has brought us to the Ritz in their honour, really, because it was here that Wyngard brought Askew for his final disastrous lunch. One of the other guests, on that occasion, we recall fondly, slid down in his chair and kicked Askew on the shin. We all try sliding down in our chairs and kicking one another on the shin.

Since that terrible first night, apparently, the audiences in Brighton have been fine, and we've had a couple of good notices. We also have a West End theatre. In fact we have a choice – the Criterion or the Garrick. We sit in Michael's office all afternoon, luxuriously discussing the advantages and disadvantages of each. Well, the others discuss. I nod wisely, entirely out of my depth. But in a very warm, blue sea.

Southsea

By the time the new play goes into the show, in Southsea at the beginning of the last week of the tour, all euphoria has long since evaporated in the awfulness of going right back to the first stage of rehearsal again. For the cast there are virtually two new plays to broach on the Monday, because John Dexter, one of our seven earlier directors, with whom Mark has worked in the past, has just spent Sunday tightening up the farce. For five hours without a break, except for occasional glasses of champagne, and imitations by Lynn of her sister in various roles, he has teased them, nagged them, reviled them, conspired with them and driven them, leaving them exhausted, and loaded with a completely new set of moves and timings.

I stay at home and hide my eyes on the Monday night. Michael reports next morning that on top of everything else a door jammed in the farce, and a man appeared to have a fit during the new play, dangling his feet over the edge of the circle and moaning throughout. But when I go down to see it later in the week, the whole show is on the upswing again. We all try to hide our cheerfulness from one another, knowing that there is nowhere to go but down. Oh dear oh dear oh dear!

London

And down indeed we go.

The first-night audience at the Garrick – largely friends of people involved, of course – laughs and claps. From the depths of despair just before the evening starts my spirits rise with the curtain, then slowly begin to sink again. 'I think it's going very well, isn't it?' says everyone I speak to in the interval, avoiding any more specific commitment. In the second half there is some barracking from the gallery. Going round to the stage door afterwards I pass three rather camp young men coming away from the gallery exit. 'That's him,' says one of them. They consult together and turn, about fifty yards behind me. 'Load of bloody rubbish!' shouts one of them.

A lot of the critics next morning seem to agree, though they put it more judicially. I feel as if I had run up hill and down dale all the way from Marathon to bring the good news to Athens, flung open the council-house door – and brought a bucket of whitewash down over my head. It has its funny side, I must admit; but I can't help feeling it would have been funnier still if it had happened to someone else instead of me. Old Askew say. Perhaps if they put Askew back in with this new scene . . .?

Observer Review, 2 August 1970

No Show

A note on the origins of *Donkeys' Years*

I wrote *Donkeys' Years* after I went back to a reunion at my own old college in the early seventies. Any resemblance between what happened on that occasion and what happens in the play is of course entirely etc., etc., but I have to confess that one of the characters in the play does have some basis in reality.

I enjoyed my time at university, but my own college and I were not on the best of terms, and I departed without leaving a forwarding address for fund-raising appeals, the College magazine, invitations to reunions, etc. So I should never have discovered that my particular year was due for its Gathering of Old Members if it hadn't been for one particular Old Member who rang me up and urged me to go to it with him.

My caller had been the most distinguished of all my contemporaries. He looked like the hero of an old-fashioned adventure story, and he had a quick mind and a sardonic sense of humour. A particular aura hung about him because he had spent his National Service as a front-line infantry officer in Korea. The College's numerous sportsmen liked him; so did its handful of alienated intellectuals. But the most striking thing of all about him was that he was a compulsive dissembler. He loved deception for its own sake, and never ceased to be amused by the endless credulity of myself and my fellow victims. It was entirely characteristic of him that he appeared in Hall in the last few days before Finals struggling to get through what even I knew were the elementary books on his first-year reading list – and that he then got a First and entered the Foreign Office.

I was not enthusiastic about his proposal to go to the Gathering, but he was very pressing. He agreed that it would be a dreadful occasion, but suggested that we could sit on the sidelines, get drunk together, and laugh at everybody else. I reluctantly allowed myself to be persuaded, and he got the College to send me an invitation. I duly went. He didn't.

Next morning I walked round Cambridge with the worst hangover since the invention of alcohol, while he sat, presumably, on some rather more remote sidelines laughing at me.

As the years went by I walked into a few more of his little boobytraps – lured, for instance, into embarrassed sympathy when a sudden downturn in his fortunes deposited him in lodgings so squalid that he was ashamed to give me the address of them; only to be informed, by someone to whom I passed on the sad news, that it was an apartment in Albany. He told me he was disillusioned with the Foreign Office and wanted to escape into journalism, so I introduced him to a newspaper editor I knew. The next time I saw the editor he would scarcely speak to me. Why, he demanded coldly, had I tried to make use of him to provide cover for a spy? My friend, he had discovered, was not in the Foreign Office at all – he was in MI6. Of course.

Some years after that my friend died, of the kind of disease that seems to afflict people of an inturned and secretive nature, and this time I think the story was true. By then I had written the play, become reconciled with my old College, and been put on the appeals list like everybody else. Now, eighteen years on from the original production, we've come to the Gathering of Old Characters. So a belated word of thanks to my late friend. I think you'll recognise which character he inspired as soon as he comes on stage.

(1992)

LATER PLAYS

Copenhagen

Where a work of fiction features historical characters and historical events it's reasonable to want to know how much of it is fiction and how much of it is history. So let me make it as clear as I can in regard to this play.

The central event in it is a real one. Heisenberg *did* go to Copenhagen in 1941, and there *was* a meeting with Bohr, in the teeth of all the difficulties encountered by my characters. He probably went to dinner at the Bohrs' house, and the two men probably went for a walk to escape from any possible microphones, though there is some dispute about even these simple matters. The question of what they actually said to each other has been even more disputed, and where there's ambiguity in the play about what happened, it's because there is in the recollection of the participants. Much more sustained speculation still has been devoted to the question of what Heisenberg was hoping to achieve by the meeting. All the alternative and co-existing explications offered in the play, except perhaps the final one, have been aired at various times, in one form or another.

Most anxious of all to establish some agreed version of the meeting was Heisenberg himself. He did indeed go back in 1947 with his British minder, Ronald Fraser, and attempted to find some common ground in the matter with Bohr. But it proved to be too delicate a task, and (according to Heisenberg, at any rate, in his memoirs) 'we both came to feel that it would be better to stop disturbing the spirits of the past.' This is where my play departs from the historical record, by supposing that at some later time, when everyone involved had become spirits of the past themselves, they argued the question out further, until they had achieved a little more understanding of what was going on, just as they had so many times when they were alive with the intractable difficulties presented by the internal workings of the atom. The account of these earlier discussions in the twenties reflects at any rate one or two of the key topics, and the passion with which the argument was conducted, as it emerges from the biographical and autobiographical record. I am acutely aware of how over-simplified my version is. Max Born described the real story as not so much 'a straight staircase upwards, but a tangle of interconnected alleys', and I have found it impossible to follow these in any detail (even where I can begin to understand them). In particular I have grossly understated the crucial role played by Born himself and by his pupil Pascual Jordan at Göttingen in formulating quantum mechanics (it was Born who supplied the understanding of matrices that Heisenberg lacked, and the statistical interpretation of Schrödinger's wave function), and of Wolfgang Pauli in Hamburg, whose exclusion principle filled in one of the key pieces in the puzzle.

But the account of the German and American bomb programmes, and of the two physicists' participation in them, is taken from the historical record; so is the fate of Danish Jewry; and Heisenberg's experiences in Germany before and during the war, his subsequent internment, and the depression that clouded his later years. I have filled out some of the details, but in general what he says happened to him – at the end of the First World War, on Heligoland, during his nocturnal walk in Faelled Park, during the Berlin air-raid and his internment, and on his ride across Germany, with its near-fatal encounter along the way – is based very closely upon the accounts he gave in life.

The actual words spoken by my characters are of course entirely their own. If this needs any justification then I can only appeal to Heisenberg himself. In his memoirs dialogue plays an important part, he says, because he hopes 'to demonstrate that science is rooted in conversations'. But, as he explains, conversations, even real conversations, cannot be reconstructed literally several decades later. So he freely reinvents them, and appeals in his turn to Thucydides. (Heisenberg's father was a professor of classics, and he was an accom-

plished classicist himself, on top of all his other distinctions.)
Thucydides explains in his preface to the *History of the Peloponnesian
War* that, although he had avoided all 'storytelling', when it came to
the speeches, 'I have found it impossible to remember their exact
wording. Hence I have made each orator speak as, in my opinion, he
would have done in the circumstances, but keeping as close as I could
to the train of thought that guided his actual speech.' Thucydides was
trying to give an account of speeches that had actually been made,
many of which he had himself heard. Some of the dialogue in my play
represents speeches that must have been made in one form or another;
some of it speeches that were certainly never made at all. I hope,
though, that in some sense it respects the Thucydidean principle, and
that speeches (and indeed actions) follow in so far as possible the original protagonists' train of thought.

But how far is it possible to know what their train of thought was?
This is where I have departed from the established historical record –
from any possible historical record. The great challenge facing the
storyteller and the historian alike is to get inside people's heads, to
stand where they stood and see the world as they saw it, to make some
informed estimate of their motives and intentions – and this is precisely where recorded and recordable history cannot reach. Even when all
the external evidence has been mastered, the only way into the protagonists' heads is through the imagination. This indeed is the substance of the play.

I can't claim to be the first person to have noticed the parallels between
Heisenberg's science and his life. They provide David Cassidy with the
title (*Uncertainty*) for his excellent biography (the standard work in
English). 'Especially difficult and controversial', says Cassidy in his
introduction, 'is a retrospective evaluation of Heisenberg's activities
during the Third Reich and particularly during the Second World War.
Since the end of the war, an enormous range of views about this man
and his behaviour have been expressed, views that have been fervently, even passionately, held by a variety of individuals. It is as if, for
some, the intense emotions unleashed by the unspeakable horrors of
that war and regime have combined with the many ambiguities, dual-

ities, and compromises of Heisenberg's life and actions to make Heisenberg himself subject to a type of uncertainty principle . . .' Thomas Powers makes a similar point in his extraordinary and encyclopaedic book *Heisenberg's War*, which first aroused my interest in the trip to Copenhagen; he says that Heisenberg's later reticence on his role in the failure of the German bomb programme 'introduces an element of irreducible uncertainty'.

Cassidy does not explore the parallel further. Powers even appends a footnote to his comment: 'Forgive me.' The apology seems to me unnecessary. It's true that the concept of uncertainty is one of those scientific notions that has become common coinage, and generalised to the point of losing much of its original meaning. The idea as introduced by Heisenberg into quantum mechanics was precise and technical. It didn't suggest that everything about the behaviour of particles was unknowable, or hazy. What it limited was the simultaneous measurement of 'canonically conjugate variables', such as position and momentum, or energy and time. The more precisely you measure one variable, it said, the less precise your measurement of the related variable can be; and this ratio, the uncertainty relationship, is itself precisely formulable.

None of this, plainly, applies directly to our observations of thought and intention. Thoughts are not locatable by pairs of conjugate variables, so there can be no question of a ratio of precision. Powers seems to imply that in Heisenberg's case the uncertainty arises purely because 'questions of motive and intention cannot be established more clearly than he was willing to state them'. It's true that Heisenberg was under contradictory pressures after the war which made it particularly difficult for him to explain what he had been trying to do. He wanted to distance himself from the Nazis, but he didn't want to suggest that he had been a traitor. He was reluctant to claim to his fellow Germans that he had deliberately lost them the war, but he was no less reluctant to suggest that he had failed them simply out of incompetence.

But the uncertainty surely begins long before the point at which Heisenberg might have offered an explanation. He was under at least as many contradictory pressures at the time to shape the actions he later failed to explain, and the uncertainty would still have existed, for us and for him, even if he had been as open, honest, and helpful as it is humanly possible to be. What people say about their own motives and intentions, even when they are not caught in the traps that entangled Heisenberg, is always subject to question – as subject to question as what anybody else says about them. Thoughts and intentions, even one's own – perhaps one's own most of all – remain shifting and elusive. There is not one single thought or intention of any sort that can ever be precisely established.

What the uncertainty of thoughts does have in common with the uncertainty of particles is that the difficulty is not just a practical one, but a systematic limitation which cannot even in theory be circumvented. It is patently not resolved by the efforts of psychologists and psychoanalysts, and it will not be resolved by neurologists, either, even when everything is known about the structure and workings of the brain, any more than semantic questions can be resolved by looking at the machine code of a computer. And since, according to the so-called 'Copenhagen Interpretation' of quantum mechanics – the interconnected set of theories that was developed by Heisenberg, Bohr, and others in the twenties – the whole possibility of saying or thinking anything about the world, even the most apparently objective, abstract aspects of it studied by the natural sciences, depends upon human observation, and is subject to the limitations which the human mind imposes, this uncertainty in our thinking is also fundamental to the nature of the world.

'Uncertainty' is not a very satisfactory word by which to come at this. It sits awkwardly even in its original context. You can be uncertain about things which are themselves entirely definite, and about which you could be entirely certain if you were simply better informed. Indeed, the very idea of uncertainty seems to imply the possibility of certainty. Heisenberg and Bohr used several different German words in different contexts. Bohr (who spoke more or less perfect German) sometimes referred to *Unsicherheit*, which means quite simply unsureness. In Heisenberg's original paper he talks about *Ungenauigkeit* – inexactness – and the most usual term now in German seems to be *Unschärfe* – blurredness or fuzziness. But the

45

word he adopts in his general conclusion, and which he uses when he refers back to the period later in his memoirs, is *Unbestimmtheit*, for which it's harder to find a satisfactory English equivalent. Although it means uncertainty in the sense of vagueness, it's plainly derived from *bestimmen*, to determine or to ascertain. This is reflected better in the other English translation which is sometimes used, but which seems to be less familiar: indeterminacy. 'Undeterminedness' would be closer still, though clumsy. Less close to the German, but even closer to the reality of the situation, would be 'indeterminability'.

Questions of translation apart, Heisenberg's choice of word suggests that, at the time he wrote his paper, he had not fully grasped the metaphysical implications of what he was saying. Indeed, he concludes that the experiments concerned are affected by *Unbestimmtheit* 'purely empirically'. He was not, as Bohr complained, at that time greatly interested in the philosophical fallout from physics and mathematics (though he became much more so later on in life), and he was publishing in a hurry, as Bohr also complained, before he had had a chance to discuss the work with either Bohr or anyone else. His paper seems to imply that electrons have definite orbits, even if these are unknowable; he talks about a quantum of light completely throwing the electron out of its 'orbit', even though he puts the word into inverted commas, and says that it has no rational sense here. The title of the paper itself reinforces this impression: *Über den anschaulichen Inhalt der quantentheoretischen Kinematik und Mechanik*. Again there are translation problems. '*Anschaulich*' means graphic, concrete, 'look-at-able'; the title is usually translated as referring to the 'perceptual' content of the disciplines concerned, which again seems to suggest a contrast with their unperceived aspects – as if Heisenberg were concerned merely about our difficulties in visualising abstractions, not about the physical implications of this.

The Copenhagen Interpretation of quantum mechanics was scientific orthodoxy for most of the twentieth century, and is the theoretical basis (for better or worse) on which the century's dramatic physical demonstrations of nuclear forces were constructed. But it has not gone unchallenged. Einstein never accepted it, though he could never find a way round it. The mathematician Roger Penrose regards the present state of quantum theory as 'provisional', and quotes Schrödinger, de Broglie, and Dirac as forerunners in this view.

An alternative to the Copenhagen Interpretation, explaining the apparent superimposition of different states that appears at the quantum level in terms of a multiplicity of parallel worlds, was developed after the Second World War by Hugh Everett III, who had been a graduate student of John Wheeler, Bohr's associate in the famous paper which opened the way to an understanding of uranium fission. David Deutsch, who proposes an extreme version of Everett's ideas in his book *The Fabric of Reality*, claims that 'hardly anyone' still believes in the Copenhagen Interpretation. I have put this view to a number of physicists. They all seemed greatly surprised by it; but maybe I have hit upon precisely the supposed handful who remain in the faith.

Another follower of Everett (though he seems to differ quite sharply from Deutsch) is Murray Gell-Mann, who with Yuval Ne'eman revolutionised elementary particle theory in the sixties with the introduction of the quark, in its three different 'colours' and six different 'flavours', as the fundamental unit of the material world. Gell-Mann believes that quantum mechanics is the fundamental tool for understanding the universe, but he sees the Copenhagen Interpretation, with its dependence upon an observer and the human act of measurement, as anthropocentric, and as characterising merely a special case that he calls 'the approximate quantum mechanics of measured systems'. I hesitate to express any reservations about something I understand so little, particularly when it comes from such an authority, but it seems to me that the view which Gell-Mann favours, and which involves what he calls alternative 'histories' or 'narratives', is precisely as anthropocentric as Bohr's, since histories and narratives are not freestanding elements of the universe, but human constructs as subjective and as restricted in their viewpoint as the act of observation.

The relevance of indeterminacy to quantum mechanics has also been challenged. A version of the famous thought experiment involving two slits has now actually been carried out in the laboratory (at the University of Konstanz). It confirms, as Bohr hypothesised, that while an unobserved particle seems to pass through both slits, so that it forms a characteristic interference pattern on a screen beyond them, any act of observation that attempts to determine which of the two paths the particle actually follows necessarily destroys the phenomenon, so that the interference pattern vanishes. But the experiment appears to suggest that, although the uncertainty principle is true, it accounts for discrepancies far too small to explain the loss of interference. The observation in the laboratory experiment, moreover, was carried out not, as in the old thought experiment, by hitting the particle involved with a photon, which transfers part of its energy to the particle and so alters its path, but by a way of marking with microwaves which has almost no effect on the particle's momentum.

Some physicists now accept that the loss of interference is caused by a much stranger and less quasi-classical aspect of the quantum world – entanglement. The notion was introduced by Schrödinger in 1935, and suggests that where quantum-mechanical entities become involved with each other (as with the particle and the photon), they form states of affairs which continue to have a collective identity and behaviour, even though their components have physically separated again. The difficulties in this are obvious, but there is no interpretation of quantum-mechanical phenomena that does not involve breathtaking challenges to the logic of our everyday experience.

For the references to all these developments see the bibliography at the end of this Postscript (p. 73).

What about my characters? Are they anything like their originals?

It's impossible to catch the exact tone of voice of people one never knew, with only the written record to go on, especially when most of what their contemporaries recall them as saying was originally said in other languages. There are also more particular problems with all three of my protagonists.

Bohr, for a start, was as notorious for his inarticulacy and inaudibility as he was famous for his goodness and lovability. He was fluent in various languages, but I have heard it said that the problem was to know which language he was being fluent in. Schrödinger, after his epic confrontation with Bohr in 1926, described him as often talking 'for minutes almost in a dreamlike, visionary and really quite unclear

48

manner, partly because he is so full of consideration and constantly hesitates – fearing that the other might take a statement of his [Bohr's] point of view as an insufficient appreciation of the other's . . .' My Bohr is necessarily a little more coherent than this – and I have been told by various correspondents who knew him that in private, if not in public, he could be much more cogent and incisive than Schrödinger evidently found him.

The problem with Margrethe is that there is relatively little biographical material to go on. She and Niels were plainly mutually devoted, and everything suggests that she was as generally loved as he was. She had no scientific training, but Bohr constantly discussed his work with her, presumably avoiding technical language – though she must have become fairly familiar with even that since she typed out each draft of his papers. I suspect she was more gracious and reserved than she appears here, but she plainly had great firmness of character – in later life she was known as 'Dronning [Queen] Margrethe'. She was always cooler about Heisenberg than Bohr was, and she was openly angry about his visit in 1941. According to Bohr she objected strongly to his being invited to the house, and relented only when Bohr promised to avoid politics and restrict the conversation to physics. Bohr himself always refused to be drawn about Heisenberg's trip in 1941, but she insisted, even after the war, even after all Heisenberg's attempts to explain, 'No matter what anyone says, that was a hostile visit.'

The problem with Heisenberg is his elusiveness and ambiguity, which is of course what the play is attempting to elucidate. The one thing about him that everyone agreed upon was what Max Born, his mentor in Göttingen, called 'his unbelievable quickness and precision of understanding'. The contrast with Bohr is almost comic. 'Probably [Bohr's] most characteristic property', according to George Gamow, 'was the slowness of his thinking and comprehension.'

As a young man Heisenberg seems to have had an appealing eagerness and directness. Born described him as looking like a simple farm boy, with clear bright eyes, and a radiant expression on his face. Somebody else thought he looked 'like a bright carpenter's apprentice just returned from technical school'. Victor Weisskopf says that he made friends easily, and that everyone liked him. Bohr, after their first meeting in 1922, was delighted by Heisenberg's 'nice shy nature, his good temper, his eagerness and his enthusiasm'. There was something about him of the prize-winning student, who is good at everything required of him, and Bohr was not the only father-figure to whom he appealed. He had a somewhat similar relationship with Sommerfeld, his first professor in Munich, and in his difficulties with the Nazis he turned to two elders of German physics for counsel, Max Planck and Max von Laue. His closest friend and colleague was probably Carl Friedrich von Weizsäcker, who was younger than him, but it is striking that during his internment the person he chose to confide his explanation of the Hiroshima bomb to was not Weizsäcker, who was interned with him (although he may well have discussed it with him already), but the sixty-six-year-old Otto Hahn.

The American physicist Jeremy Bernstein says that 'he had the first truly quantum-mechanical mind – the ability to take the leap beyond the classical visualising pictures into the abstract, all-but-impossible-to-visualise world of the subatomic . . .' Cassidy believes that a great part of his genius was his 'ability to adopt a serviceable solution regardless of accepted wisdom'. Rudolf Peierls stresses his intuition. He would 'almost always intuitively know the answer to a problem, then look for a mathematical solution to give it to him'. The obverse of this, according to Peierls, is that 'he was always very casual about numbers' – a weakness that seems to have contributed to his downfall – or his salvation – in the atomic-bomb programme.

Margrethe always found him difficult, closed, and oversensitive, and this propensity to be withdrawn and inturned was exacerbated as life went on – first by his political problems in the thirties, and then by his efforts to reconcile the moral irreconcilables of his wartime work. His autobiographical writing is rather stiff and formal, and his letters to Bohr, even during the twenties and thirties, are correct rather than intimate. Throughout the period of their closest friendship they addressed each other with the formal *Sie*, and switched to *Du* only when Heisenberg also had a chair.

The conversations that Heisenberg claimed such freedom to recreate in his memoirs are stately. Much more plausibly colloquial is the transcript of David Irving's long interview with him for *The Virus House*, Irving's history of the German bomb programme, though he is still (naturally) watchful. In the transcripts of the relatively unguarded conversations that the German atomic team had among themselves during their internment, where Heisenberg emerges as the dominant figure, both morally and practically, a certain hard-headed worldliness can be detected. He is much concerned with professional prospects, and with how they might make some money out of their wartime researches. When one of the others says that if they agree to work on atomic matters under Allied control they will be looked down upon as traitors 'in the eyes of the masses', Heisenberg replies: 'No. One must do that cleverly. As far as the masses are concerned it will look as though we unfortunately have to continue our scientific work under the wicked Anglo-Saxon control, and that we can do nothing about it. We will have to appear to accept this control with fury and gnashing of teeth.'

There was always something a little sharp and harsh about him, something that at its best inspired respect rather than love, and that after the war occasioned really quite astonishing hostility and contempt. Even Samuel Goudsmit turned against him. Goudsmit was an old friend and colleague; when the investigators of the Alsos mission, the Allied agency for gathering intelligence on German atomic research, for which he was working, finally broke into Heisenberg's office in 1945, one of the first things they saw was a picture of the two of them together that Heisenberg had kept there as a memento of happier days. But when Goudsmit subsequently interrogated Heisenberg he found him arrogant and self-involved. Goudsmit had understandably bitter feelings at the time – he had just discovered the record of his parents' death in Auschwitz. Heisenberg was also caught in a false position. Confident that his team had been far ahead of the Americans, he offered Goudsmit his services in initiating them into the secrets of uranium fission. (Goudsmit did nothing to correct his misapprehension, which gave Heisenberg, when the truth finally came out, grounds for returning Goudsmit's bitterness.) In his superficial and strangely unimpressive book on Alsos, Goudsmit wrote about Heisenberg and his team with contemptuous dismissal, and in the year-long correspondence in the American press that followed its publication, accused him of self-importance and dishonesty.

Weisskopf gave a reception for Heisenberg during his trip to America in 1949, but about half the guests – including many people from the Los Alamos team – failed to appear, explaining to Weisskopf that they didn't want to shake the hand of the man who had tried to build a bomb for Hitler. Even Cassidy, who gives full measure to Heisenberg as a physicist, is notably cool and cautious in his assessment of Heisenberg's role in the German bomb programme. Ronald Fraser, the British Intelligence officer who escorted Heisenberg back to Copenhagen in 1947 (the British seem to have been frightened that he would defect to the Russians, or be kidnapped by them), replied to Irving's enquiry about the trip in tones of patronising contempt that seem slightly unhinged. 'The whole story of "a kind of confrontation",' he wrote to Irving, 'in the matter of his 1941 natter with Bohr in the Tivoli Gardens [sic] is a typical Heisenberg fabrication – maybe a bit brighter than a thousand others, but like them all a product of his *Blut und Boden* guilt complex, which he rationalises that quickly that the stories become *for him* the truth, the whole truth, and nothing but the truth. Pitiful, in a man of his mental stature.'

The historian Paul Lawrence Rose, who has focussed upon Heisenberg as an emblem for what he regards as the general failings of German culture, also takes a remarkably high moral tone. In a paper he wrote in 1984, entitled *Heisenberg, German Morality and the Atomic Bomb,* he talked about Heisenberg's 'guff', his 'self-serving, self-deluding claims', and his 'elementary moral stupidity'. After a further fourteen years' research Professor Rose returned to the subject in 1998 in a full-length book which was published after the play was produced, and which has attracted considerable attention, *Heisenberg and the Nazi Atomic Bomb Project: A Study in German Culture*. His contempt for Heisenberg remains unmoderated. He believes that Heisenberg failed, in spite of his perfect readiness to serve the Nazi regime, because of his arrogance and wrong-headedness, and because he embodied various vices of German culture in general, and of the Nazi regime in particular, whose values he had absorbed.

It is a difficult book to read – Rose can scarcely quote a word of

Heisenberg's without adding his own disparaging qualification. Here is a selection of his interjections on two facing pages taken more or less at random: '. . . self-incriminating . . . a somewhat inadequate explanation . . . this inconsistency . . . the falseness of these lame excuses . . . a characteristic Heisenberg lie . . . Heisenberg's usual facile rationalising ability . . . Heisenberg then went on glibly to recollect . . . the delusory nature of Heisenberg's memory . . .'

You wonder at times whether it wouldn't look better if it were handwritten in green ink, with no paragraph breaks. Rose seems to be aware himself of the effect he is producing. He realises, he says, that some readers may 'find distasteful the recurrent moral judgments passed on Heisenberg'. They may also, he thinks, be put off by what seems a 'lack of sympathy with German culture' – he cannot say, he confesses, that his 'British background' has made him entirely sympathetic to it. He is at pains to distance himself from any unfortunate echoes that this attitude may awaken: he hopes that readers will not accuse him of 'unthinkingly preaching a crude view of German "national character", whatever that term may mean'. What he is concerned with, he explains, is not that at all, but 'the enduring nature of what one might call the "deep culture" of Germany . . . In this book I have tried to penetrate into how Germans think – or rather, perhaps, used to think – and to show how radically different are German and what I have termed "Western" mentalities and sensibilities.' It is this that underlies what he calls, without apparent irony, 'the Heisenberg problem'.

Some of his evidence induces a certain dizziness. He quotes without comment, as the epigraph to a chapter, a remark by Albert Speer, the Nazi Minister of Armaments: 'I do hope Heisenberg is not now claiming that they tried, for reasons of principle, to sabotage the project by asking for such minimal support!' It's true that any claim to have sabotaged the project, particularly for reasons of principle, would represent an astonishing departure from Heisenberg's habitual caution on the subject. But the question is not what Speer hoped, but whether Heisenberg *did* make such a claim.

So did he or didn't he? Rose doesn't tell us, and the only reference he gives is Gitta Sereny's new book, *Albert Speer: His Battle with*

Truth. The allusion is to the crucial meeting at Harnack House in 1942, mentioned in the play. Speer said in his memoirs that he was 'rather put out' by the very small amount of money that Heisenberg requested to run the nuclear research programme. In an earlier draft of the manuscript (the 'Spandau draft'), says Sereny, he had added in brackets the remark that Rose quotes – and Heisenberg, she says, 'did in fact try precisely that after the war'.

So he *did* make the claim! But when and where? Sereny doesn't tell us. The only references to the smallness of the sums of money he asked for that I can find in the record are the one quoted, by Speer himself, and another by Field Marshal Milch, Goering's deputy in the Luftwaffe, who was also present at the meeting. There's certainly nothing about it in Heisenberg's memoirs, or in Robert Jungk's book, *Brighter than a Thousand Suns*, or in Heisenberg's long interview with Irving, or in the other two obvious places, his interview with *Der Spiegel* in 1967, when Irving's book was published, or his review of the book in the *Frankfurter Allgemeine Zeitung*. I hardly like to put myself forward to fill the gap, but so far as I know the only reference he made to the subject was posthumously and fictitiously in my play.

Sereny, like Rose, is markedly unenthusiastic about Heisenberg in general. She goes on to argue that Heisenberg's claims about his intentions in meeting Bohr in 1941 'are now shown by Speer's Spandau account to be false', though quite how this is so she doesn't explain. About what she calls 'the facts' of the Copenhagen meeting she is remarkably brisk. In the conversation '. . . which Bohr subsequently reported to his associates at the Niels Bohr Institute, Heisenberg had made his political stand crystal clear. His team, he told Bohr, had gone some way towards discovering a way to produce an atom bomb. Germany was going to win the war, probably quite soon, and Bohr should join them now in their efforts.'

The idea that Heisenberg was inviting Bohr to work on the German bomb is on the face of it the least plausible out of all the possible interpretations that have been offered. It is completely at odds with what Weisskopf recalls Bohr as saying in 1948, and with what Bohr is on record as telling Chadwick at the time. In any case, the suggestion that Heisenberg thought he might be able to import someone half-Jewish into the most secret research programme in Nazi Germany is frankly preposterous.

So what is Sereny's evidence for her account of the meeting? At this point the sense of vertigo returns, and one begins to have the feeling that one is in an Escher drawing, where the stairs up to the floor above somehow lead back to the floor one is already on, because the only reference she gives is . . . Powers, Heisenberg's great champion, in *Heisenberg's War*.

And it's true – Powers *does* quote an opinion to this effect (and it's the only possible source for it anywhere, so far as I know). He says he was told by Weizsäcker that some person or persons unnamed in Copenhagen, forty-four years after the event, had told *him* that this is what Bohr had said he had believed Heisenberg's intention to be. One might think that this is rather faint evidence. In any case, even if it really is what Bohr believed, it is of course not what Weizsäcker believed, or Powers either. They are reporting Bohr's alleged belief as a possible misapprehension on his part which might have explained his anger. Indeed, Powers's own reading of the situation is precisely the one that Sereny claims to be discredited by Speer's remark.

Goudsmit gradually modified his opinion, and his final judgement on Heisenberg, when he died in 1976, was a generous one which goes some way to expunging the dismissive tone of his book: 'Heisenberg was a very great physicist, a deep thinker, a fine human being, and also a courageous person. He was one of the greatest physicists of our time, but he suffered severely under the unwarranted attacks by fanatical colleagues. In my opinion he must be considered to have been in some respects a victim of the Nazi regime.'

Robert Jungk, one of the few authors who have ever attempted to defend Heisenberg, modified his opinion in the opposite direction. In *Brighter than a Thousand Suns*, originally published in 1956, he suggested that the German physicists had managed to avoid building nuclear weapons for conscientious reasons, and quoted Heisenberg as saying that 'under a dictatorship active resistance can only be practised by those who pretend to collaborate with the regime. Anyone speaking out openly against the system thereby indubitably deprives himself of any chance of active resistance.' But Jungk later changed his mind, and described the notion of passive resistance on the part of the German physicists as a 'myth'. He had contributed to spreading it, he said, out of an 'esteem for those impressive personalities which I have since realised to be out of place'.

For a really spirited and sustained defence Heisenberg had to wait until Powers published his book in 1993. It is a remarkable piece of work, journalistic in tone, but generous in its understanding and huge in its scope. A little too huge, perhaps, because Powers is unable to resist being side-tracked from the main narrative by the amazing byways that he perpetually finds opening off it. I recommend it particularly to other dramatists and screenwriters; there is material here for several more plays and films yet.

His central argument is that the Allied bomb programme succeeded because of the uninhibited eagerness of the scientists to do it, particularly those exiles who had known Nazism at first hand, and who were desperate to pre-empt Hitler, while the German programme failed because of the underlying reluctance of scientists in Germany to arm Hitler with the bomb, however strong their patriotism, and however much they wanted to profit from the possibilities for research. 'Zeal was needed,' he says; 'its absence was lethal, like a poison that leaves no trace.'

But he goes further, and argues that Heisenberg 'did not simply withhold himself, stand aside, let the project die. He killed it.' He tries to show that at every point Heisenberg was careful to hold out enough hope to the authorities to ensure that he and his team were left in charge of the project, but never enough to attract the total commitment and huge investment that would have offered the only real hope of success. 'Heisenberg's caution saved him. He was free to do what he could to guide the German atomic research effort into a broom closet, where scientists tinkered until the war ended.'

Cassidy, reviewing the book in *Nature*, described it as a good story, but insisted that 'as history it is incredible'. Rose dismisses it as 'entirely bogus' and 'a scholarly disaster'. Powers acknowledged ruefully, in a recent letter to the *Times Literary Supplement*, that he had failed to convince any historian who had pronounced upon the matter.

The play is not an attempt to adjudicate between these differing views of Heisenberg's personality, or these differing accounts of his activities. But it would have been impossible to write it without taking *some* view of Powers's version of events, so here, for what it is worth, is a brief summary of the case, and of my own hesitant view of it. The evidence is confused and contradictory, and making any sense of it involves balancing probabilities and possibilities almost as indeterminable as Heisenberg found events inside the atom.

Some of the evidence undoubtedly appears to support Powers's thesis in its stronger form, that Heisenberg deliberately sabotaged the project.

In the first place there are two scraps of direct testimony. One is a message brought to America in 1941 by a departing German Jewish academic called Fritz Reiche. It was from Fritz Houtermans, the German physicist who had just realised that if they could get a reactor going it would produce plutonium, and that plutonium would be a fissile alternative to the U235 that they could not separate. Reiche testified later that he had passed it on to a group of scientists working at Princeton, including Wolfgang Pauli, John von Neumann, and Hans Bethe. As Rudolf Ladenburg, the physicist who arranged the meeting, recorded it afterwards, Houtermans wanted it to be known that 'a large number of German physicists are working intensively on the problem of the uranium bomb under the direction of Heisenberg', and that 'Heisenberg himself tries to delay the work as much as possible, fearing the catastrophic results of a success'.

Rose dismisses Houtermans as a proven liar, and records that Reiche later appeared to withdraw his belief in Heisenberg's opposition to the project. But neither of these objections seems immediately relevant to the consistency of Reiche's and Ladenburg's testimony.

The second scrap of evidence is even more direct, but much more dubious. Heisenberg's American editor, Ruth Nanda Anshen, records receiving a letter from him in 1970 in which he claimed that 'Dr Hahn, Dr von Laue and I falsified the mathematics in order to avoid the development of the atom bomb by German scientists'.

The letter itself has apparently vanished from the record. Rose nonetheless accepts it as beyond doubt genuine, and sees it as a yet more blatant attempt at self-justification. It is not, however, called into evidence by Powers, even though it would appear to support his case, and he mentions it only in his notes, and with the greatest reserve. Jeremy Bernstein, who seems to me the best informed and most fair-minded of all Heisenberg's critics, and whose book *Hitler's Uranium Club* will be relied upon in understanding the scientific considerations that follow, dismisses it as 'incredible' and 'a chimera'. It is entirely at odds with Heisenberg's careful moderation in all his other references to the matter, and the inclusion of Hahn and von Laue in the plot is nonsensical. Hahn was a chemist, not a physicist, and, as will be plain from what comes later, had no knowledge whatsoever of the relevant mathematics, while von Laue is famous as an outspoken opponent of Nazism who never worked on the German nuclear programme at all.

So much for the direct evidence, true or false. All the rest of the evidence is indirect, and relates to whether Heisenberg did actually have some understanding of the relevant physics and concealed it, or whether he failed out of ignorance. It centres on the question of critical mass, the amount of fissile material ($U235$ or plutonium) large enough to support an explosive chain reaction. An estimate of this amount was crucial to the decision about proceeding with a serious nuclear weapons programme because of the enormous difficulty and expense of separating the $U235$ from the $U238$ that makes up the vast bulk of natural uranium, and the length of time it would take to develop a reactor capable of transmuting the uranium into plutonium. At the beginning of the war it was believed by scientists on both sides that the answer would be in tons, which put the possibility of producing it beyond practical consideration. The idea became imaginable only when two scientists working in Britain, Rudolf Peierls and Otto Frisch, did the calculation and realised quite how fast the reaction would go with fast neutrons in pure $U235$, and consequently how little fissile material you would need: not tons but kilograms. (The various ironies associated with this are explored in the play, and I will not repeat them here.)

Powers argues that the idea never became imaginable in Germany because Heisenberg 'cooked up a plausible method of estimating critical mass which gave an answer in tons'. He believes that Heisenberg 'well knew how to make a bomb with far less, but kept the knowledge to himself'.

There is a certain amount of evidence that the German team did at one point arrive at a much lower figure for the critical mass – indeed, for one in kilograms, that bore some relation to the estimate made by Frisch and Peierls, and to the actual mass of the Hiroshima bomb (56 kg). Manfred von Ardenne, who was running an alternative nuclear programme for the German Post Office, later claimed in his memoirs that in the late autumn of 1941 he was informed independently by both Heisenberg and Hahn that they had worked out the critical mass for a $U235$ bomb and found it to be about ten kilograms. This information was subsequently withdrawn by Weizsäcker, who told him that he and Heisenberg had decided that a $U235$ bomb was impossible (because the heat of the reaction would expand the uranium too fast for it to continue). But Heisenberg, so far as I know, never commented on this, and Weizsäcker, according to Bernstein, 'essentially denied' that any such conversation ever took place.

As Bernstein says, it is difficult to know what to make of all this – it is 'one of several brick walls anyone who studies this subject runs into'. I think it's difficult to take von Ardenne's recollection entirely literally. Hahn, as I noted before, plainly had no understanding of the mathematics, nor of any of the other issues involved, and, as we shall see, had to have them explained to him by Heisenberg later. On the other hand (and this story has more other hands than a Hindu god), in Weizsäcker's report on the possibility of an American bomb programme, written in September 1941, he talked about the destructive effects of a bomb weighing 5 kg. Then again, in February 1942 a brief progress report for German Army Ordnance, authors unnamed, suggested without further explanation a critical mass of between 10 and 100 kg. And at the crucial meeting with Speer at Harnack House in June 1942, when Field Marshal Milch asked him how large an atomic bomb would have to be to destroy a city, Heisenberg replied, or so he said in his interview with Irving, that it, or at any rate its 'essentially active part', would have to be 'about the size of a pineapple'.

In the end, though, I believe that the crucial piece of evidence lies elsewhere, in a source that was denied to everyone who wrote about

Heisenberg until recently – the transcripts of the Farm Hall recordings. Bernstein, Powers, and Rose were the first commentators to have
access to them.

Though of course they still don't reach the same conclusions from
them.

The story of Farm Hall is another complete play in itself. Sir Charles
Frank, the British atomic physicist, in his admirably fair and clear
introduction to the text of the transcripts that was published in
Britain, regrets that they were not released in time for Dürrenmatt to
make use of.

At the end of the war troops of the Alsos mission, to which
Goudsmit was attached, made their way through what was left of the
German front line and located the remains of the German reactor at
Haigerloch, with the intention of finally reassuring themselves that
Germany would not be able to spring some terrible nuclear surprise at
the last moment. They also seized the team of scientists themselves,
making a special armed sortie to Urfeld, in Bavaria, to collect
Heisenberg from his home. Hechingen, the nearby town where the
team was based, and Haigerloch itself were in the French sector. The
scientists were abstracted secretly, from under the noses of the French,
and brought back to Britain, where they were held, under wartime
laws and without anyone's knowledge, in a former Intelligence safe
house – Farm Hall, near Cambridge. The intention seems to have been
partly to prevent their passing on any atomic secrets to either of our
other two allies, the Russians and the French; partly to forestall any
discussion of the possibility of nuclear weapons until we had completed and used our own; and partly, perhaps, to save Heisenberg and the
others from the alternative solution to these problems proposed by
one American general, which was simply to shoot them out of hand.

They were detained at Farm Hall for six months, during which time
they were treated not as prisoners but as guests. Hidden microphones,
however, had been installed, and everything they said to each other
was secretly recorded. The existence of the transcripts from these
recordings was kept as secret as that of the prisoners. General Groves,
the head of the Allied bomb programme, quoted from them in his

memoirs (1962), and Goudsmit plainly had access to them, which he drew upon in his book on Alsos, but the British government, perhaps to protect the feelings of the former detainees, some of them now prominent in post-war German science, perhaps merely out of its usual pathological addiction to secrecy, continued to block the release of the papers themselves. Even Margaret Gowing was refused access when she wrote her official history of British atomic policy in 1964, and David Irving was refused again, in spite of strenuous efforts, for *The Virus House* in 1967. The ban was maintained until 1992, when the government finally gave way to a combined appeal from leading scientists and historians.

The German originals are lost, and the translation was plainly done under pressure, with little feeling for colloquial nuance, but the transcripts are direct evidence of what Heisenberg and the others thought when they were talking, as they believed, among themselves. The ten detainees represented a wide range of different attitudes. They ranged from Walther Gerlach, the Nazi government's administrator of nuclear research, and Kurt Diebner, who had been a member of the Nazi party, to Max von Laue, who had been openly hostile to the regime, who had never worked on the atomic programme, and whose inclusion in the party seems on the face of it mysterious. Their conversations over the six-month period reflect a similarly wide range of attitudes and feelings. The general tone is pretty much what one might expect from any group of academics deprived of their liberty without explanation and cooped up together. There is, as one might suppose, quite a lot of complaining, scheming, and mutual friction.

One thing, though, seems to me to emerge quite clearly: for all practical purposes German thinking had stopped at a reactor, and there had been no eagerness at all to look beyond this to the possibility of weapons. Their shocked comments in the moment of unguarded horror that followed the announcement of Hiroshima are particularly revealing. The internees had been given the news by their (almost) endlessly sympathetic and urbane gaoler-cum-host, Major Rittner, at dinner-time, but Heisenberg had not believed it until he had heard it with his own ears on the BBC nine o'clock news. 'They were completely stunned', reported Rittner, 'when they realised that the news was genuine. They were left alone on the assumption that they would discuss the position . . .'

'I was absolutely convinced', says Heisenberg, in the conversation that followed, 'of the possibility of our making an uranium engine [reactor] but I never thought that we would make a bomb and at the bottom of my heart I was really glad that it was to be an engine and not a bomb. I must admit that.' Weizsäcker says that he doesn't think that they should make excuses now for failing, 'but we must admit that we didn't want to succeed'. Gerlach: 'One cannot say in front of an Englishman that we didn't try hard enough. They were our ene- mies, although we sabotaged the war. There are some things that one knows and one can discuss together but that one cannot discuss in the presence of Englishmen.'

In a letter written fourteen years later von Laue complained that, during their conversations at table in the following weeks, 'the version was developed that the German atomic physicists really had not want- ed the atomic bomb, either because it was impossible to achieve it dur- ing the expected duration of the war or because they simply did not want to have it at all.' Von Laue's account of the elaboration of this sanitised 'version' (*Lesart* in German) has been seized upon by unsym- pathetic commentators, and contrasted with the encouraging prospects for atomic weapons that some of the physicists had undoubtedly held out to the Nazi authorities at various times during the earlier part of the war.

Well, we all reorganise our recollections, consciously or unconscious- ly, as time goes by, to fit our changed perceptions of a situation, and no doubt Heisenberg and his fellow detainees did the same. But Bernstein locates the origins of the *Lesart* in those immediate reactions to the announcement of Hiroshima on the nine o'clock news. If this is so then I can only say that the team began to get their story together with quite remarkable spontaneity, speed, presence of mind, and common pur- pose. If they all thought as fast as this, and co-operated as closely, it's even more surprising that they didn't get further with the bomb.

To me, I have to say, those immediate and unprepared reactions sug- gest quite strongly that the first part of Powers's thesis, at any rate, is right, and that there *had* been the fatal lack of zeal that he diagnosed.

Perhaps Gerlach's claim, unchallenged by the others, that they had actually 'sabotaged the war' suggests at the very least a consciousness that quite a lot of stones had been left unturned.

But do the transcripts support Powers's contention that Heisenberg 'cooked up a plausible method of estimating critical mass which gave an answer in tons', and that he 'well knew how to make a bomb with far less, but kept the knowledge to himself'?

One preliminary point needs to be cleared out of the way first: the question of whether Heisenberg understood an even more fundamental point, the difference between a reactor (which is operated by slow neutrons in natural uranium, or some other mixture of $U238$ and $U235$) and a bomb (which functions with fast neutrons in pure $U235$ or plutonium). Goudsmit, who plainly had access to the transcripts when he wrote his book on Alsos, seems to have thought they supported his view that Heisenberg didn't. Before the transcripts were published Rose shared Goudsmit's dismissive view.

But, according to the transcripts, what Heisenberg tells Hahn that same night, when Gerlach has retired to sob in his room, and they are finally alone together, is that 'I always knew it could be done with 235 with fast neutrons. That's why 235 only [presumably = 'only 235'] can be used as an explosive. One can never make an explosive with slow neutrons, not even with the heavy water machine [the German reactor], as then the neutrons only go with thermal speed, with the result that the reaction is so slow that the thing explodes sooner, before the reaction is complete.'

Bernstein (unlike Goudsmit) reads this and what follows as showing that Heisenberg *did* understand the difference between a reactor and a bomb, 'but that he did not understand either one very well – certainly not the bomb'. Rose now seems to accept that Heisenberg's remarks do indicate that he realised the bomb would have to be fissioned with fast neutrons (though he shows that in the past Heisenberg had been toying with the idea of some kind of vast exploding reactor).*

---

* Bernstein takes the trouble to explain in his book what few other commentators do – the difference between slow and fast neutrons: 'By definition, slow neutrons move with speeds of the order of a few kilometers a second, about the speeds that

This same conversation between Heisenberg and Hahn, when they were alone together on that terrible night, seems to me also to resolve the question of Heisenberg's understanding of the critical mass beyond any reasonable doubt. He takes Hahn through what he believes to be the relevant calculation and tells him that the answer is 'about a ton'. I can't see any earthly reason why he should be rehearsing a fabricated calculation or a fabricated answer at this stage, in a private conversation with someone he seems to have trusted, after the German team are out of the race and in custody, and after someone else has in any case already built the bomb. If he had had the right calculation and the right answer up his sleeve all the time, now would surely have been the moment to produce them. I find it much more plausible that he was telling the simple truth when he said to Hahn just before this that 'quite honestly I have never worked it out as I never believed one could get pure 235'.

Earlier on in the evening, it's true, when everyone was present during the conversation immediately after the news bulletin, Hahn says to Heisenberg: 'But tell me why you used to tell me that one needed fifty kilograms of 235 in order to do anything.' (To which Heisenberg replies that he wouldn't like to commit himself for the moment.) This does seem to suggest that he *had* made a calculation of some sort earlier, as von Ardenne claimed – though it also surely destroys once and for all the improbable proposition that Hahn had been involved in it, or had made some kind of estimate of his own. Perhaps Heisenberg had made not so much a calculation as some kind of guess or estimate. Even if it *was* a serious calculation, it seems most unlikely that it was the right calculation, or that it was one he had adhered to.

This is made clear to me (at last) by Jeremy Bernstein. I should explain that when I first read the Farm Hall transcripts, before I wrote the play, I was using the bare uncommented text published in Britain, unaware that there was also a completely different edition published in the US, incorporating Bernstein's detailed commentary. After the play was produced and published he was kind enough to send me it,

---

molecules at room temperature move in a gas. That is why these neutrons are also referred to as thermal. Fast neutrons, the kind that are emitted in many nuclear processes, move at speeds of tens of thousands of kilometers a second.

and it illuminated a great many matters that I had not understood before. These are after all scientists talking to scientists, and they are reported verbatim with all the ellipses of spoken conversation, and with a further haze cast over the proceedings by translation. Bernstein is both a distinguished journalist and a professor of physics, and he has a long acquaintance with the history of atomic research. (He recalls being given the bare plutonium core of a bomb to hold on the Nevada test site in 1957; 'it was slightly warm to the touch, since plutonium is marginally radioactive'.) He has a thorough understanding of the scientific issues involved, and is the ideal guide to the physics – though a slightly less percipient one, I think, to the psychology of the physicists.

I'm pleased to discover for a start that he takes the same view of Heisenberg's admission to Hahn about never having worked out the critical mass. He believes that it has to be taken at its face value, and he asks how it can be reconciled with the figure of 50 kg recalled by Hahn. He demonstrates that when Heisenberg attempts to do the calculation for Hahn he 'gets it wrong at every level' – he does the arithmetic wrong, and is in any case doing the wrong arithmetic. 'Knowing how scientists work,' says Bernstein, 'I find it implausible that he ever did the calculation correctly before. One can imagine even a Heisenberg forgetting a number – he was, in any case, not very good with numbers – but it is very difficult to imagine his forgetting a general method of calculation, a method that once led him to a more reasonable answer.'

The calculation of the critical mass is not the only thing that Heisenberg got wrong that night. Even when he revealed to Hahn that he understood how the critical mass could be reduced by the use of a reflective shield he suggested a material, carbon, that would have had the opposite effect to the one intended. Carbon is a good moderator for a reactor, and Heisenberg's proposing it for the 'tamper' in a bomb, says Bernstein, 'shows he was thinking like a reactor physicist, which, for the last two years, he was'.

These were of course Heisenberg's first thoughts off the top of his head in the wake of Hiroshima. A week later, with the help of what few details the newspapers had given of the two bombs, Heisenberg offered all his fellow-internees a lecture in which he presented a complete and considered account of how the Allies had done it. The inclusion in the lecture of quite fundamental matters, argues Powers, together with the questions which his hearers asked, makes it clear that it was all news to everyone present except his closest associates. 'What the Farm Hall transcripts show unmistakably', he says, 'is that Heisenberg did not explain basic bomb physics to the man in charge of the German bomb program [Gerlach] until after the war was over.' They 'offer strong evidence that Heisenberg never explained fast fission to Gerlach'. At the end of the lecture, says Powers, 'the German scientists, given a second chance, would have been ready to start building a bomb.'

Bernstein sees the lecture very differently. He demonstrates that Heisenberg's exposition is still marred by quite fundamental misconceptions. Heisenberg now seems to have 'the first inkling' of how to calculate the critical mass (though he still does the arithmetic wrong), but is not much nearer to the practicalities of building a bomb than his audience. What the novelty of a lot of this material suggests to Bernstein is simply that communications between the different sections of the German project were very poor.

As a non-scientist I can't offer any opinion on the physics. To my eyes, I have to say, Heisenberg does seem to have come a remarkably long way in a week – if, that is, he was starting more or less from scratch. And he surely must have been. It's really not plausible that he hadn't recollected more by this time if he actually had done the work. The conclusion seems to me inescapable: he hadn't done the calculation. If he had kept the fatal knowledge of how small the critical mass would be from anyone, as Powers argues, then it was from himself.

In the end, it seems to me, your judgement of Heisenberg comes down to what you make of his failure to attempt that fundamental calculation. Does it suggest incompetence or arrogance, as his detractors have claimed? It's possible. Even great scientists – and Bernstein agrees that Heisenberg was one of them – make mistakes, and fail to see possibilities that lesser men pick up; Heisenberg accepted that he had made a mistake in the formulation of uncertainty itself. And I think we have to accept Bernstein's judgement that, although he was the first person to be able to grasp the counter-intuitive abstraction of quantum mechanics, he was not so good at the practicalities of commonsense estimates and working arithmetic.

Or does the failure suggest something rather different? An unconscious reluctance to challenge the comforting and convenient assumption that the thing was not a practical possibility? Comforting and convenient, that is, if what he was trying to do was *not* to build a bomb. Is it all part of a general pattern of reluctance, as the first and more plausible part of Powers's thesis suggests? If so, you might wonder whether this reluctance was a state definite enough to be susceptible of explanation. Heisenberg was trapped in a seamless circle which explains itself: he didn't try the calculation because he didn't think it was worth doing – he didn't think it was worth doing because he didn't try it. The oddity, the phenomenon that requires explaining, is not this non-occurrence but its opposite – the escape of Frisch and Peierls from that same circle. It seems almost like a random quantum event; in which case, of course, it is no more explainable than its not happening.

After the war, certainly, Heisenberg was not just passively reluctant about any military application of nuclear power, but very actively so. In the 1950s, when there was a proposal to arm Federal Germany with nuclear weapons, he joined forces with Weizsäcker and others to fight a vigorous campaign that entirely and permanently defeated it.

There is also one small piece of evidence about his attitude during the war that Powers rather curiously doesn't comment on: the question of the cyclotron.

At the crucial meeting between Heisenberg and Speer in 1942, which seems finally to have scuppered all possibility of a German bomb, Heisenberg is reported to have emphasised the need to build a cyclotron. A cyclotron could have been used, as the cyclotrons in America were, for isotope separation, the great sticking-point in the German programme. In the account of this meeting in his memoirs Speer says: 'Difficulties were compounded, Heisenberg explained, by the fact that Europe possessed only one cyclotron, and that of minimal capacity. Moreover, it was located in Paris and because of the need for secrecy could not be used to full advantage.' Powers mentions this, but does not go on to the obvious corollary: that if Speer's recollection is accurate, then Heisenberg was plainly lying, because he knew perfectly well that there was a second cyclotron to hand – at Bohr's institute in Copenhagen. This would suggest that his apparent anxiety to lay his hands on a machine that might actually separate some U235 was not quite what it seemed. Or, at the very least, that he placed Germany's war aims below his desire to protect Bohr's institute.

Perhaps Speer is simply wrong. It seems uncharacteristic of Heisenberg to have risked such a blatant falsehood, and he makes no mention of it in his own accounts of the meeting. All the same, when he went back to Copenhagen in 1944, after Bohr had fled, to adjudicate a German proposal to strip the institute of all its equipment, presumably including the cyclotron, he seems to have contrived to leave it even then still in Danish hands.

One of the forms of indeterminacy touched upon in the play is the indeterminacy of human memory, or at any rate the indeterminability of the historical record. There are various examples which I left out, for fear of making the play even more tangled than it is. Some, such as the difficulties about the amazingly realistic figure for the critical mass that von Ardenne recollected being given by Heisenberg and Hahn in 1941, I have already mentioned in this Postscript (see above, p. 59). There were others. A minor one concerns whether there were two ships sent to load the Jews of Copenhagen for deportation, as some witnesses recall, or a single one (named as the *Wartheland*). A more significant point of dispute is the drawing which Heisenberg did or didn't make for Bohr during their meeting in 1941.

According to Hans Bethe, who was one of the team at Los Alamos, Heisenberg drew a rough sketch to show Bohr the work that was being done in Germany. Bohr evidently took it to Los Alamos with him when he went, because Bethe (and others) recall it being passed around at a meeting there. Bethe told Powers that Bohr believed it represented a bomb; but the consensus of opinion at the meeting was that it was a reactor. However, Aage Bohr, Niels's son, a physicist himself (and another Nobel prizewinner), who was with his father in

Copenhagen during Heisenberg's visit, and with him again in Los Alamos, was absolutely insistent that there was no drawing.

If the story is true it might help to explain Goudsmit's insistence, in the teeth of the evidence from Farm Hall, that Heisenberg couldn't tell the difference between a reactor and a bomb. It would certainly cast doubt on Heisenberg's recollection that the entire discussion with Bohr in 1941 took place during the walk, and that Bohr broke off the conversation almost as soon as it was broached. It seems improbable to me that Heisenberg would have risked putting anything down on paper, and if even so he had then I can't see why he didn't seize upon it after the war, to support his claim that he had hinted to Bohr at the German research on a bomb. I suppose it's possible that Bohr made the sketch himself, to illustrate to his colleagues at Los Alamos what he thought Heisenberg was getting at, but the truth of the matter seems to be irretrievable.

I have had many helping hands with this play, both before it was produced in London and since. Sir John Maddox kindly read the text for me, and so did Professor Balázs L. Gyorffy, Professor of Physics at Bristol University, who made a number of corrections and suggestions. I am also indebted to Finn Aaserud, the Director of the Niels Bohr Archive in Copenhagen, and to his colleagues there, for much help and encouragement. Many scientists and other specialists have written to me after seeing the play on the stage. They have mostly been extraordinarily generous and supportive, but some of them have put me right on details of the science, for which I am particularly grateful. They also pointed out two mathematical errors so egregious that the lines in question didn't make sense from one end to the other – even to me, when I re-read them. All these points have now been addressed, though I'm sure that other mistakes will emerge. So much new material has come to hand, in one way or another, that I have extensively overhauled and extended this Postscript to coincide with the production of the play in New York.

One matter of dispute that I have not been able to resolve completely concerns the part played by Max Born in the introduction of quantum mechanics. The matter was raised (with exemplary temperance) by his son, Gustav Born, who was concerned about the injustice he felt I had done to his father's memory. I was reluctant to make the play any more complex than it is, but I have since made adjustments both to the play itself and to this Postscript which go at any rate some way to meeting Professor Born's case. We are still at odds over one line, though, in which Heisenberg is said to have 'invented quantum mechanics'. I am quoting the judgement of other physicists here (including one not especially sympathetic to Heisenberg), but I realise that it is a huge over-simplification, and that it seems to compound the original injustice committed when Heisenberg was awarded the Nobel Prize in 1932 'for the creation of quantum mechanics', while Born had to wait another twenty-two years to have his part acknowledged in the same way. The trouble is that I have not yet been able to think of another way of putting it briefly enough to work in spoken dialogue.

The American physicist Spencer Weart, in a letter to Finn Aaserud, very cogently pointed out that the calculation of the critical mass was much harder than I've made it seem for Heisenberg once Bohr has suggested it to him. 'Perrin failed to get it and his publication of a ton-size critical mass subtly misled everyone else, then Bohr and Wheeler failed, Kurchatov failed, Chadwick failed, all the other Germans and Russians and French and British and Americans missed it, even the greatest of them all for such problems, Fermi, tried but missed, everyone except Peierls . . . Physics is hard.'

Some correspondents have objected to Heisenberg's line about the physicists who built the Allied bomb, 'Did a single one of them stop to think, even for one brief moment, about what they were doing?', on the grounds that it is unjust to Leo Szilard. It's true that in March 1945 Szilard began a campaign to persuade the US government not to use the bomb. A committee was set up – the Committee on Social and Political Implications – to allow the scientists working on the project to voice their feelings, and Szilard also circulated a petition among the scientists, sixty-seven of whom signed it, which mentioned 'moral considerations', though it did not specify what exactly these were.

But the main stated reasons for Szilard's second thoughts were not to do with the effects that the bomb would have on the Japanese – he was worried about the ones it would have on the Allies. He thought (presciently) that the actual use of the bomb on Japan would precipitate an atomic arms race between the United States and the Soviet Union. The committee's report (which Szilard himself seems to have written) and the petition stressed the same points. By this time, in any case, the bomb was almost ready. It had been Szilard who urged the nuclear programme in the first place, and at no point, so far as I know, while he worked for it (on plutonium production) did he ever suggest any hesitation about pursuing either the research or the actual manufacture of the bomb.

I think the line stands, in spite of Szilard's afterthoughts. The scientists had already presented their government with the bomb, and it is the question of whether the German scientists were ready or not to do likewise that is at issue in the play. If Heisenberg's team *had* built a bomb, I don't think they would have recovered very much moral credit by asking Hitler to be kind enough not to drop it on anyone – particularly if their objection had been the strain it might place upon post-war relations among the Axis powers.

One looming imponderable remains. *If* Heisenberg had made the calculation, and *if* the resulting reduction in the scale of the problem had somehow generated a real eagerness in both the Nazi authorities and the scientists, could the Germans have built a bomb? Frank believes that they could not have done it before the war in Europe was over – 'even the Americans, with substantial industrial and scientific advantage, and the important assistance from Britain and from ex-Germans in Britain did not achieve that (VE-Day, 8 May 1945, Trinity test, Alamogordo, 6 July 1945).' Speer (who as armaments minister would presumably have had to carry the programme out) suggests in his memoirs that it might have been possible to do it by 1945, if the Germans had shelved all their other weapons projects, then two paragraphs later more cautiously changes his estimate to 1947; but of course he needs to justify his failure to pursue the possibility. Powers makes the point that, whatever the timetable was, its start date could have been much earlier. Atomic energy in Germany, he argues, attracted the interest of the authorities from the first day of the war. 'The United States, beginning in June 1942, took just over three years to do the job, and the Soviet Union succeeded in four. If a serious effort to develop a bomb had commenced in mid-1940, one might have been tested in 1943, well before the Allied bomber offensive had destroyed German industry.'

If this 'serious effort' had begun only after Heisenberg's visit to Copenhagen, as the play suggests might have happened if the conversation with Bohr had gone differently, then even this timetable wouldn't have produced a bomb until late 1944 – and by that time it was of course much less likely that German industry could have delivered. In any case, formidable difficulties remained to be overcome. The German team were hugely frustrated by their inability to find a successful technique for isolating $U235$ in any appreciable quantity, even though the experimental method, using Clusius-Dickel tubes, was of German origin. They could have tried one of the processes used successfully by the Allies, gaseous diffusion. This was another German invention, developed in Berlin by Gustav Hertz, but Hertz had lost his job because his uncle was Jewish. (It was, incidentally, the delays in getting the various American isotope-separation plants to function which meant that the Allied bomb was not ready in time for use against Germany.)

The failure to separate $U235$ also held up the reactor programme, and therefore the prospect of producing plutonium, because they could not separate enough of it even for the purposes of enrichment (increasing the $U235$ content of natural uranium), so that it was harder to get the reactor to go critical. The construction of the reactor was further delayed because Walther Bothe's team at Heidelberg estimated the neutron absorption rates of graphite wrongly, which obliged the designers to use heavy water as a moderator instead. The only source of heavy water was a plant in Norway, which was forced to close after a series of attacks by Norwegian parachutists attached to Special Operations Executive, American bombers, and the Norwegian Resistance. Though perhaps, if a crash programme had been instituted from the first day of the war, enough heavy water might have been accumulated before the attacks were mounted.

If, if, if . . . The line of ifs is a long one. It remains just possible, though. The effects of real enthusiasm and real determination are incalculable. In the realm of the just possible they are sometimes decisive.

SOURCES

Anyone interested enough in any of these questions to want to sidestep the fiction and look at the historical record should certainly begin with:

Thomas Powers, *Heisenberg's War* (Knopf 1993; Cape 1993)
David Cassidy, *Uncertainty: The Life and Science of Werner Heisenberg* (W. H. Freeman 1992)
Abraham Pais, *Niels Bohr's Times* (Oxford University Press 1991). Pais is a fellow nuclear physicist, who knew Bohr personally, and this, in its highly eccentric way, is a classic of biography, even though Pais has not much more sense of narrative than I have of physics, and the book is organised more like a scientific report than the story of someone's life. But then Bohr notoriously had no sense of narrative, either. One of the tasks his assistants had was to take him to the cinema and explain the plot to him afterwards.
Werner Heisenberg, *Physics and Beyond* (Harper & Row 1971). In German, *Der Teil und das Ganze*. His memoirs.
Jeremy Bernstein, *Hitler's Uranium Club, the Secret Recordings at Farm Hall,* introduced by David Cassidy (American Institute of Physics, Woodbury, New York, 1996). Or the British edition of the transcripts: *Operation Epsilon, the Farm Hall Transcripts*, introduced by Sir Charles Frank (Institute of Physics Publishing 1993).

ALSO RELEVANT
Werner Heisenberg, *Physics and Philosophy* (Penguin 1958)
Niels Bohr, *The Philosophical Writings of Niels Bohr* (Oxbow Press, Connecticut 1987)
Elizabeth Heisenberg, *Inner Exile* (Birkhauser 1984). In German, *Das politische Leben eines Unpolitischen*. Defensive in tone, but revealing about the kind of anguish her husband tended to conceal from the world; and the source for Heisenberg's ride home in 1945.
David Irving, *The German Atomic Bomb* (Simon & Schuster 1968). In the UK, *The Virus House* (Collins 1967). The story of the German bomb programme.
Paul Lawrence Rose, *Heisenberg and the Nazi Atomic Bomb Project* (University of California Press 1998)
Records and Documents Relating to the Third Reich, II: German Atomic Research, Microfilms DJ29–32 (EP Microform Ltd, Wakefield). Irving's research materials for his book, including long verbatim interviews with Heisenberg and others. The only consultable copy I could track down was in the library of the Ministry of Defence, London.
Archive for the History of Quantum Physics, microfilm. Includes the complete correspondence of Heisenberg and Bohr. A copy is available for reference in the Science Museum Library, London. Bohr's side of the correspondence is almost entirely in Danish, Heisenberg's in German apart from one letter.

73

Leni Yahil, *The Rescue of Danish Jewry* (Jewish Publication Society of America, Philadelphia 1969)

There are also many interesting sidelights on life at the Bohr Institute in its golden years in French & Kennedy, eds: *Niels Bohr, A Centenary Volume* (Harvard 1985), and in the memoirs of Hendrik Casimir, George Gamow, Otto Frisch, Otto Hahn, Rudolf Peierls, and Victor Weisskopf.

For the subsequent challenges to the Copenhagen Interpretation:

David Deutsch, *The Fabric of Reality* (Allen Lane 1997)

Murray Gell-Mann, *The Quark and the Jaguar* (W. H. Freeman 1994; Little, Brown 1994)

Roger Penrose, *The Emperor's New Mind* (Oxford University Press 1989)

The actual 'two-slits' experiment was carried out by Dürr, Nonn, and Rempe at the University of Konstanz, and is reported in *Nature* (3 September, 1998). There is an accessible introduction to the work in the same issue by Peter Knight, and another account of it by Mark Buchanan (boldly entitled 'An end to uncertainty') in *New Scientist* (6 March, 1999).

Post-postscript

I made a number of changes to the text of the play, as I have explained above, in response to suggestions and criticisms I received during the run of the play in London, and to new material I came across. The production in New York, however, opened up a much broader and more fundamental debate. A number of commentators expressed misgivings about the whole enterprise. Paul Lawrence Rose, the most outspoken of the play's critics, even managed to detect in it a 'subtle revisionism . . . more destructive than Irving's self-evidently ridiculous assertions – more destructive of the integrity of art, of science, and of history'.

One of the most frequent complaints about the play in America was that I should have laid more stress on the evils of the Nazi regime, and in particular upon the Holocaust; it was pointed out that Heisenberg's visit to Copenhagen in 1941 coincided with the Wannsee Conference. It was argued that I should have put the visit in the context of a number of subsequent trips he made during the course of the war to other occupied countries. It was also felt that I should have laid more stress than I did on Heisenberg's stated view that Germany's conquests, at any rate in Eastern Europe, were justified, and that her victory over Russia was to be welcomed.

With hindsight I think I accept some of these criticisms. I should perhaps have had Heisenberg justify Germany's war aims on the Eastern Front direct, instead of having Bohr refer to his arguments in one angry but passing aside. I should perhaps have found some way to make the parallel with all the other trips that were found offensive, and about whose purpose there was none of the mystery which had seemed to attach to the one to Copenhagen.

About a greater stress on the evil of the Nazi regime I'm not so sure. I thought that this was too well understood to need pointing out. It is after all the *given* of the play; this was precisely why there was (or should have been) a problem facing Heisenberg, and us in understanding him. In any case the play returns to the persecution of Jews in Nazi Germany again and again, from the suppression of so-called 'Jewish physics' (relativity) to the enforced flight of all the Jewish physicists, the death of Goudsmit's parents in Auschwitz, and the attempt by the SS to deport the Jewish population of Denmark to the death camps, which Margrethe Bohr describes as 'that great darkness inside the human soul . . . flooding out to engulf us all'.

Some of the criticisms were even more radical. The play turns on the difficulty of determining why Heisenberg made his trip. For a number of commentators there was no problem at all – they knew the correct explanation for certain; though what that explanation was varied from one to another. For some it was Heisenberg's desire to persuade Bohr of the rightness of Germany's war aims and of its inevitable victory; for Rose and others he was on a spying mission, to find out through Bohr if the Allies were also working on an atomic bomb.

I agree that Heisenberg may have wished to present the German case to Bohr; but he surely didn't go all the way to Copenhagen *just* to do that. I also agree about the spying. But then so does my Heisenberg. He tells Bohr that he wanted 'some hint, some clue' about whether there was an Allied nuclear programme. This seems to me to be commonsense; he would have had to be insanely incurious not to seize any chance he could to find out whether the Allies might drop atomic bombs on his country. There is surely no contradiction at all with what he himself claimed his purpose was – to discuss whether the German team were justified in working on a German weapon. Any information he could get about the other side's intentions would have been a prerequisite for deciding what to do.

Some criticisms I reject, and I should like to put the record straight. Professor Rose suggested that I had 'fantasised' Heisenberg's fear that he was in danger of his life from the Gestapo for talking to Bohr. Not so – I was simply expanding upon what the real Heisenberg said. Jonothan Logan, a physicist writing in *American Scientist*, dismissed as misleading the fictitious Bohr's assertion that in June 1942 Heisenberg had been slightly ahead of Fermi in Chicago. The context makes plain that this was in terms of neutron multiplication, and the claim was based on what David Cassidy says in his biography of Heisenberg. The correctness of Cassidy's assessment was verified for me, after much enquiry on my part, by Al Wattenberg, one of the editors of Fermi's *Collected Papers*.

All these are at any rate debatable points. Other criticisms I found extremely difficult to make sense of – some even to credit. Professor Rose, who detected the subtle revisionism of the play, found a particularly sinister significance in one detail – the fictitious Heisenberg's remarking upon the neatness of the historical irony whereby the crucial calculation (of the critical mass), which persuaded the Allies of the possibility of building a nuclear weapon, was made by a German and an Austrian, driven into exile in Britain because they were Jewish. This Professor Rose saw as an attempt to blame 'the Jews' for the bomb's invention.

A little more extraordinary still was the view of the play taken by Gerald Holton, Professor of Physics and Professor of the History of Science Emeritus at Harvard. He saw it as being 'structured in good part' to reflect the thesis advanced by Powers, that Heisenberg had correctly calculated the critical mass, but concealed it by 'cooking up' a false result. By the time the play was produced in New York, he believed, I had been forced (by Bernstein) to lay this idea aside, so that I now had an 'unsolvable problem' with the motivation of the play.

I can only suppose that Professor Holton was misled because in the

Postscript I speak warmly and gratefully about Powers's book. It has been much attacked, but I continue to admire the generosity of its tone, and the range of Powers's research. I also agree with the first part of his thesis (lack of zeal). But then so does Holton himself, and so, he says, does everyone else who has studied the matter. In the Postscript, however, I make abundantly clear that I don't accept Powers's view about the 'cooking up' and never did.

But you don't even need to read the Postscript to discover this, because it's all over the play itself. The central argument turns on Heisenberg's confession to Otto Hahn that he had *not* attempted the calculation. By my count there are something like thirty-five speeches devoted to establishing this, to asking why he hadn't attempted it, and to suggesting what might have happened if he had. How anyone could give the play even the most cursory glance and fail to notice this is difficult to understand.

Even harder to credit was the reaction in some quarters to the 'strange new quantum ethics' proposed by the fictitious Heisenberg. I suppose I should have erected a flashing 'IRONY' sign in front of it. The allusion is to his insight, in his original introduction of quantum mechanics, that physics should be limited to the measurement of what we could actually observe – the external effects of events inside the atom. We should need a similar kind of ethics, he suggests in my play, if we judged people purely on the external effects of their actions, without regard to their intentions. According to Professor Holton, Heisenberg 'exults' that under the new dispensation there would be a place in heaven even for him. Professor Holton fails to mention that Heisenberg also 'exults' that, under the new quantum ethical rules, there would also be a place in heaven for the SS man who seemed ready to murder him in 1945, simply because in the end he settled for a pack of American cigarettes instead. Jonothan Logan manages to believe that I am seriously proposing even the SS man's assumption into heaven.

Let me make it absolutely unambiguous: my Heisenberg is saying that we *do* have to make assessments of intention in judging people's actions. (The epistemology of intention is what the play is about!) He is saying that Bohr will continue to inspire respect and love, in spite of his involvement in the building of the Hiroshima and Nagasaki bombs; and that he himself will continue to be regarded with distrust in spite of his failure to kill anyone. The reaction of Holton, Rose, and others to the play is perhaps an oblique testimony to the truth of this judgement.

One of the most striking comments on the play was made by Jochen Heisenberg, Werner Heisenberg's son, when I met him, to my considerable alarm, after the premiere of the play in New York. 'Of course, your Heisenberg is nothing like my father,' he told me. 'I never saw my father express emotion about anything except music. But I understand that the characters in a play have to be rather more forthcoming than that.'

This seems to me a chastening reminder of the difficulties of representing a real person in fiction, but a profoundly sensible indication of the purpose in attempting it, which is surely to make explicit the ideas and feelings that never quite get expressed in the confusing onrush of life, and to bring out the underlying structure of events. I take it that the nineteenth-century German playwright Friedrich Hebbel was making a similar point when he uttered his great dictum (one that every playwright ought to have in pokerwork over his desk): 'In a good play everyone is right.' I assume he means by this not that the audience is invited to approve of everyone's actions, but that everyone should be allowed the freedom and eloquence to make the most convincing case that he can for himself. Whether or not this is a universal rule of playwriting it must surely apply to this particular play, where a central argument is about our inability, in our observation of both the physical world and the mental, ever to escape from particular viewpoints.

I suppose that this is what sticks in some people's throats – that my Heisenberg is allowed to make a case for himself – even to criticise others. His claims about his intentions are strongly contested by another character in the play, Margrethe Bohr. Neither Heisenberg nor Margrethe Bohr, so far as I can see, is presented as winning the argument. I don't see why my Margrethe shouldn't be allowed to express her suspicions of Heisenberg much more sharply and woundingly than the real Margrethe's habitual courtesy would ever have permitted, and

I don't see why my Heisenberg shouldn't be free to express the deeper feelings that the real Heisenberg remained silent about. Why shouldn't he have the same conflicting loyalties and the same mixed motives and emotions that we all have? Why shouldn't he try to juggle principle and expediency, as we all do? Why shouldn't he fear his country's defeat, and its destruction by nuclear weapons? Why shouldn't he lament its ruin and the slaughter of its citizens?

I can imagine it being asked how far I think this principle should be carried. Do I believe that a fictitious Hitler should be accorded the same privileges? I can see all the problems of exhibiting Hitler on the stage, but I can't see any point in attempting it at all if he is to be simply an effigy for ritual humiliation. Why should we be asked to endure a representation of his presence if he doesn't offer us some understanding of what was going on inside his head from his own point of view? The audience can surely be trusted to draw its own moral conclusions.

The most surprising result of the debate set off by the production of the play, though, has been the release of the Bohr documents.

I was told privately about the existence of at any rate one of the documents at a symposium on the play organised in Copenhagen by the Niels Bohr Archive in the autumn of 1999. Heisenberg had made public his own version of the 1941 meeting with Bohr, chiefly in two places: a memorandum written in 1957 to Robert Jungk, who was preparing the material for *Brighter than a Thousand Suns*, and his memoirs, published in 1969. Bohr, however, had never publicly given his side of the story, and historians had been obliged to rely upon what other people (chiefly his son Aage – also a physicist, and later a Nobel prizewinner himself – and his colleague Stefan Rozental) recalled him as saying about it.

In 1957, however, Bohr had apparently been so angered by Heisenberg's version, when he read it in Jungk's book, that he had written to Heisenberg dissenting, and giving his own account. He had never sent the letter, though, and at his death in 1962 it had been placed in the Archive by his family, not to be released for another fifty years. This was all my informant was prepared to tell me.

I said nothing about this because I believed that I had been told in confidence. The existence of the letter was first publicly mentioned, so far as I know, by Professor Holton, at a further symposium on the play organised in New York in March 2000 on the occasion of its production there. He said that he had actually seen the letter – he had been shown it by the Bohr family. He felt bound not to divulge its contents, but I recall him as promising that when it was finally made public, in 2012, it would entirely change our view of the meeting.

Now the cat was out of the bag, and at yet another symposium on the play, at the Niels Bohr Archive in September 2001, it was announced that the Bohr family had decided to release the letter early. It also turned out that there was not just the one letter but various alternative drafts and notes relating to it. When they were finally published on the web in February 2002 (http://www.nba.nbi.dk/papers/introduction/htm) the whole question of the visit was accorded wider attention in the press than ever before.

The documents seem to me to bear out remarkably well the very detailed reconstruction made of Bohr's attitude by Powers from other sources. The most surprising thing to me in Bohr's first attempt at the letter is its remarkably sharp tone – particularly coming from a man so celebrated for his conciliatoriness:

> I think that I owe it to you to tell you that I am greatly amazed to see how much your memory has deceived you . . .
>
> Personally, I remember every word of our conversations, which took place on a background of extreme sorrow and tension for us here in Denmark. In particular, it made a strong impression both on Margrethe and me, and on everyone at the Institute that the two of you spoke to, that you and Weizsäcker expressed your definite conviction that Germany would win and that it was therefore quite foolish for us to maintain the hope of a different outcome of the war and to be reticent as regards all German offers of co-operation. I also remember quite clearly our conversation in my room at the Institute, where in vague terms you spoke in a manner that could only give me the firm impression that, under your leadership, everything was being done in Germany to develop atomic weapons and that you said

that there was no need to talk about details since you were completely familiar with them and had spent the past two years working more or less exclusively on such preparations. I listened to this without speaking since [a] great matter for mankind was at issue in which, despite our personal friendship, we had to be regarded as representatives of two sides engaged in mortal combat.

It is a revelation to have all this in Bohr's own voice, and I wish it had been available when I wrote the play. I recognise that the real Bohr remained much angrier for much longer than my character, that he claimed to have paid much closer attention to what Heisenberg said, and that he claimed to recall it much more clearly.

Does it really modify our view of what Heisenberg said, though, and of what his intentions were?

Slightly, I think, but not fundamentally. There has never been any disagreement, for a start, that Heisenberg publicly told various people at the institute that Germany was going to win the war, and that her aims, at any rate in the East, were justified. Then again, Aage and Rozental were both already on record as recalling Bohr's saying that Heisenberg had talked about the military applications of atomic energy. According to Aage: 'My father was very reticent and expressed his scepticism because of the great technical difficulties that had to be overcome, but he had the impression that Heisenberg thought that the new possibilities could decide the outcome of the war if the war dragged on.' According to Rozental: 'I can only remember how excited Bohr was after that conversation and that he quoted Heisenberg for having said something like, "You must understand that if l am taking part in the project then it is in the firm belief that it can be done."'

The letter, however, is the first direct confirmation that Bohr believed he was being urged to accept German 'offers of co-operation', which is what Weizsäcker suspected he may have understood Heisenberg to be suggesting. It's not clear from the letter what Bohr thought this 'co-operation' would entail, and the recollection may not be entirely at odds with what Weizsäcker recalls Heisenberg as telling Bohr – that he ought to establish contact with the staff of the German Embassy for his own safety.

Some of the differences between Bohr's account of the meeting and Heisenberg's are less clear-cut than Bohr's indignation makes them appear. According to Heisenberg, in his memorandum to Jungk, he told Bohr he knew that the use of uranium fission for making weapons was 'in principle possible, but it would require a terrific technical effort, which one can only hope cannot be realised in this war'. Bohr, he said, was shocked, 'obviously assuming that I had intended to convey to him that Germany had made great progress in the direction of manufacturing atomic weapons'. This is not all that different in substance, it seems to me, from what Bohr recalls.

The same is true when Bohr goes on to dispute Heisenberg's interpretation of his reaction:

> That my silence and gravity, as you write in the letter, could be taken as an expression of shock at your reports that it was possible to make an atomic bomb is a quite peculiar misunderstanding, which must be due to the great tension in your own mind. From the day three years earlier when I realised that slow neutrons could only cause fission in Uranium 235 and not 238, it was of course obvious to me that a bomb with certain effect could be produced by separating the uraniums . . . If anything in my behaviour could be interpreted as shock, it did not derive from such reports but rather from the news, as I had to understand it, that Germany was participating vigorously in a race to be the first with atomic weapons.

The difference between the 'shock' that Heisenberg diagnosed and the more dignified 'silence and gravity' that Bohr himself recalled dissolves a little in a later draft of the letter, where Bohr refers to his reaction as 'alarm'. His assertion that he already understood about the possibility of producing a weapon based on fission is moreover a simplification which is not quite supported by his subsequent behaviour. He had in fact up to that moment believed that it was a practical impossibility, because of the difficulty of separating the fissile U235, and Heisenberg could not tell him why the balance of probability had now changed – because of the German team's realisation that a reactor, if they could get one going, would produce plutonium as an alternative. After Heisenberg's visit, according to Rozental, he was sufficiently shaken by Heisenberg's confidence to go back to the blackboard and rework all his calculations. Even so he seems to have remained unconvinced when he got his guarded report on the meeting through to Chadwick, his contact with British Intelligence, and said: 'Above all I have to the best of my judgement convinced myself that in spite of all future prospects any immediate use of the latest marvellous discoveries of atomic physics is impracticable.'

The real kernel of the apparent disagreement about the meeting emerges only in later drafts of the letter, where Bohr says that 'there was no hint on your part that efforts were being made by German physicists to prevent such an application of atomic science'. This appears to be a rebuttal of some claim made by Heisenberg. The belief that Heisenberg made some such claim seems to be widespread. Professor Holton suggests that my play is 'based in large part on Heisenberg's published claim that for him an impeding moral compunction may have existed about working on atomic energy'.

But nowhere, so far as I know, did Heisenberg ever make the claim that Bohr seems to have attributed to him. There is no mention of it in the memorandum to Jungk. Even in the expanded account of the meeting that he gave in his memoirs he remained extremely cautious: 'I hinted that . . . physicists ought perhaps to ask themselves whether they should work in this field at all . . . An enormous technical effort was needed. Now this, to me, was so important precisely because it gave physicists the possibility of deciding whether or not the construction of atom bombs should be attempted. They could either advise their governments that atom bombs would come too late for use in the present war, and that work on them therefore detracted from the war effort, or else contend that, with the utmost exertions, it might just be possible to bring them into the conflict. Both views could be put forward with equal conviction . . .'

One might think this sounds a quite implausibly judicious rendering of anything he might have said. The fact remains, however, that he is not claiming to have made any efforts to prevent work on weapons. He is not even claiming that up to this point the German team had exercised the option of offering discouraging advice, only that they might at some point if they so chose. In any case, Heisenberg says that Bohr 'was so horrified by the very possibility of producing atomic weapons that he did not follow the rest of my remarks'.

Some reports on the release of the documents have suggested that they refute a claim made by Heisenberg to have offered Bohr a 'deal', whereby the German physicists would discourage their government from proceeding with nuclear weapons if Allied physicists would do likewise. I suppose the implication of Heisenberg's indeterminate phrase 'the physicists' is that this applied to the physicists on both sides, but the only evidence I can find for Heisenberg having made any more definite suggestion than this is in a part of the memorandum to Jungk which is quoted by Powers: 'I then asked Bohr once again if, because of the obvious moral concerns, it would be possible for all physicists to agree among themselves that one should not even attempt work on atomic bombs . . .' This might perhaps be interpreted as a tentative hint at some possible arrangment, though in the interview he gave to David Irving for *The Virus House* in 1965 he seems to be retreating even from this, and says merely that Bohr 'perhaps sensed that I should prefer it if physicists in the whole world would say: We will not make atom bombs.' The remark to Jungk was not quoted by him in his book, and so presumably not seen by Bohr in 1957. In his letter, in any case, Bohr makes no reference to any such claim, or to having understood any such offer at the time.

There are discrepancies in every other aspect of the evidence relating to this meeting, and it is scarcely surprising that there are some to be found between the two participants' own accounts. In both cases they are attempting to recollect something that happened sixteen years earlier, and their perceptions are inevitably coloured by strong feelings and conflicting loyalties. On the whole, I think, it's surprising how slight the differences of substance are, and how readily most of them can be understood in the circumstances.

The most remarkable point of agreement, it seems to me now that I have had time to reflect upon it, was missed by everyone who wrote about the letters at the time of their release, myself included: Bohr's confirmation of Heisenberg's claim to have overriden all normal obligations of secrecy. Heisenberg did indicate to him, he agrees, that there was a German atomic programme; that he himself was involved in it; and that he now believed it in principle possible to build atomic weapons.

Whatever Heisenberg was officially licensed or ordered to do in Copenhagen, I cannot believe that it included revealing the existence of one of the most secret research programmes in Germany – least of all to an enemy alien who was known to be in contact with Allied scientists (Bohr was at this point still contributing to the US journal *The Physical Review*), and also to be under observation because of his hostile attitude to Nazism and his extensive help for its victims. Heisenberg must have done this of his own initiative, and he must have been aware that Bohr would pass the information on, if he possibly could, to his contacts in Britain or the US. This, it seems to me, goes a considerable way to supporting the account that Heisenberg subsequently gave of his intentions.

The only really clear-cut disagreement between the two accounts is about a circumstantial detail – where the meeting took place. Bohr talks about 'our conversation in my room at the Institute'. Heisenberg, on the other hand, recalls in his memoirs visiting the Bohrs' home in Carlsberg, and finally broaching 'the dangerous subject' on their evening walk. This version is reinforced by what he recalls of his attempt to reconstruct with Bohr the 1941 meeting when he returned to Copenhagen in 1947. He was convinced, he said, that the conversation had taken place during 'a nocturnal walk on Pile Allé', which is very close to Carlsberg, and four kilometres away from the institute. (Bohr at the time, according to Heisenberg, thought it had been in his study – but in his study at home in Carlsberg.)

Bohr himself lends some colour to the Carlsberg version by a remark in the letter that 'every word of our conversations . . . made a strong impression both on Margrethe and me'. It seems highly unlikely that Margrethe would have been present at any of the various meetings in the institute; I don't think that any of the other participants mention her. Jochen Heisenberg recalls his father showing him the street where he said he had walked with Niels Bohr in 1941, though he can't now remember the name of it, only that it was tree-lined (which Pile Allé is).

There is a secondhand account of the meeting given to Thomas Powers by Ruth Nanda Anshen, Heisenberg's American editor, who said that she was told it by Bohr, and that his assistant Aage Petersen confirmed it. According to Powers, in *Heisenberg's War*, Bohr told Anshen that 'the invitation had cost him much agony – he wanted to sit down to dinner with Heisenberg, but his wife, Margrethe, object-ed, and Bohr couldn't make up his mind what to do. Finally his assis-tant Aage Petersen suggested that Bohr should write down his objections to Heisenberg's visit, then read them carefully a day or two later, and decide. This Bohr did; the old friendship seemed to him stronger than the objections, and he told his New York friend that he finally obtained Margrethe's agreement with a solemn promise to dis-cuss only physics with Heisenberg – not politics.'

On the other hand Abraham Pais, Bohr's biographer, after making enquiries among Bohr's surviving colleagues just before his own death in 2000, concluded that Heisenberg had never been to the Bohrs' home. Even Heisenberg's own testimony is not entirely consistent. According to his biographer, David Cassidy, he made an earlier state-ment in which he 'remembered that his most important talk with Bohr occurred one evening as they strolled along a tree-lined path in the large and secluded Faelledpark, just behind Bohr's institute'. Weizsäcker, who recalled that he met Heisenberg only ten minutes after the meeting with Bohr was over (the two men had parted com-pany, he said, 'in a friendly way', but Heisenberg had immediately told him: 'I'm afraid it's gone completely wrong'), agreed that it had taken place in the open air, but introduced another location altogether – Langlinie, the raised walk beside the harbour, miles from either Carlsberg or the institute.

Some light on this question has now been cast, nine months after the release of the Bohr documents, by the emergence of yet another letter. This one was written by Heisenberg, and revealed by Dr Helmut

Rechenberg, the director of the Werner Heisenberg Archive in Göttingen. The Heisenberg family, who seem not to have taken in its implications earlier, have now published it.*

It makes no direct reference to the disputed conversation itself, but is a much more reliable guide to the circumstances surrounding it than the accounts we have had so far, because it was written not sixteen years after the event but during the week that Heisenberg was actually there. In fact it's in three sections, dated respectively to three different evenings – Tuesday (September 16, the day after he arrived), Thursday, and Saturday – and it was posted to his family in Leipzig as soon as he got back to Berlin.

It clears up one small point of dispute completely. Heisenberg *did* go to the house – and more than once. He also records various visits to the institute, and the sheer number and variety of meetings that the two men had during the week supports the claim that Heisenberg's chief reason for making the trip was to see Bohr. The conflation of the different occasions in the participants' memories also probably explains some of the later discrepancies.

The first visit to the Bohrs was late on the Monday evening, as soon as Heisenberg had got off the train from Berlin. The sky, he recorded, was clear and starry, but in the Bohrs' house he found rather darker weather. 'The conversation swiftly turned to the human questions and misfortunes of our time; about the human ones there was spontaneous agreement; on the political questions I found it difficult to cope with the fact that even in a man like Bohr thoughts, feelings, and hatred cannot be completely separated.'

It's just possible that the fateful conversation occurred at this first meeting, either in the house – where, said Heisenberg, 'later I sat for a long time alone with Bohr' – or later still, after midnight, when Bohr saw him to the tram. But they were accompanied to the tram-stop by Hans, one of Bohr's sons, who would surely have remembered it and remarked upon it if it had happened then. And if Weizsäcker's recollection is even remotely accurate then the conversation can't have

---

* In *Liebe Eltern! Briefe aus kritischer Zeit, 1918 bis 1945* (ed. Anna Maria Hirsch-Heisenberg, 2003), and posted on the Internet, in both German and English, at http://werner-heisenberg.unh.edu.

occurred at any point during this first meeting, because he himself arrived in Copenhagen only on the Wednesday.

The most likely occasion was two days later, during Heisenberg's second visit, on the Wednesday evening. (This time there was a young Englishwoman present, who 'decently withdrew' during 'the unavoidable political conversations, in which the role of defending our system of course automatically fell upon me'.) Dr Rechenberg suggests plausibly that Bohr accompanied Heisenberg alone part of the way back to his hotel, where Weizsäcker was waiting for him.

The real surprise of the letters, though, is that Heisenberg was invited back to the Bohrs' home for a *third* time, on the Saturday evening, three days after this (and the conversation can't have occurred during this visit, because this time Weizsäcker was accompanying him.) 'It was in many ways particularly nice,' wrote Heisenberg later that same night. 'The conversation turned for a great part of the evening around purely human problems. Bohr read something aloud, I played a Mozart sonata (A major).'

The immediate rupture of the two men's friendship is almost the only aspect of the story which has up to now seemed reasonably unambiguous (I certainly take it for granted in the play). Now even this turns out to be as clouded as everything else.

Rechenberg suggests that it may have been at this farewell meeting that Heisenberg and Weizsäcker urged Bohr to maintain contact with the German Embassy. If so it could have been Bohr's anger at this that coloured his recollection of the earlier conversation. It is in any case clear that the quarrel took the form it did only later, in the recollection of the participants, as they reflected upon it – probably also as the circumstances of the war got worse, as the deepest horrors of the Nazi period were uncovered, and as the actual development of nuclear weapons called into question the two men's participation.

History, in other words, is not what happens when it happens, but what seems to people to have happened when they look back upon it.

I can't help being moved by the picture of Bohr drafting and redrafting his letter over the last five years of his life – and still never sending it. He was famous for his endless redrafting of everything he wrote, and here he was trying not only to satisfy his characteristic concern for the precise nuance, but also to reconcile that with his equally characteristic consideration for Heisenberg's feelings. There is a sad parallel with the account which Professor Hans-Peter Dürr gave, at the Heisenberg Centenary symposium in Bamberg, of Heisenberg's rather similar efforts to understand what had happened.

Professor Dürr, who worked for many years with Heisenberg in Göttingen after the war, said that Heisenberg had contined to love Bohr to the end of his life, and he recalled his going over the fatal meeting again and again, trying to work out what had happened. Professor Dürr offered what seems to me the most plausible commonsense estimate of Heisenberg's intentions that has yet been advanced. He thought that Heisenberg had simply wanted to have a talk. Heisenberg and Bohr had been so close that they could finish each other's sentences, and he assumed that he would have only to hint at what was on his mind for Bohr to grasp the significance of it. What he had entirely failed to grasp was that the situation had changed, and that Bohr's anger about the German occupation would make the old easy communication entirely impossible.

Whatever was said at the meeting, and whatever Heisenberg's intentions were, there is something profoundly characteristic of the difficulties in human relationships, and profoundly painful, in that picture of the two ageing men, one in Copenhagen and one in Göttingen, puzzling for all those long years over the few brief moments that had clouded if not ended their friendship. It's what their shades do in my play, of course. At least in the play they get together to work it out.

(1998–2003)

Democracy

1972 marked the high summer of Willy Brandt's brief but remarkable career as German Chancellor. It was also, as it happened, the year in which I made my first serious visit to Germany, and first became fascinated by it – particularly by its evolution since the Second World War. Perhaps this is why the complex and painful story of Brandt's downfall two years later captured my imagination at the time, and has been lurking at the back of my mind ever since.

Brandt was one of the most attractive public figures of the twentieth century, who won people's trust and love not only in Germany but all over the world. He first became a national and international celebrity in the 1950s, when he was Governing Mayor of West Berlin, and led the city's resistance to the efforts of the Soviet Union to undermine and intimidate it so that it could be absorbed into the East German state surrounding it. After his resignation from the Federal chancellorship in 1974 he won himself a completely new reputation with yet another career as an internationalist and champion of the Third World. His greatest achievements, though, were in Federal politics. The first of them was to help reform his party, the SPD (the Social Democrats), so as to make it electable by the cautiously conservative German voters. The second was single-handedly to seize the chance, when it was at last offered by a modest improvement in the party's share of the vote in 1969, of forming an SPD-led coalition – the first left-of-centre coalition in Germany, with the first left-of-centre Chancellor, since Hitler had crushed parliamentary democracy in the early thirties. His real triumph, though, was the use to which he put the power he had gained:

to secure what had hitherto seemed a politically impossible goal – a reconciliation with Germany's former enemies in Eastern Europe.

The difficulty was that this could be done only by at last recognising the painful realities created by the outcome of the war. One of these was the loss of nearly a quarter of Germany's territory in the east. The other was the existence within the remaining German lands of the second state that had grown out of the Soviet zone of occupation – the German Democratic Republic, alien in its political character, bound hand and foot to the Soviet instead of the Western power block, and sealed off behind closed frontiers that sundered all natural family and social connections. There was entrenched and embittered opposition to accepting either fact, particularly from those most directly involved – the eight million Germans who had been expelled from the former German territories east of the Oder and Neisse rivers, which had now been divided up between the Soviet Union and Poland, plus the four million who had fled from East Germany, and the millions more who had relatives still trapped there. But Brandt succeeded in doing it, and succeeded totally. The consequences of this reconciliation reached far beyond Germany. They changed the face of Europe, and of the world, by making possible the gradual scaling down of the Cold War – and thereby, eventually, an event that Brandt never foresaw: the end of the very state whose existence he had recognised, followed by the collapse of the entire Soviet empire.

In the summer of 1972, when I arrived in Germany, Brandt's government was in the middle of this great work. In spite of the severe difficulties it was encountering at home because of its small and steadily vanishing majority in the Bundestag, it was already ratifying the treaties it had negotiated with the Soviet Union and Poland. I can't say that I paid very much attention to these triumphs at the time. Federal politics happened in Bonn, and Germany for me that summer was Berlin, the once great city I had come to Germany to write about, now only notionally the capital, left marvellous but functionless deep inside East Germany, like a luxury liner that had somehow become beached in the sandy wastes of the Mark Brandenburg.

The city compelled the imagination in all kinds of ways. Its greatest fascination, though, was undoubtedly its greatest monstrosity – the

Wall, the hideous concrete barrier, enforced by armed guards and a complex series of lethal mantraps, that the East German government had been forced to erect in 1961 to stop the massive haemorrhage of its citizens to the West. Another much longer wall, from the Baltic to Thuringia, divided the German Democratic Republic from West Germany proper, but the Berlin Wall obtruded more on the consciousness because it closed in the Western half of the city as tightly as the fence round a suburban garden. Wherever you went you came face to face with it barring the street you were in, and defining the geography of Berlin even more sharply than the Hudson river does the geography of New York.

Somewhere out of sight behind it that summer Egon Bahr and Michael Kohl, the representatives of the Federal and Democratic German Republics respectively, were negotiating the terms of the Basic Treaty by which the West was at last to recognise the East, and by which relations between the two states were at last to be given some semblance of normality. Already a new agreement on Berlin itself, signed by the four former allies, was for the first time making it possible for West Berliners to visit the Eastern half of their city. Friends of mine came back to the modern wonderland of West Berlin stunned by the different kind of wonderland that they had found on the other side of the Wall: cobbled streets, unlit villages, pockmarked tenements, snorting steam-trains – the long-lost old Germany of the Weimar Republic and the Third Reich, magically preserved in all its nostalgic dullness and shabbiness, as if in some vast grey heritage park, by the conservatism of the Communists and the backwardness of their economy.

The existence of this other Germany, and the endless puzzle of its relations with the Federal Republic, was part of what made modern German politics the most interesting in Europe. How even to refer to it officially without seeming to acknowledge that it was a separate state? The right-wing press stuck with 'the Soviet Zone', or even simply 'the Zone', long after it had acquired a government of its own. The usual official euphemism was 'the other part of Germany'. Kiesinger, Brandt's predecessor as Chancellor, described it as not a state but a 'phenomenon'. Brandt was prepared to concede that it was a state, but refused to see it as a foreign one. As he famously said, in the statement of his new government's policies in 1969: 'Even if two states exist in Germany they are not foreign to each other; their relations to each other can only be of a special sort.'

Whatever West Germans called it, there were endless practical difficulties in coping with a hostile next-door neighbour that was obsessed with spying on every aspect of life, not only internally but externally – particularly since all its fifteen million citizens were potential agents because they spoke exactly the same language – and since a further four million of them were inside the gates already. What could such close cousins, who found themselves upon such different paths in life, make of each other? How would they behave as their relationship began to change?

The complexities of the situation were made painfully personal in the story of Willy Brandt and Günter Guillaume. Guillaume, who had crossed over from East Berlin thirteen years earlier, joined the Chancellor's office as a junior aide within weeks of Brandt's election in 1969. For the next four years he served Brandt with devotion and efficiency, and rose to become the personal assistant who organised his travels and accompanied him wherever he went. He was also spying on him, it turned out, with equal devotion and efficiency, on behalf of his employers in the East German Ministry of State Security, and his arrest in 1974 precipitated Brandt's resignation.

Exactly why it did, though, is by no means obvious. In his official letter of resignation Brandt said that he assumed political responsibility for negligence in connection with the affair. The security services had indeed committed a catalogue of errors in failing to vet Guillaume properly before his appointment, and in allowing him to continue even after the first serious suspicions had been raised against him. In private some of Brandt's colleagues told him that he was open to blackmail by the East German government, because Guillaume had presumably supplied them with a list of Brandt's extra-marital activities. But historians tend to agree that the unmasking of Guillaume was more the occasion of the Chancellor's downfall than its cause. It took its place among a complex of factors arising from the political situation inside the Federal Republic, from the internal conflicts of the SPD

and its leaders, from Brandt's own character and physical condition –
even from the very success that he had achieved.

Peter Merseburger, Brandt's most recent biographer, mocks sup-
porters of Brandt who detect treachery and see his fall as a kind of
regicide. 'As if, in the respectable republican court at Bonn there had
been Shakespearean dramas, opponents are demonised as Brutus figures who carried daggers under their robes, even as dark Nibelung
warriors who had nothing in mind but to assassinate the Chancellor's
character.' Politics, as Merseburger says, is mostly 'terribly banal', and
the events of 1974 were no exception. Among the banalities, nevertheless, were many strands of powerful personal feeling, of loyalty and
jealousy, of courage and despair. It was really the sheer complexity of
this mixture that finally decided me to write the play. Complexity is
what the play is about: the complexity of human arrangements and of
human beings themselves, and the difficulties that this creates in both
shaping and understanding our actions.

The only part of German history that seems to arouse much interest in
the British is the Nazi period. That brutal holiday from the moral
restraints under which West European societies normally labour pos-
sesses a kind of corrupt glamour for even the most timid and law-
abiding. The half-century that has followed Germany's awakening from
the sick dream is thought to be a time of dull respectability, with the
Federal Republic characterised by nothing much except material prosperity, and formed in the image of the peaceful and provincial Rhineland
town which was the seat of its government for most of the period.

To me, I have to say, that material prosperity, that peacefulness,
even that supposed dullness, represent an achievement which I never
cease to marvel at or be moved by. It's difficult to think of parallels for
such an unlikely political, economic, and moral resurgence. What
other nation, even Japan, has risen so swiftly from beginnings as
abject as the physical ruin, moral degradation, and political paralysis
in which Germany found itself in 1945? Federal Germany began life as
a graveyard in which almost every city had been reduced to rubble,
and almost every institution and political resource contaminated by
complicity in the crimes of National Socialism; yet from this utter des-

olation, without recourse to despotism or military means, its citizens constructed one of the most prosperous, stable, and decent states in Europe, the cornerstone of a peace which has endured now, at least in Western Europe, for nearly sixty years.

The process was greatly assisted, it's true, by some of the consequences of defeat itself. It was in the first place the presence of the occupying armies that probably saved Germany from the revolutions and counter-revolutions by which it was ravaged after the First World War. Then there were the refugees from the East. By 1950 nearly eight million of the twelve forced out of the lost provinces of East Prussia and the Sudetenland flooded into the Western zones of occupation. How the shattered country ever absorbed them beggars the imagination. A further three million arrived over the years, plus another four million from East Germany. This flood of immigrants, though, provided the Federal Republic with the labour it needed to rebuild. Recovery was also helped by Marshall Aid, provided to the Western zones of occupation by America even while the Russians were still pillaging their own zone (though the net value of it, when offset against reparations and occupation costs, has been queried by some historians; and in any case Germany received less of it than Britain and other European countries).

Even the famous currency reform of 1948, which gave birth to the mighty Deutschmark, and which first kicked the moribund economy into life again, was sprung upon Germans not by Ludwig Erhard, their economics minister, as is generally supposed, but by the Americans (and hijacked by Erhard in a spectacular double double-cross which would provide the material for another play). The currency reform also precipitated the splitting of the nation, because the Soviet Union refused to accept the Deutschmark in its zone of occupation. But this, too, had its positive effects for West Germany, because it marked a further step in the division of the entire world into two competing empires, whose confrontation in the ensuing Cold War swiftly transformed America's defeated enemy into its crucial front-line ally.

German politicians were reluctant to endorse the dismemberment of their nation, and the concept of West Germany as a separate political entity seems to have originated once again with the Americans (according to Dean Acheson, it was first proposed by the US Military Governor, General Lucius Clay). The new state even acquired the constitution that has served it so well ever since (more properly called the Basic Law, so as not to imply any constitutional acceptance of the country's division) only because it was instructed by the occupying powers to compose one.

In the end, though, the success of the new state was created by the efforts of its own citizens – by the sheer hard labour of its workers, by the crafts that were lying dormant in people's fingertips and the professional and entrepreneurial skills in their brains, by the readiness of so many people to put the public good at least as high as their own personal profit – and by the political skills of the leaders it found. The Basic Law was signed into effect, and the first Federal election held, in 1949, but there was already a complex political landscape in place: the *Länder*, the patchwork of provinces that make up the German nation (eleven of them at the time), together with their governments. Their heterogeneity reflects the very different characters and histories of the various German states that were assembled to compose Imperial Germany in 1871, and the combination of their individual politics with their participation in the Federal politics of Bonn created the characteristic complexity of modern Germany.

Since that first election in 1949, which brought the wily Konrad Adenauer to power, the Federal Government has gone through many crises and scandals. It has survived many revelations that its members or officers had been implicated in the crimes of the past, or were working for East German Intelligence, and many alarms when the nationalistic right seemed to be resurgent, or when the electorate seemed to be still nostalgic for past glories. In the last decade the longed-for reunification with the Eastern *Länder* has plunged the nation into its most severe and prolonged difficulties yet. But the Federal Republic has worked. It has proved stable and moderate. It has even survived its dependence upon coalition as a way of life – something which appears unworkable to British and American eyes, which has caused endemic weakness in France and Italy – and which indeed destroyed the Weimar Republic and opened the door to Hitler. Every West German government since the Federal Republic was founded has been a coalition, usually between the CDU/CSU (the conservative alliance formed by the Christian Democratic Union of the northern *Länder* and the Christian Social Union of Bavaria) on the one hand and the tiny FDP, the Free Democratic Party (aka the Liberals), on the other.

In 1966, though, coalition politics reached its bizarre apotheosis in the so-called Grand Coalition, when the junior partner of the CDU/CSU became not the FDP but the SPD, their principal antagonist, hitherto apparently doomed to serve as the permanent opposition. Willy Brandt was bounced into the arrangement against his wishes by his colleagues Herbert Wehner and Helmut Schmidt, because the plane bringing him from Berlin to the crucial meeting was delayed by fog. But, once again, the arrangement worked. Brandt himself, with his charm, his fluency in other languages, and his impeccable political past, made a natural Foreign Minister. And although he loathed Georg Kiesinger, the CDU Chancellor and a former member of the Nazi Party, to the point where he claimed to feel physically ill in his presence, the Coalition lasted for three years, and is regarded by some commentators as one of the most successful governments in the history of the Federal Republic.

The elections in the autumn of 1969 transformed the politics of coalition once again. Although it still trailed the Christian Democrats, the SPD picked up enough seats to raise the possibility of securing a slim majority in the Bundestag by going into coalition with the FDP. Wehner and Schmidt were against it; they wanted to continue with the existing arrangement. With entirely uncharacteristic decisiveness Brandt seized his chance. Wehner and Schmidt had bounced him into the Grand Coalition; now he bounced them out of it. Without a word to either of them he went on television on election night and announced that he would seek to form a new government with the FDP. He succeeded, and three weeks later the new Bundestag elected him Chancellor.

Which is where my play begins.

Two mutually contradictory developments had conspired to bring the SPD and the electorate somewhat closer together. The first was the change in the nature of the party that had begun at its conference in Bad Godesberg ten years earlier, when Brandt, Wehner, and Schmidt had persuaded it to dump its residual Marxism in favour of the so-called social market economy. The second was the change in the nature of the electorate brought about by the events on the streets of Germany in the previous year.

The 'student movement' of 1968 swept right the way across Europe and the US. But it began the year before in Berlin. The trigger was a demonstration against a visit by the Shah of Iran, and its heavy-handed suppression by the police, during which they shot and killed a student called Benno Ohnesorg. The wave of demonstrations, strikes, and sit-ins that ensued all over the world was like the long-stored energy released in an earthquake. It came from a huge idealism that had found little outlet in the cautious compromises of parliamentary democracy. In Germany there were two additional causes of frustration. One was the new generation's realisation that the apparently solid fabric of German society rested upon foundations built out of the rubble of its National Socialist past, and which were by unspoken common consent not to be inspected too closely. The second was the extreme expression of the consensuality of post-war German politics in the Grand Coalition, which left all the functions of an opposition to the tiny, impotent, and far from radical FDP.

So the radical left had constituted itself as an informal 'extra-parliamentary opposition'. This chaotic grouping was, needless to say, far more disparate than any official coalition could ever be, and it was the spectacular array of its fission products that caught my eye when I arrived in Berlin in 1972. Some of its factions were rigidly subservient to the SED (the 'Socialist Unity Party' which ruled East Germany), some of them were Maoist, some of them nostalgic throwbacks to the KPD, the old Communist Party of the Weimar years, some of them engaged in increasingly brutal terrorism. A wide range of idealistic lifestyles and business enterprises had sprung up in the city, a kaleidoscope of 'left-oriented' communes, of pubs and cafes selling drinks and hot cakes at 'comrades' prices'.

The movement produced a sympathetic shift to the left among many voters who were never part of it. A number of its most active and effective adherents, in any case, decided to pursue their battle within the framework of practical politics. They proclaimed 'the long march through the institutions', including the unions and the SPD, with the intention of bringing them under their control by constitutional means. All this helped to earn the Party the small increase in its vote in 1969 (3.4 per cent) that put it within reach of real power. The pressures it produced inside the Party, though, and the expectations that the Party's success aroused in its new adherents, created great difficulties for Brandt. It also produced a backlash among voters, particularly since left extremists in the Baader-Meinhof group, now reconstituted as the Red Army Faction, had taken to robbing banks and murdering judges. Brandt's proposal to encourage yet another manifestion of the left by offering concessions to Soviet Communism and by recognising its client regime in East Germany became even more alarming than it had been before. He had to find ways of reassuring people. One attempt was the proclamation of the so-called 'Radicals Edict' of January 1972, more usually known abroad as the *Berufsverbot* ('bar to the professions'), designed to exclude radicals from teaching and other public services. If Brandt's greatest achievement was the Ostpolitik (and the Deutschlandpolitik, as the part of it relating to *Deutsch-Deutsche* relations was more properly called), then his greatest mistake – or so he said himself – was this reactionary domestic counterpoise to it.

All politics is necessarily complex, since its essence is the practical resolution of differences of interest and outlook which are in principle irreconcilable. All human beings, too, are complex – but Brandt (like German politics) was perhaps more complex than most. He was certainly more complex than he seemed. In public there was something engagingly open and straightforward about him, even when he was at his most devious – something recognisably decent and human, to which many people in many different parts of the world responded. Even the new leftists were charmed by him. Even the personal assistant who was spying on him. His associates, though, often complained about the weaknesses he showed in private: his indecisiveness, his avoidance of confrontation, his uncommunicativeness, his proneness to depression, and his vanity. He made many conquests, but had few real friends. He extended a personal intimacy to a hall full of people, but not to many individuals taken on their own.

He *did* it, though; he achieved his great goal. This is the most difficult thing of all to understand about him. He performed that one single act that makes its mark upon the world, that defines and validates
a life, and that eludes almost everybody.

With this play as with an earlier one of mine, *Copenhagen*, the question arises as to how much of it is fact and how much of it fiction. The
division there, it seemed to me, was reasonably clear, since the characters were all shades returning from beyond the grave – and in any case
almost every aspect of the real event that they were discussing was
open to dispute. Even so I found myself being solemnly asked by prob-
ing interviewers if audiences might not be misled into thinking they
were watching 'the truth'.

This play is open to more reasonable objections. The characters are
all shown as being alive, the events in which they are participating as
unfolding in the present tense. Very few of the words that these characters speak, however, were ever actually spoken by their real counterparts. What the feelings and ideas of those counterparts were, and
whether the feelings and ideas expressed by my characters have anything in common with them, is a matter of interpretation and conjec-
ture. The events themselves, and the world in which they take place,
are hugely over-simplified. Any librarian should unhesitatingly file the
play under fiction.

But, for anyone who is interested, this fiction does takes its rise
from the historical record. All the political events referred to are real
ones: the trips to Erfurt and Warsaw, the vanishing majority and the
no-confidence vote, the triumph in the 1972 election and the gathering difficulties that followed it. The personalities of the protagonists
are very much those attributed to their real counterparts by observers
and historians. Brandt's drinking and womanising are not in dispute,
nor are his 'feverish colds' and his taste for jokes. (Almost all the jokes
that Brandt makes in the play are taken from a written collection he
assembled.*) All the circumstances of his childhood that Brandt
recalls, and all his adventures when he was operating underground in

---

* For the reference to this and all other books mentioned in the Postscript, see the
list of sources on p. 120.

the thirties for the Socialist Workers' Party, are taken from his memoirs and the standard biographies. The picture of life in the Palais Schaumburg, where the Federal Chancellor's office was housed, comes from various recorded accounts. So does that of life aboard the special train (which was indeed built for Reichsmarschall Goering, and which you can see now preserved in the historical musum in Bonn).

Two of the murkier topics touched upon in the play are factual. The first is the bribery that perhaps saved Brandt in the no-confidence vote. The truth about this began to come to light a year later, in the summer of 1973, when a CDU deputy called Julius Steiner confessed to having received fifty thousand marks for withholding his vote against Brandt. He claimed that the money had come from Karl Wienand, the business manager of the Parliamentary SPD, who notoriously assisted Herbert Wehner in many of the shadier dealings on behalf of the Party for which Wehner enjoyed taking the credit. The money came from the Stasi, the East German Ministry of State Security.* Or so it is claimed in his memoirs by Markus Wolf, the legendary head of the Stasi's foreign intelligence service ('Mischa' to his colleagues, and said to be the model for John le Carré's Karla), and the allegation was accepted by the court that tried him in 1994, though Wienand, for what it's worth, denied it. The name of a second Christian Democrat deputy has since come to light in the Stasi files.

The other topic is the Federal Republic's secret ransoming of the Democratic Republic's political prisoners, and the equally secret payments it made to have people allowed out of East Germany to rejoin their families in the West. The DDR† carried on this cynical extortion at arm's length, through an East German lawyer called Wolfgang Vogel. When I stumbled across the trade in 1972 I was begged by officials of Amnesty International not to refer to it in the articles I was

---

* More properly the MfS, the *Ministerium für Staatssicherheit*, which was responsible both for internal surveillance and for the foreign intelligence service. The latter, the HVA, the *Hauptverwaltung Aufklärung* (Chief Reconnaissance Directive), was the arm controlling Guillaume.

† Often known in English as the GDR, but this seems as awkward to me as it would be if in German the USA became the VSA.

writing, for fear of jeopardising it. The income was so vast that it covered something like twenty per cent of the DDR's chronic balance-of-payments deficit in 'inter-German' trade. According to Vogel's own records, between 1964, when the trade started, and 1989, when the Wall came down, the Federal Republic bought out 33,755 prisoners and 215,019 people to be reunited with their families, at a total cost of 3,436 million Deutschmarks.

The most fictitious-looking aspect of the play is the role played by Günter Guillaume. Once again, though, I have followed the outline of the story fairly closely. His career in the Chancellor's office did begin almost simultaneously with Brandt's own. The doubts that were raised about his background were dismissed much as described in the play. Brandt did repeatedly ask his chief of staff Horst Ehmke (and later Günter Grabert, Ehmke's successor) to replace him; but somehow instead he did indeed get promoted from one position to another until, at the start of the 1972 election campaign, he took over as Brandt's personal assistant, with access to his files and in charge of organising the Chancellor's special train. On the train journeys he also accompanied Brandt as his valet, among other things, and was in charge of all his communications with Bonn and the rest of the world.

There are plenty of photographs of him, because he's in a lot of the pictures that were taken of Brandt. He's at the side of the room, or in the background, or walking a few paces behind the Chancellor, his hands folded respectfully behind his back, a dull, cosy, chubby figure in horn-rimmed spectacles and polite smile. He was known for his endless capacity for work and his equally endless good humour. He was always described as *kumpelhaft* (matey), a characteristic that was thought to be typically *berlinisch*. According to *Die Zeit*, he 'never lost the fried-food smell of the Berlin *Hinterhof*'. A lot of the journalists around the Chancellor's office seem to have appreciated his easy-going chumminess. Brandt didn't; he found him servile. In some ways he was a kind of dim reflection of Brandt himself, with the same taste for the good life, and the same eye for women. Wibke Bruhns, a brilliant journalist on *Der Stern*, and one of the women with whom Brandt was said to have been involved, wrote memorably of Guillaume that he was 'nothing . . . a servant – not a person but a part of the place. You'd find him there just as you'd find a chair in the room.' Marianne Wichert-Quoirin, a local journalist who had known Guillaume at the time, described him to me as quite visibly the type of man that the DDR sent over – slightly old-fashioned and formal, given to wearing suits and buying flowers for ladies and helping them on with their coats.

His job as Brandt's assistant was a demanding one. The working day ended only when he laid out the last batch of papers on Brandt's night-table, and began again when he collected them first thing next morning, marked up with Brandt's annotations in green pencil. His few hours off each day must have been largely taken up with copying or photographing documents for his other employer. His home life was bleak. Wibke Bruhns caught the anonymity of the apartment where he and his wife Christel lived with her observation that it was furnished with the kind of potted plants that people give as presents; 'no one likes them, but no one throws them away.' Christel (somewhat too loud, sharp-tongued, and rather charmless, according to Bruhns) was also a spy, and had been seen by their employers as the star until Günter had been so unexpectedly catapulted into the Chancellor's office. Their marriage was on the rocks. His only consolations were good lunches and dinners with his controller, an undetermined number of extra-marital liaisons, his teenage son Pierre, and the great secret that he nursed.

Apart from a conviction for drunken driving in 1972, there seems to be only one moment recorded when he showed any sign of the strain that he must have been living under. This was on a trip he made with Brandt in the following year to the South of France. Brandt was informed later, according to his memoirs, that Guillaume had fallen asleep after he had been drinking, and dropped a notebook out of his pocket. When the security men accompanying the Chancellor thoughtfully tried to put it back, Guillaume awoke and mumbled: 'You swine! You won't catch me, though!'

There were evidently more Günter Guillaumes than the two who played out their simultaneous parts in the Palais Schaumburg. When he finally appeared in court, the summer after his arrest, a number of journalists noted the change in his manner and appearance. *Der Spiegel* decided that he had been underestimated. The new Guillaume, said the magazine, was visibly endowed with 'judgement, vitality and willpower'. He radiated an extraordinarily direct and intense warmth that made his successes with women understandable. And in a long television interview he gave much later, after he had been released from prison and returned to the DDR, he has changed once again. It's difficult to make any connection between the pudgy little man in Bonn and the slim, bearded figure on the television screen, whose alert dryness and sharp tongue suggest the retired senior administrator rather than the willing dogsbody.

All the aspects of the surveillance on Guillaume which seem hardest to credit come from the record. Brandt was indeed informed of the suspicions against his assistant and sworn to silence. He was indeed encouraged to take Guillaume off to Norway with him as his only assistant, because Wilke and his deputy Schilling had holiday arrangements of their own, and Guillaume was indeed allowed to handle all the teleprinter traffic between Norway and Bonn, unchecked and unobserved. Guillaume and his wife did indeed throw a party for all the security staff. Also taken from the record is the even more farcical confusion between 'the second son' and 'the second man', and the belatedness of its resolution.

About other details I have to sound a note of caution. The ticking of an unseen insect in the rafters of the Palais Schaumburg* and various other colourful touches are certainly taken from a published source. But the source in this case is Guillaume's own memoirs – and these have to be treated with a great deal of reserve.

They were ghosted, and first published in 1988 in the DDR – not for sale to the public but 'for official use only' (by the East German security services) – then reissued in the Federal Republic two years later. Markus Wolf, in *his* memoirs (also, of course, to be treated with circumspection), says that Guillaume's book was 'written in part to rub

---

* Guillaume calls it a woodworm, but I'm informed by experts on infestation that if it knocked or ticked it must have been a death-watch beetle.

in the embarrassment of the affair to Bonn (after careful combing and adaptation by my service as disinformation – to protect other sources – and as positive PR for our work and its necessity) . . .'

Guillaume's book is curiously engaging, in spite of (or perhaps because of) its dubious provenance. But, some time between the collapse of the DDR in 1989 and his death in 1995, he gave a long interview to the journalist Guido Knopp, who was preparing a television programme about him, in which he cast even further doubt on it as a source. The ghost, he says, was 'a very nice journalist' supplied by the Stasi, who encouraged him to improve his stories somewhat. One of them, which had always puzzled me, about a meeting Guillaume claimed to have had in the Picasso Museum in Vallauris with 'a high-ranking man' in the intelligence service – presumably Wolf himself – he now disavowed completely. He also confessed to having built up the story of persuading Bauhaus to take the wrong despatch-box back to Bonn at the end of the holiday in Norway. There were a whole series of boxes, he admitted, not just two, and he hadn't intended any deceit in getting Bauhaus to take one full of left-over souvenirs. I confess in my turn to having kept to Guillaume's first version of the story, for the same reasons as he first told it.

Wolf in his memoirs is rather disparaging about Guillaume and his vanity, and he confesses frankly that he sees the downfall of Brandt through his agent's actitivities as 'the greatest defeat we suffered up to that time . . . equivalent to kicking a football into our own goal'. This may go some way to accounting for another discrepancy between Guillaume's book and the later interview. In the book Guillaume speaks about Wolf with the greatest warmth and respect. In the interview his tone has grown much sharper. 'Herr Wolf', he says, 'shouldn't say things today that were not so. Just because it doesn't suit him in retrospect to accept responsibility. He was very quick to excuse himself before God and the world.'

Guillaume's attitude to his other employer, too, has become a little more critical. In the book he speaks of him with nothing but admiration (and his attitude was remarked upon at the time by Bruhns and others). Now he says that Brandt was not always easy to work with. He would much rather have been personal assistant to Helmut

Schmidt, whom he regards as the Federal Republic's greatest Chancellor.

I have in any case exercised a good deal of licence in other directions, though I think this is in most cases fairly obvious. The continuous contact that my Guillaume has with his controller is plainly a dramatisation of their discrete monthly meetings. The conversations that Guillaume has with Brandt on the train go much further in this direction. In his memoirs Guillaume says that Brandt became another man on his travels. 'Other cities, other faces, other thoughts, other problems – he discovered a new impetus towards them. Suddenly he seemed free and relaxed . . . He became talkative, excited by every good joke . . . En route he tanked up, and I made it my business to give him as much chance as possible to do it.' When there were no election trips in prospect, Guillaume invented the excuse of 'information journeys' instead. He alleges that on their travels together Brandt sometimes called him '*du*', and he felt obliged to return the compliment. Nowhere, though, does he claim that Brandt ever carried this intimacy as far as conversations about his childhood or his personal feelings.

I have extended my licence even further in the case of the holiday in Norway. The two families *were* together, and they did have a certain amount of social contact. The story of the relaxed mushrooming with Bauhaus, and of the games that Matthias and Pierre played together in the woods, come from Guillaume's memoirs. He says he was convinced that Brandt had long since suppressed the memory of the allegations against him – probably because he simply didn't want to spoil the holiday. In the interview with Knopp, however, a rather different picture emerges. Guillaume says that Brandt was unusually silent with him in Norway, partly because they both felt constrained by the presence of their families. (Christel seems to have done most of the talking when they were all together.) It is in any case unlikely that Brandt had forgotten the allegations. Klaus Harpprecht, Brandt's speechwriter, told Knopp that Brandt had made an effort of his own before they left Bonn to get evidence against Guillaume. He had 'touchingly' left threads on his desk overnight, and carefully arranged files and pencils; 'he'd probably read about this in novels when he was a boy.' His attempts in the play to sound Guillaume out while they are in Norway by telling him about his own involvement in underground activities before the war are my purely invented equivalent to the threads and pencils (though what Brandt recalls from those years is based very closely on what he says himself in his memoirs).

I can only say that fact has subsequently outstripped any fiction of mine in sheer implausibility. Brandt's son Matthias, who is said to have played so happily in the Norwegian woods with Guillaume's son Pierre, is now an actor. A German television company has recently produced a dramatised reconstruction of the case, and Matthias has entered the story once again. Playing the part of Günter Guillaume.

Further licence with the narrative: I have made the emergence of the Ostpolitik seem rather more clear-cut than it was. Brandt had already been pursuing a policy of rapprochement with the East as Foreign Minister in the Grand Coalition. The desirability of improving relations with the Soviet Union and its allies was a matter of general agreement; the stumbling-block was the precondition for this – acceptance of the Oder–Neisse frontier and recognition of the DDR. What Brandt says on the subject in the early stages of Act One is based closely upon various speeches he made, but I'm not aware of any occasion where he articulated it as completely as he does here, or where he laid quite as much emphasis on it in a general context. In later years he saw the Ostpolitik as his life's work, and historians agree that it was the core programme and real achievement of his government. But he knew only too well how sensitive the subject was with a large proportion of the voters, and in his declaration of the new government's policy that followed the 1969 election he gave more prominence to security, continuity, and internal reform ('daring more democracy' – a famous phrase said to have been contributed by Günter Grass). There are certain parallels, one might think today, with the British government's handling of entry into the European currency.

No one knows exactly what Brandt, Wehner, and Schmidt said to each other the night before the Chancellor's decision to resign, and it notoriously happened not in Bonn but at a party conference in the resort of Münstereifel; the name has become part of SPD mythology, like Erfurt (where in 1891 the party adopted Marxism), and Bad Godesberg (where in 1959 it abandoned it). I have also shifted some actions from offstage characters to onstage ones. According to Guillaume's memoirs it was not Ehmke who gave Guillaume his promotion to be Peter Reuschenbach's replacement but Reuschenbach himself. Then again, Bauhaus didn't volunteer his information about Guillaume's knowledge of Brandt's womanising to Nollau personally but to his interrogators. The general absence of police and security men from the play is symptomatic of the staff shortages imposed by the economics of drama (both literal and metaphorical). Real politics is a labour-intensive business, and the Bundestag should have been teeming with deputies, the Palais Schaumburg with ministers, advisers, and civil servants – not to mention Germany as a whole with Germans.

For similar reasons I have sacked even a number of the principal protagonists in the story. The dismissal I regret most is that of Egon Bahr. Bahr was Brandt's closest confidant, a former radio journalist who had become his press representative back in the Berlin days. He was Brandt's trusted representative in the gruelling process of negotiating all the Eastern treaties (fifty meetings with the Russians alone). Brandt joked that Bahr didn't even know where France was, but he had a fascination with power politics and a natural bent for secret negotiation. Guillaume called him 'the sly fox', others 'Tricky Egon' (in English, presumably by analogy with the Tricky Dicky who was forced out of the White House three months after Brandt was out of the Palais Schaumburg).

He was an engaging and somewhat eccentric figure, who began his career as a pianist, but who was unable to pursue it in the Nazi period because one of his grandmothers was Jewish. In his retirement he took up one of the oddest hobbies I've ever heard of – travelling around the world with his wife as the only passengers aboard container ships, from one grim depot to another. When Wehner stood up in front of the Party leadership after Brandt's resignation and talked about his love for Brandt's person and politics, Bahr put his hands over his face and wept. (Though it has to be said that this was on camera, and Karl Wienand remarked coldly that he'd seen Bahr weep before.) The dramatic problem is that, while he was away negotiating, his role in Bonn was more or less duplicated by Brandt's other confidant, Horst Ehmke, who coaxed Brandt out of his depressions (and got sidelined for his pains), and who as Brandt's chief of staff was much more closely involved in the events surrounding Guillaume.

Also missing is another confidant of Brandt's, the publisher Klaus Harpprecht, whom Brandt brought into his second government as a speechwriter, and whose diary supplies a lot of the atmosphere in the Palais Schaumburg during those last eighteen months. I also wish I could have found a way of introducing a most remarkable man who made a marginal appearance earlier in *Copenhagen* – Georg Duckwitz. In the 1940s, as the shipping specialist in the German Embassy in Copenhagen, he had warned the Danes exactly when the SS were to begin their round-up of the Jews, which enabled almost all of them to be saved. After the war he went back to Copenhagen as German Ambassador, and was greatly honoured by the Danes, before finishing his career as head of the Eastern Department in the Foreign Office. Brandt was a personal friend, and when he was still Foreign Minister in the Grand Coalition brought him back from retirement, then as Chancellor moved him to his personal staff to work on the Ostpolitik.

The oddest economy of all, one may think, is the exclusion of the entire female sex – particularly since it was Brandt's relations with women that undid him. German parliamentary politics at the time, though, was a man's world; the story of Brandt's government might have been rather different if it hadn't been so closed off from normal demographic reality. There were a few women in the Bundestag (and by the time Helmut Schmidt took office one of them was President of it), but only one in the Cabinet. In general, though, as was often noted, the only women whom German politicians saw during the course of the working week in Bonn were wives, secretaries, and journalists, and there are no women at all who are recorded as playing any significant role in the arguments and struggles that form the background to the play.

Two remarkable women stand on the fringes of it, though, and there are other plays to be written about both of them. One of them is Brandt's wife, Rut. He had been married before during his time in

Norway, and he married for a third time in his late sixties. But for almost the whole of his career his partner was Rut. She was a Norwegian who had been involved in distributing material for the Resistance during the German occupation, and he met her in Stockholm in 1943. She was as attractive and charming as her husband, the kind of wife that every traditional male politician must dream of having at his side, and she behaved with great dignity, generosity, and humour throughout their trials in 1974, and in their later divorce. The account she gives in her memoirs of her escape as a girl from occupied Norway, through the mountains into Sweden, is compelling; so is her description of the devastation and misery that she found in Berlin when she arrived with Willy at the end of the war. By 1974 their marriage seems to have been reduced more or less to a social arrangement, and during the crisis she says that when Brandt was at home he went around 'like a stranger in the house'. He subsequently blamed her (along with Wehner) for his resignation, because she had agreed with him that he should take responsibility for the situation, and had made no attempt to dissuade him.

The other remarkable woman is Guillaume's wife, Christel. She might have been created as Rut's antithesis – cold, charmless, and unapproachable. She was thought by the journalists who met her to be much more intelligent than her husband, and for a long time it was she who had the starring role as a spy, because she had managed to get a job in the Chancellery of Hesse, in Wiesbaden. She must have had to make a painful readjustment when Guillaume leapfrogged over her into the Federal Chancellery and she was ordered to act as his courier – though by the time they were both unmasked she seemed to be about to recover some of the lost ground by getting a job in the Ministry of Defence.

At no point, though, did she have much control over her own destiny. She was not consulted about the Stasi's plan to send her with her husband to the West – merely informed about it and told to keep quiet and co-operate – while her mother, who had Dutch nationality, was used as the lever for getting permission for the three of them to settle in the Federal Republic. She put on a great performance of marital solidarity at their trial, because, she said much later, she didn't want to appear weak. But the marriage had long been dead, and kept in being only because the Stasi required them to be a married couple. Many years later, after the collapse of the DDR, she gave a long and desolating television interview. Her life, she said, had been a series of uprootings. She had been taken out of her own country and dumped in the West to live a life of fiction. Then dumped in prison, where she served over five years of the eight to which she was sentenced, during which time she lost contact with her son Pierre (another victim who could step forward to claim a play about his own story). Then she was dumped back in the DDR, and, as soon as her husband was also exchanged and arrived to join her six months later, dumped by him. Then dumped again, by the collapse of the DDR, in yet another new and alien society. At the end of the interview she sat in silence for some moments, thinking back over it all. '*Ein verpfuschtes Leben*,' she said eventually – 'a botched life'.

There is a third, more shadowy woman missing from the play: Nora Kretschmann, the wife of Guillaume's controller. But then my Arno Kretschmann himself is a simplification of reality. At the beginning of his career in the Federal Chancellery Guillaume had other controllers whom he does not name. In his interview with Guido Knopp, Guillaume says that Kretschmann took over at the time of the election campaign in the autumn of 1972. In his memoirs, though, Guillaume dates his arrival a year earlier, and gives so many circumstantial details that I suspect this version is more likely to be the correct one. Although Kretschmann was younger than him they seem to have hit it off immediately. They had lunch together at their first meeting and found themselves enjoying 'a conversation about God and the world as completely unconstrained as any two men who wanted to spend a stimulating afternoon with beer foam under their noses'. After this he remained controller until the Guillaumes were arrested.

It was proposed for a start that their meetings should take place in a secluded boat-house, but this meant that Guillaume would have to take up sailing, which he thought would be found to sort oddly with his known aversion to sporting activities, and in the end they agreed to meet quite openly in and around Bonn. So openly, in fact, that Kretschmann would occasionally come to the Chancellery and have

Guillaume summoned on the house phone. But usually they met in restaurants and bars, often for convivial evenings with their wives present. Guillaume says that Christel and Nora got on well together, and if this is true then these occasions must have been one of the brighter spots in his wife's bleak life.

The Kretschmanns had been fictionalised long before I got near them. They were a married couple, names unknown, who had been sent separately to the West, as 'Franz Tondera' and 'Sieglinde Fichte', and they had begun by establishing separate and very different cover stories. According to Guillaume in his memoirs, Franz travelled for a well-known firm in the motor industry (he doesn't say which), while Sieglinde, having given up her training as a vet in the DDR, worked on a factory production line with Turkish and Greek women guest-workers. They were then directed to make each other's acquaintance by chance on a ski-ing course, fall in love, conduct a bashful courtship, and get married all over again. So now Sieglinde Fichte of Ulm, otherwise Ursula Behr of Stuttgart, was Sieglinde Tondera of Cologne. Except that the Tonderas for some reason became Arno and Nora Kretschmann (their given names were extracted, according to the *Spiegel*, from a rearrangement of the letters in 'Tondera'.) When the Guillaumes were arrested, the Kretschmanns, in all their shifting avatars, vanished, and even the most diligent searches since the collapse of the DDR in the files of the Stasi, the source of so many revelations about so many people, have so far uncovered no trace of them.

A number of other questions about the case remain unanswered. Exactly what information, for a start, did Guillaume pass on? He preferred to report to his controller orally, and his information – certainly before the election campaign of 1972, when he first had access to documents – came by his own account chiefly from office gossip. Files and notes, Brandt is reported to have said when he gave evidence at the Guillaumes' trial,* were much less important than the insights he

---

* Any account of the case has to rely heavily upon press reports (often remarkably divergent) because in German law there is no such thing as an official transcript of the proceedings, only a summary of the evidence made by the court as part of its judgement.

could have got from informal functions. Various journalists covering the case filled in the likely circumstances. 'Lunch with a minister president, coffee with a city mayor – on such occasions not every word is carefully weighed. What relations do leading politicians have to one another . . . ? When, for example, after a session at a Party conference, Schmidt, Wehner, and Brandt visited a *Weinstube* and went on talking – Guillaume would be at the next table . . . In the car after long sessions of the Party Executive, when Brandt gave vent to "expressions of displeasure", or "characterised" somebody . . . When the SPD chiefs talked over a cup of coffee or – at the end of the day – over something stronger, about who was going to be renominated or not and where . . . He could catch the nuances of what was said, and hear confidential briefings to journalists on matters that might later make the headlines. He knew much more than any state secret – he knew about the moods, connections, and developments that could lead to the decisions taken later.'

As Bahr said in evidence, 'He was always there, but people weren't aware of him.' Wilke recalled him as always wanting to be in on everything, whether it concerned him or not. Guillaume himself said in his interview with Knopp that he couldn't remember what he'd passed on, but agreed that it included everything he could lay his hands on about the negotiations with Moscow and East Berlin. Stephan Konopatzky, a researcher working on the Stasi files now held in a massive archive in Berlin, can find relatively little information credited to XV/19142/ 60 and XV/11694/60, aka Hansen and Heinze, aka Günter and Christel Guillaume – and less still that was regarded as of any great value. He concedes that Guillaume's reports may, because of their importance and sensitivity, have been handled by some special channel as yet unexplored in the archive, but thinks it more likely that he was being used very cautiously to protect his unique position. When one thinks of all those monthly debriefings by Arno aka Franz, though . . . What happened to everything that was said? Was it the supportive Arno who thought it wasn't worth passing on?

If Wolf is telling the truth in his memoirs he must have received much more material than the files reveal. He says that before Brandt's visit to Erfurt in March 1970 – i.e. even at the very beginning of

Guillaume's employment in the Chancellor's office, when he was still concerned with nothing more than trade union liaison – he 'gained access to some of the West German plans, which, combined with information from other sources, gave us a clearer idea of Brandt's intentions and fears'. He also says that Guillaume's 'real importance for us in East Berlin lay in his political instincts. Through Guillaume's judgements we were able to conclude sooner rather than later that Brandt's new Ostpolitik, while still riven with contradictions, marked a genuine change of course in West German foreign policy. As such, his work actually aided détente by giving us the confidence to place our trust in the intentions of Brandt and his allies.'

There is a further striking discrepancy between the files and Wolf's account. The files contain nothing about Brandt's extra-marital affairs. In his memoirs, though, Wolf claims to know that 'Guillaume soon realised that Brandt's adultery was frequent and varied'. Then again, after Guillaume was unmasked, and the head of the Federal Criminal Police wrote his report on Brandt's private life, cataloguing what Wolf calls 'his affairs with journalists, casual acquaintances, and prostitutes', he claims that 'Guillaume had of course been telling us about this kind of behaviour all along.' So perhaps the surviving files don't record the whole story.

The range of material on which the court case was based was narrow. The charge brought against the Guillaumes was the most serious possible: 'schwerer Landesverrat' – high treason. It would have been impossible to secure a conviction on this merely for passing on gossip and unspecified overheard remarks – or even documents, if no one knew what the documents were. So the case depended largely upon Guillaume's spontaneous admission at the moment of his arrest to being an 'officer' of the DDR, and also upon the only specific documents that he was known for certain to have handled – the teleprinter traffic on the Norwegian holiday.

There remains some doubt, however, as to whether any of this material ever reached East Berlin. In his memoirs Guillaume says that he didn't attempt to contact his controller during the holiday, but gives a very graphic and circumstantial account of how he arranged for the copies of all the documents in his possession to be photographed by a courier while he was making an overnight stop at a hotel in Sweden on the way back to Bonn. In the interview with Knopp, as we have seen, he withdraws his claim to have deliberately fooled Bauhaus into thinking that he was carrying the documents himself, but doesn't modify any other part of the story. All this is cast into doubt by Markus Wolf's memoirs, however. Wolf says that the copies were handed over by Christel to a courier called Anita at the Casselsruhe restaurant in Bonn, and that Anita, realising she was being followed, threw them into the Rhine. So he never received them, though he kept this fact from Guillaume so as not to hurt his pride. Konopatzky agrees that there is no trace of any of the Norwegian messages in the files.

Oddly, though, Wolf makes no reference at all to Guillaume's version of the handover, by way of the courier in the Swedish hotel. Even more oddly, perhaps, he recounts in some detail the contents of the three most important messages that Guillaume copied, but doesn't explain where the information came from; not from the Guillaumes' trial, plainly, where the evidence relating to this was given in camera. More oddly still, in a television interview with Guido Knopp for his programme on Guillaume, he says that the documents in the despatch-box *did* reach East Berlin, though he refuses to say what happened to them.

The story of Christel's meeting at the Casselsruhe restaurant, incidentally, is recounted in Guillaume's book. As in Wolf's version, her lunch companion realised she was being kept under observation, and found herself being tailed when she left the restaurant. Guillaume, who calls the woman not Anita but Thomin, purports to be much amused by his interrogators' suspicion later that she had been a courier. She thought, he says, that the watchers were private detectives employed by her husband because she was having an affair.

There are a number of other points of dispute in the record, where I have had to choose one version or another. According to Brandt's notes on the case (see the later part of this section), his bodyguard Ulrich Bauhaus came to him 'with tears in his eyes' and assured him that he had given his interrogators information about Brandt's women only under pressure; he was astonished at how much had already been collected. In a television interview much later, however, Karl Wienand says that Bauhaus went voluntarily to offer his evidence, because he and the other security people, as ordinary citizens in bowler hats and umbrellas, were genuinely shocked by the Chancellor's behaviour. Neither Wienand's record nor his appearance incline one to place much confidence in anything he says, but *someone* must have first brought up the question of the women, and of Guillaume's awarenesss of them, and I have followed Wienand's version.

I have also given expression to some of the many conspiracy theories that have been aired. Most of them have centred on the role played by Herbert Wehner, the Chairman of the Parliamentary Party of the SPD and its *éminence grise*. There is general agreement that Wehner was a Machiavellian figure, and relations between him and Brandt had always been difficult; even during the Grand Coalition they had been reduced to communicating through an intermediary. Brandt's single-handed 'cavalry charge' to the chancellorship in 1969 was perhaps, among other things, a declaration of independence from Wehner, and in no way improved Wehner's low assessment of Brandt's suitability for the job. He thought Brandt a lightweight. The publisher Rudolf Augstein once overheard him saying that Brandt and Walter Scheel (the Foreign Minister and leader of the FDP, therefore Brandt's coalition partner – another central character missing from the play) were both gigolos – '*Sie können nicht regieren, sondern erigieren.*' ('Their forte is not so much government as erection.') Wehner went to quite extraordinary lengths to undermine Brandt during his second term, and to prepare the way for Helmut Schmidt to succeed him. But, only a few weeks before Brandt's resignation, when Schmidt at last made an open bid for the chancellorship, Wehner seems to have had a sudden belated realisation of how much he needed Brandt's appeal to both voters and party members, and the two men had a bizarre rapprochement (which I reluctantly cut out of the play as one complication too many) – a long meeting at Brandt's home, with many pauses for thoughtful silence and the consumption of red wine, conspiring together against Schmidt.

This odd turn of events, however, did nothing to allay the suspicions of both Brandt and the press later that Wehner had played some kind of underhand role in the Chancellor's resignation. The version in the press was that Wehner had conspired in one way or another with his protégé, Günther Nollau, the President of the Federal Office for the Protection of the Constitution (the counter-espionage service). It was suggested that in 1973 Nollau had informed Wehner of the suspicions against Guillaume before he told Hans-Dietrich Genscher, the Minister of the Interior, to whom he was formally responsible. Nollau always vehemently denied this. He insisted that he had told Genscher on 29 May, and Wehner not until 4 June. He remembered the latter date very clearly, he said, because it was his own birthday. Genscher, however, seems a little sceptical of this in his memoirs. 'What did worry me', he says, 'was that Nollau kept Wehner informed of the investigation. What would Wehner do with this knowledge, since as everyone knew, he was increasingly critical of Willy Brandt's chancellorship?' Arnulf Baring, the standard historian of the period, is inclined to agree. Nollau's forewarning of Wehner, which might have been on May 23, the very day that the file landed on Nollau's desk, he finds 'exceedingly likely'.

Genscher didn't like Nollau, and blamed him afterwards for telling untruths about the amount of information he had passed on about the case. His behaviour, he said, 'confirmed many of the prejudices raised against him previously'. Brandt didn't like him, either, and refers to him sarcastically in his memoirs as 'supposedly able'. Nollau certainly pursued the case with remarkable ineptitude and desuetude, if nothing worse. His appearance in subsequent television interviews inclines one to share all the prejudices and suspicions that were expressed against him; just as well, you feel, as with Wienand, that he was not in the secondhand car trade, or he might not have got as far as he did.

Guillaume also came to believe that there was a conspiracy – but in his version Wehner, Nollau, and Genscher were all in it together. Nollau, he is reported to have said in the evidence he gave when his old employer Markus Wolf was in his turn tried for treason in 1993,*

---

* He was convicted, but two years later the judgement was overturned by the Federal Constitutional Court, which ruled that former officers of the DDR intelligence service could not be prosecuted for treason and espionage. Whether he was at all grateful for this expression of the rule of law, or even amused by the irony

was the confidant of Genscher as well as of Wehner, and both of them wanted to force Brandt out. 'Nollau held out the knife, and Genscher gave Brandt the necessary push to make him run on to it.' He himself, he said, in a slightly different version of the metaphor, had been used as the club with which Brandt had been struck.

Brandt himself was obsessed with suspicions of a rather different conspiracy against him – between Herbert Wehner and the East German leadership. He recorded them in a series of cryptic notes, written at some point after his retirement but not published until 1994, and held to them for the rest of his life. They centred on Wehner's known contacts in East Berlin. Wehner reported to Brandt two meetings there. The first was with Erich Honecker, the East German party leader, and its purpose, according to Wehner, was to relaunch the secret trade in political prisoners and family reunions, which had ironically been brought to an end by the regularisation of relations between the two states in the newly signed Basic Treaty. The second was with Wolfgang Vogel, the middleman in this trade, though the subject in this case was said by Wehner to be economic collaboration in general. The timing of both meetings was unsettling – the first on the evening of 29 May 1973, the day that Nollau told Genscher, and Genscher told Brandt, about the suspicions against Guillaume, and the second on 3 May 1974, the day that Nollau told Wehner about the list of Brandt's women. In any case Brandt believed that Wehner had had additional contacts with East Berlin which had gone unreported. In the course of them, he suspected, Wehner had been told that Guillaume was a spy, and had also been primed to launch his extraordinary attack on him from Moscow in the autumn of 1973.

Brandt's information was provided by Egon Bahr, who had obtained it from the Russians. It had come by way of the secret system of communication that Bahr had established with the Soviet leader Leonid Brezhnev, in imitation of the 'back-channels' used by Henry Kissinger to negotiate with the Soviet Union. The historian August H.

of it, in the Federal Germany of which he now found himself a citizen, and which he had worked so hard and so skilfully to undermine, he does not say in his memoirs. Brandt, incidentally, was one of the people who had spoken out against his prosecution in the first place.

Leugers-Scherzberg has recently cast more light on this dark corridor, and the allegations against Wehner that it was used to convey. What neither Bahr nor Brandt realised, says Dr Scherzberg, is that the chain of communication led through Yuri Andropov, later Brezhnev's successor, but at that time head of the KGB. Andropov had reasons to want Wehner discredited in Brandt's eyes, because Wehner distrusted the 'back-channel', and wanted to replace it with a more direct link, while Andropov himself naturally wished to preserve it as an instrument for his own influence. Wehner also dissented from Brandt's belief that an understanding with the Soviet Union was the key that would unlock relations with East Germany, and wanted to distribute the Federal Republic's efforts at reconciliation more broadly around Eastern Europe.

Whatever Wehner did or didn't do behind the scenes, however, his assurance of support for Brandt at the crucial moment in Münstereifel seems to have been less than whole-hearted, and Brandt always held him responsible (together with Rut) for failing to dissuade him from a decision that he never ceased to regret.

I've had much help with this project. First of all (once again) from Sarah Haffner, who got me off on the right foot as soon as I told her what I had in mind, by recommending me to read Arnulf Baring's *Machtwechsel*, and who subsequently supplied me with further parcels of books and help in translating a number of particularly awkward phrases. Peter Merseburger, the political journalist, who was working in Bonn during the Brandt chancellorship and whose own biography of Brandt has since appeared, gave me a great deal of patient advice. He also introduced me to Klaus Harpprecht, Brandt's speechwriter, and asked his old colleague Fritz Pleitgen to open the film archives of Westdeutscher Rundfunk in Cologne for me.

Eva Giesel, a colleague of my German play agent Ursula Pegler, spent much time, energy, and ingenuity making contacts and enquiries on my behalf. I originally expected the play to lay more emphasis on the Guillaumes' trial, and Frau Giesel worked particularly hard at putting me in touch with officials of the court where it took place, the Oberlandesgericht in Düsseldorf. My thanks, too, to Herr

Bundesanswalt Lampe, in the office of the Generalbundesanwalt in Karlsruhe, who explained some of the basics of German law to me, and to Professor Peter Brandt, Willy Brandt's eldest son, who most kindly offered to see me, though in the end I decided it might inhibit me; to Frau Gertrud Lenz in the Friedrich-Ebert-Stiftung in Bad Godesberg, where the Brandt papers are lodged; to Fritz Pleitgen at WDR; to ZDF for the text of Guido Knopp's interview with Guillaume; to Frau Marianne Wichert-Quoirin, who covered Federal politics in Bonn and the Guillaume trial in Düsseldorf for the *Kölner Stadt-Anzeiger*; and to Finn Aaserud for the Norwegian.

The amount of material available turned out to be oceanic, and for the first time in my life, when I finally had to recognise that I was drowning, I got the help of a research assistant. My choice – Stefan Kroner, the dramaturg who had worked on one of the German productions of *Copenhagen* – turned out to be inspired. He was not only unbelievably quick and industrious, but had an uncanny ability to guess what I should find useful. He plunged into the archive of the Friedrich-Ebert-Stiftung, and of WDR in Cologne, and reduced the tons of press-cuttings and weeks of newsreel to proportions I could just about manage. He found books long out of print, and trawled information from the huge deposits of old Stasi files in Berlin (still not fully explored, and a rich potential source of fossil fuel). We also had a delightful trip around the Rhineland together, to see where it all happened and to visit the various archives.

SOURCES

For anyone interested in finding out more about the case itself, or the personalities and politics of the period, the following is a short list of the more easily available material:

GENERAL

Baring, Arnulf, *Machtwechsel, die Ära Brandt-Scheel* (1983, 1998). The standard history of the period. Long (nearly a thousand pages), but boldly and incisively written. The chapters on the Guillaume affair and Brandt's resignation are relatively brief and particularly fine.

Harpprecht, Klaus, *Im Kanzleramt: Tagebuch der Jahre mit Willy Brandt* (2000). Harpprecht is a well-known publisher who joined Brandt's office at the beginning of 1973 as a speechwriter and adviser. He was also a personal friend of Brandt's, and provided him with a holiday house in the South of France which gave him some respite from the political storms of that difficult year. His diary of life in the Palais Schaumburg is sharp, worldly, and observant – and a salutary corrective to the schematic over-simplification of my picture.

Rehlinger, Ludwig A., *Freikauf* (1991). For the rate of ransom per prisoner charged by the DDR.

Whitney, Craig R., *Advocatus Diaboli: Wolfgang Vogel – Anwalt zwischen Ost und West* (1993). For the complete figures of the trade in prisoners and family reunions, as given in Vogel's own files.

BRANDT'S OWN WRITINGS

Brandt, Willy, *Erinnerungen* (1989). The 1994 edition also contains the *Notizen zum Fall G*, the notes about the Guillaume affair that he made around the time of his resignation. There is an English edition, *My Life in Politics* (1992), but it doesn't include the *Notizen*.

A complete collection of Brandt's works is in the course of publication (the *Berliner Ausgabe*). The volume relating to the domestic and social policy of his government is Volume 7, *Mehr Demokratie wagen: Innen- und Gesellschaftspolitik 1966–1974* (2001). The volume relating to his government's foreign policy (including relations with East Germany) is Volume 6, *Ein Volk der guten Nachbarn, Außen- und Deutschlandpolitik 1966–1974*. This has not yet appeared, however, and for his speeches and other statements on foreign policy I have used:

Brandt, Willy, *Reden und Interviews 1968–1969* (German government publication, undated), and *Bundeskanzler Brandt: Reden und Interviews* (1971).

Brandt, Willy, *Lachen hilft – Politische Witze* (2001). A collection of jokes, mostly but not exclusively political, assembled by Brandt over the course of the years. It was completed and published after his death by his widow, Brigitte Seebacher-Brandt. This is the source of most of Brandt's jokes in the play.

BIOGRAPHIES OF BRANDT

Merseburger, Peter, *Willy Brandt 1913–1992, Visionär und Realist* (2002). The most recent. Well-written and comprehensive, unashamedly partisan, with a foreword that gives a particularly brilliant overview of Brandt's achievements.

Koch, Peter, *Willy Brandt* (1998). Colourful, journalistic, gossipy, and highly readable.

Marshall, Barbara, *Willy Brandt, a Political Biography* (1993). In English. Short but to the point.

Schöllgen, Gregor, *Willy Brandt – die Biographie* (2001). Compact and serviceable.

GUILLAUME

Guillaume, Günter, *Die Aussage*. The original edition, described as '*protokolliert von Günter Karau*', was published by the East German military publishing house in 1988 for the benefit of the security organs and the National People's Army, marked 'for official use only'. In 1990 it was reissued in West Germany in a revised form, as *Die Aussage – wie es wirklich war* ('The Testimony – how it really was'. The implication is presumably that the book is a substitute for the testimony which Guillaume refused to give at his trial). For the reserve with which this source should be treated see above. It should really be read in conjunction with:

Knopp, Guido, *Top Spione* (1997), and the TV programme that this was published in association with (ZDF 1994); or, better still, the transcript of the interview conducted with Guillaume by Knopp and Steinhauser that was obtained for me from ZDF (TV2) by Stefan Kroner, though this seems not to have been published. It appears to be the full text of a conversation from which only excerpts have been used in the programme itself, though it has no date or other indication of its provenance.

The assessment of Guillaume's reports as it appears in the files of the Stasi comes from a contribution by Stephan Konopatzky to a conference on the role of the Stasi in the West, in November 2001, organised under the auspices of the organisation that now holds the archive, the office of *Die Bundesbeauftragte für die Unterlagen des Staatssicherheitsdienstes der ehemaligen DDR* (The Federal Commissioners for the Documents of the State Security Service of the Former DDR).

OTHER CHARACTERS IN THE STORY

Wolf, Markus, with Anne McElvoy, *Man Without a Face* (1997). His memoirs, in English. Very lively and absorbing, and apparently frank about many things, though reserving the right to silence on others.

Genscher, Hans-Dietrich, *Erinnerungen* (1995). Memoirs. In English as *Rebuilding a House Divided* (1995).

Brandt, Rut, *Freundesland* (1992). Her memoirs, and as engaging as Frau Brandt herself.

Schmidt, Helmut, *Weggefährten* (1996). Memoirs.

Leugers-Scherzberg, August H., *Die Wandlungen des Herbert Wehner, von der Volksfront zur Großen Koalition* (2002). This is the standard biography of Herbert Wehner, but it takes him only as far as the Grand Coalition. Until the next volume appears:

Leugers-Scherzberg, August H., *Herbert Wehner und der Rücktritt Willy Brandts am 7.Mai 1974* (in the *Vierteljahreshefte für Zeitgeschichte* 2.Heft, April 2002).

Nollau, Günther, *Das Amt* (1982). Memoirs. Relevant extracts in *Der Stern* (11 Sept 1975).

Ehmke, Horst, *Mittendrin* (1994). Memoirs.

Bahr, Egon, *Zu meiner Zeit* (1996). Memoirs.

(2003)

Afterlife

The genesis of this play was its setting – Schloss Leopoldskron, the great baroque palace on the outskirts of Salzburg.

It is by any standards what an estate agent would call an imposing residence. It was built in the middle of the eighteenth century by the Prince Archbishop of Salzburg, and its white stucco facades, in the Austrian rococo style, crowned by the Prince Archbishop's coat of arms, give it the appearance of an enormous wedding-cake. It looks northwards towards the Festung, the great fortress that dominates Salzburg, southwards across a lake towards the even vaster backdrop of the Alps.

A huge portrait of its builder, Prince Archbishop Leopold Anton Freiherr von Firmian (one of whose successors, a few years later, was the patron of the young Mozart), hangs in the galleried Marble Hall of the Schloss. It looks down now upon the scholars who come from all over the world to attend the academic conferences organised by the present occupants of the palace, the Salzburg Seminar. I stayed there with my wife, who was speaking at one of them, and I was astonished to discover that for eighteen years, from 1920 until 1938, this princely establishment had been the private home of someone who was in a sense a professional colleague of mine – the great Austrian producer and director Max Reinhardt.

There is a theatricality about all baroque and rococo architecture, and the perfect setting of Leopoldskron almost suggests a painted backcloth. I could see why it might have appealed to a man of the theatre. The sheer scale of it, though, indicated a breathtaking level of social grandeur. There have been many princes (and princesses) of the entertainments industry, from the nineteenth century onwards, who have housed themselves pretty lavishly, but even by the most extravagant standards of show-business Leopoldskron seemed remarkable – particularly when I discovered that Reinhardt had owned two other properties at the same time: one, in Berlin, a wing of the Bellevue Palace, the official residence of the former German Crown Prince (and now of the Federal President), and the other, in Vienna, an apartment in the Hofburg, the official residence of the former Austrian Emperor.

The theatre is a notoriously uncertain way of earning a living, and it's always encouraging to find that there are at any rate some people in the business who have managed to keep their heads above water. Reinhardt had been able not only to buy the palace and maintain it in the style to which it was accustomed but to go far beyond. When he acquired it, in 1918, it was in a sadly decayed state, and he devoted himself to restoring it – then went on to raise it to heights of glory that it had never known, even in the days of Firmian. It was his passion. He ransacked the great houses of Austria and south Germany for statuary and pictures – trans-shipped complete rooms – scoured Europe for antique furniture and books – filled the gardens with exotic plants and creatures – employed the finest craftsmen to carve and gild, to refurbish and replace, to copy the furnishings that could not be bought. Of all his many productions, said Helene Thimig, his companion and eventually his second wife, Leopoldskron was the one he was proudest of. Reinhardt and Thimig had no children together. Leopoldskron was their child, and together they loved it and nurtured it with parental intensity.

And then they lost it.

Reinhardt had made an unwitting early mistake in life that had re-emerged, as in a Greek tragedy, to break him. He had been born a Jew. In 1938, when Hitler absorbed Austria into the German Reich, Leopoldskron was 'aryanised' – expropriated – and Reinhardt was forced into exile.

As my wife and I walked through the gardens that Reinhardt and Thimig had created, she read out to me, from the Seminar's brochure on the history of Leopoldskron, this paragraph in a letter he wrote to Thimig in 1942, the year before he died:

I have lived in Leopoldskron for eighteen years, truly lived, and
I have brought it to life. I have lived every room, every table,
every chair, every light, every picture. I have built, designed, dec-
orated, planted and I have dreamt of it when I was not there. I
have always loved it in a festive way, not as something ordinary.
Those were my most beautiful, prolific and mature years . . .
I have lost it without lamenting. I have lost everything that I
carried into it. It was the harvest of my life's work.

I was moved by this noble expression of resignation. I walked straight
into the centre of Salzburg and bought all the books relating to
Reinhardt that I could find.

Max Reinhardt today is probably not much remembered outside
Germany and Austria. I asked a number of normally well-informed
friends in London if they knew anything about him. One recalled the
British publisher of the same name. Most of the others confessed ignorance. For the first forty years of the twentieth century, though, he was
a world celebrity.

Outside the German-speaking lands his reputation derived partly
from a legendary *Midsummer Night's Dream* which he staged in various places, and which eventually became a Hollywood film (his only
one), with the young Mickey Rooney as Puck. He was probably
known mostly, though, for his spectacular international stagings of a
play called *The Miracle*. This (as even serious theatre historians may
now need to be reminded) was the story of a medieval nun who falls
in love with a knight, and is first abducted from her nunnery and then
abandoned by him. But God takes pity on her and sends a miracle. A
statue of the Virgin comes to life and takes on the identity of the fall-
en sister to conceal her absence.

This heart-warming tale was told with a lavishness that far outdid
any modern musical or rock show. The Vienna production in 1912
had a cast of 1,500 and an orchestra of 150, the London one a cast of
2,000 and and orchestra of 200. In New York in 1924 the parts of the
Nun and the Virgin were alternated between two noted society beau-
ties – Lady Diana Duff Cooper representing the British aristocracy and
Rosamond Pinchot its American equivalent. (The latter, like the Nun,

went to the bad, apparently as result of her sudden stardom. The Virgin in this case failed to intervene, and she ended up taking her own life.)

In 1937 Reinhardt outdid this with an even more stunning excursion into show-business piety – this time Judaic rather than Christian, a Broadway show called *The Eternal Road*, which covered the entire history of the Jews, through the forty centuries of the Old Testament and on through the twenty centuries of the Diaspora. It's true that it had only a modest cast – 350 – but between them they wore 1,700 costumes, and the sets, which were four storeys high and covered almost an acre, required the rebuilding of the theatre. The result was a sell-out – and beggared all who had been cajoled to invest in it.

Before the First World War Reinhardt was said to be the third most popular personality in Germany after the Kaiser and Count Zeppelin, and in Germany and his native Austria his name remains a familiar one. The tide of theatrical fashion, though, long ago turned against him and everything he represented, in favour of the kind of theatre associated with Brecht and Piscator. Even at the height of his success he was often dismissed as a mere showman, and his son Gottfried accepts, in his memoir of his father, that 'a slight whiff of charlatanism' has always hovered about him. Some commentators on the German theatre, however, now believe that there are signs of a reassessment.

And so, it seems to me, there should be. The spiritual force of his great religious extravaganzas may have become a little dimmed by time, but his real achievements were on no less a scale. In 1905 he took over the direction of the Deutsches Theater in Berlin, rebuilt it, and bought out its previous owner. Without any state or city subsidy he turned it into an institution that, in its scope, ambition, and output, came to occupy the same kind of position that the National Theatre now does in London. He did the great classics, and he introduced the most interesting new writers of the day to German audiences – Chekhov, Ibsen, Strindberg, Pirandello, Shaw, Galsworthy, Hauptmann. By the time he gave up the running of the theatre in 1932 it had produced over 450 plays – and he had directed about 170 of them himself. It was the only private art theatre in the world, he claimed, that had managed to support itself, without subsidy and without political or party connection, out of its own resources.

His energy and ambition were boundless. In 1923 he took on, in addition to the Deutsches Theater, the lease of the beautiful Theater in der Josefstadt in Vienna, and did for his native city what he had already done for Berlin. By this time he had also helped found the Salzburg Festival, in the teeth of considerable local reluctance, and was responsible for all the drama that was produced there. By the end of his life he had directed some 340 productions and built or rebuilt no fewer than thirteen theatres.

He was born Max Goldmann, in 1873. The Goldmann family had for generations eked out a modest living as small businessmen in the little town of Stampfen (aka Stomfa, aka Stupava, depending upon which of the local languages was in the ascendant) near Pressburg (aka Bratislava), then in Hungary, in a district which had served historically as a dumping ground for Jews driven out of Austria on the other side of the Danube. By the middle of the nineteenth century, though, the Jews of Austria had been emancipated – and the German-speaking Jews of Hungary subjected to pogroms and forced magyarisation. In 1869 Max's father moved to Vienna, where he set up a firm trading in cotton goods and married a woman from Moravia. At first the business seems to have prospered, but by the time Max, their first child, was born, the stock market had collapsed, the firm had gone bankrupt, and the Goldmanns had had to move into more modest quarters. As the family grew so its fortunes declined. Another bankruptcy followed. Max's father sold bed-springs and bedding feathers for someone else; took over the business; went bankrupt again; became a corset-maker. In the course of Max's childhood the family moved seven times. At the end of his life, after he had lost everything and was struggling to survive in exile, Reinhardt said that he had gone through the torment of sudden impoverishment before, in his parents' home as a child. It was, he said, incomparably worse than poverty itself.

From this shifting and straitened world he escaped into the theatre. When he wrote later, as he often did, about his boyhood passion for the Burgtheater, the vast imperial court theatre of Vienna (claimed to be the second oldest in the world after the Comédie Française), you get the feeling that he saw it as providing him with not just an alternative world to inhabit for a few hours in the evening but a complete alternative biography – 'I always say that I was born in the gods. There I saw for the first time the light of the stage. There I was nourished (for 40 crowns an evening) on the rich artistic fare of the Imperial-Royal institution, and there the famous actors of the day sang their classic speech-arias around my cradle.' In Vienna at the time, he says, theatre was based exclusively on the spoken word. 'The stage was completely primitive, there were the bare necessities of furniture; everything else was the actor and his word . . . The Burgtheater was full of voices, that formed an incomparably well-toning orchestra, like old and precious instruments.'

He goes on to give a brilliantly evocative account of the excitement that theatre can sometimes generate:

The sound came to us out of the remote distance, pressed together as we were, up in the highest point of the house . . . My neighbours . . . were almost exclusively young people . . . I knew no one among them and in any case little was said. It was much too exciting . . .

As soon as it got dark and the curtain rose we melted together into one mysterious unity . . . Suddenly 250 faces broke into a single smile, then a giggle ran through the rows of people – and suddenly a ringing laugh broke out like a storm. You were swept irresistibly away, and you rejoiced that all the others were as drunk on merriment as you were. Then gradually it would become quieter and ever more still. The actors heard every stirring, just as we heard theirs. They would wait until we had settled . . . Things would become serious. Hundreds bent to the left, where someone had entered. The couple on the stage didn't see him. We were in the secret. Hearts beating. Breathing in time together. Two companies: the company of actors and the company of the audience.

The actors at the Burg tended to be elderly, and Reinhardt describes how they forgot their lines and had to be prompted – and were so remote that you could scarcely see them. But even this he saw as a kind of virtue. It meant that 'you had to play along with them yourself up there. The distance from the stage was so great . . . that you had to fill everything out for yourself.' He saw them as the real rulers of Vienna. 'The way they dressed influenced the way the aristocracy dressed. When one of the actors drank chocolate on the stage people watched with bated breath.' At the age of seventeen he became an actor himself, and adopted a new name, 'Reinhardt', to go with the new persona he was creating; and he became rather famous at the age of twenty, perhaps as a result of watching all those ancients at the Burg, for his ability to glue on a false beard and become an old man.

He worked in small theatres around Vienna, and in 1894 played a summer season in Salzburg. It was here that he got his first big break – a contract to join Otto Brahm's company in Berlin that autumn. Berlin was a relatively new theatrical centre, and Brahm was establishing for the first time its pre-eminence over Vienna. He had taken over the direction of the Deutsches Theater, accommodated in an old operetta house and now having a *succès de scandale* with the innovative naturalism of productions that introduced middle-class audiences for the first time to the social realities of poverty and sexual hypocrisy (Hauptmann's *The Weavers*, for example, and Ibsen's *Ghosts*).

Reinhardt's feelings about the revolution in which he now began to play a part were mixed. 'I was always acting in torn clothes, dirty and smeared,' he wrote later. 'Night after night I had to eat sauerkraut on stage. I wanted for once to play something else as well, something more beautiful and more enjoyable. At that time we had a club with merry and talented members. We allowed ourselves a good deal of professional fun at the expense of all the gloom in the art we practised.' The mockery was channelled into a kind of satirical cabaret, *Schall und Rauch* ('Sound and Smoke' – i.e. appearance without substance), which fought a running battle against the censors and was a great popular success. The team took over a small theatre to house the shows, and went on to produce first one-act straight plays in it, then full-length ones. Although one of these, Wilde's *Salome*, was seen as marking a decisive break with naturalism, it was a naturalistic production that propelled Reinhardt to the next stage of his career. He read about the opening of Gorky's *The Lower Depths* at the Moscow Arts Theatre, sent a friend to Russia to see it and fetch the text, then produced it with such enormous success that he was able to take over a second theatre as well.

Here, in the Neues Theater in 1905, he first did the *Midsummer Night's Dream* that he was to direct over and over again in the following years, and that became the signature of his style. The production of a play is an event in time that vanishes once the run is over as surely as youth or summer, and it is impossible to reconstruct it or to know why it should have caught the audience's imagination. As Gottfried Reinhard recalls in his memoir of his father, the play itself was only too familiar in Germany, where it was regarded as a rather tedious fairy-tale fit only for school matinees.

'What had made this tired warhorse a winning racer?' he asks. 'How could this drug on the repertory market suddenly transform itself into a smash hit and make its producer Europe's number one theatre man?' Not the text, evidently, nor even Mendelssohn's music, which had already been used to accompany many German productions. Not the actors, excellent as they were, nor the set, even though it was based on the novelty of a revolving stage. 'It was the *sum total* of all these elements,' says Gottfried, in a striking passage of critical description, 'or, to put it another way, the new element that made out of all of them a conceptual whole; the single idea to which all participants bent plus the generating force behind them; the unfamiliar ingredient of a new type of *direction*. The woods *acted*. The actors were a botanical part of the woods. Trees, shrubbery, mist, moonlight intermingled with the lovers, the rehearsing artisans, the trolls, the elfs, the spirits. The music, the wind, the breathless running, the clowning, the fighting were all of one key and came from one and the same source. So did the calm, the sweep, the dream, the poetry. Nothing was background, nothing foreground. Passion, humour, lyricism, bawdiness, nobility, fantasy did not have their allotted moments side by side or consecutively. They were ever-present, simultaneous, feeding on one another in multiple symbiosis.'

To achieve this Reinhardt exercised total control over everything, including the actors' performances. In the autobiographical notes that he wrote later in his life he describes how he worked, reading and working over a text until

> Finally you have a complete optical and acoustic vision. You see
> every gesture, every step, every piece of furniture, the light, you
> hear every intonation, every rise in emotional temperature, the
> musicality of the idioms, the pauses, the different tempi. You feel
> every inward stirring, you know how it is to be concealed and
> when it is to be revealed. You hear every sob, every intake of
> breath. The way another character listens, every noise onstage
> and backstage. The influence of light.
>
> And then you write it down, the complete optical and acoustic
> vision, like a score. You can scarcely keep up, so powerfully are
> you driven, mysteriously in fact, without discussion, without
> labour. Justification you find later. You write it chiefly for your-
> self. You have no idea why you see and hear it this way or that.
> Difficult to write down. No notation for speech. You invent
> your own signs.

I've never met any modern director who works like this. But then nor have I met one who wears the kind of clothes in which Thimig dressed Reinhardt – handmade suits of tastefully restrained grey English flan-nel (though Michael Blakemore, who has directed so many of my plays, including *Afterlife*, wears handmade shoes). The style has changed. Styles of dressing and directing, as of everything else, come and go. Alan Bennett, in *Writing Home*, remembers when he was a boy in Leeds seeing members of the Yorkshire Symphony Orchestra going home on the tram after the concert, 'rather shabby and ordinary and often with tab ends in their mouths, worlds away from the Delius, Walton and Brahms which they had been playing. It was a first lesson to me that art doesn't have much to do with appearances and that ordinary middle-aged men in raincoats can be instruments of the sub-lime.' So, on occasion, can extraordinary men in handmade suits.

As Reinhardt's notes on his methods continue, and he begins work in the rehearsal room, he sounds for a moment as if he is prepared to set his carefully prepared battle plans aside and to work collaboratively with the actors, as most modern directors do, in a joint effort to discover what the text has to offer. 'You talk to the actors about their parts,' he says. 'You listen, you get new ideas . . . Some actors have their own ideas. They insist on playing cheerful devils as fallen angels. Tragically, magnificently. You nod in an interested way, agreeing with them.' This collaboration, however, soon turns out to be not quite what it seems. 'The individual opinions rarely have any importance,' he says, 'but you take them seriously. You allow yourself to be convinced.'

Modern directors, of course, also feign deference in this way more often than they would be prepared to admit. Once rehearsals begin in earnest, though, Reinhardt's methods are again quite openly autocratic. 'You play all the parts,' he says. This is something that no modern director, in my experience, would dare to attempt. According to Thimig in her biography of her husband, however, it is precisely what Reinhardt's actors loved about him – that at rehearsals he was himself an actor, and one who could demonstrate every kind of part – old men (of course) but also 'children, eccentrics, women, girls, and lovers'. One actor who worked with him remembers him having the same line repeated over and over again, then saying it over and over again himself; another as guiding the player, 'without saying much, on invisible threads. With a look, a nod of the head, and then with one or two brief words, he leads him where he wants.' Then, when it comes to bringing an ensemble scene to life, 'he jumps in himself, takes actors waiting for their entrance by the hand, rushes them forwards into the middle of the stage, throws them (in one rehearsal it did actually happen) down on their knees, raises their hands – in a word, is now the leader who rushes into the battle ahead of everyone.'

One of Reinhardt's innovations, after he had moved on to the Deutsches Theater, had perhaps a more profound influence than even the revolving stage that he had introduced in *A Midsummer Night's Dream*: he added to the main house a studio theatre, the Kammerspiele. The auditorium of this smaller house comprised 292 seats – little bigger than the stage, and separated from it only by a couple of steps. This smallness and closeness allowed actors to develop a more intimate style, better suited to the new plays that Reinhardt was doing. It also created a luxuriously furnished space, closed off from the outside world, in which actors and audience felt themselves to be a single entity. 'Since I first came into the theatre,' wrote Reinhardt in a letter to Thimig, 'I was pursued and finally guided by one clear thought: to bring actors and audience together – pressed up against each other as closely as possible. Why? Theatre consists in essence of both these partners.'

Most major producing theatres now have a Kammerspiele of one sort or another attached, and in them (particularly in the National Theatre's Cottesloe) some of my best evenings in the theatre have been spent (and some of the best productions of my own plays done). Reinhardt himself, though, later changed his mind. 'I found that it was all a mistake,' he wrote in his autobiographical notes. 'The small house, the nearness of the stage, the all-too-comfortable seats. The Kammerspiele held too few people, and the quality of the audience grows with its quantity.' And also declines with its metropolitan sophistication: 'The so-called "good" audience is in reality the worst. Dulled unnaive people. Unobservant, blasé . . . Only the gallery is good.'

He seemed to be hankering for the kind of theatre that had first captured his imagination as a child in Vienna. But he went further. He turned his back, as other directors did later, on the concept of theatre as illusion, as an animated peepshow. His intentions remained the same: to dissolve the traditional boundaries between stage and house, and to involve the audience, the essential second company in which he had himself so memorably played at the Burgtheater. But now he thought that it could best be done as it had been in classical Greece, or in the medieval market-place – by creating dramas that served as religious, or quasi-religious, experiences for a mass audience in a vast open arena. He conceived the idea of 'the Theatre of the Five Thousand' whose numbers were to be drawn not from *die oberen Zehntausend*, as the upper crust are called in Germany (and who, if they have been counted correctly and had all bought tickets, could presumably have supported only two performances of a production) but from the ranks of 'upwardly-striving workers and craftsmen' hungry for art and culture.

He tried the idea out at a summer festival in Munich in 1910, with a production of *Oedipus Rex,* in a new adaptation by Hugo von Hofmannsthal, before an audience of 3,000. The experiment was judged a success (though quite how many of the audience were upwardly striving workers is not clear). He took over a 3,000-seat circus hall in Berlin and moved the production in, then next year followed it up with the *Oresteia.* That December he found time to go to London and produce *The Miracle* at Olympia, with a cast of 2,000 – and an audience of 20,000.

And in the same month, back in Berlin, he created his production of *Everyman,* the play to which he was going to find himself tied for most of the rest of his life.

By this time he had begun to construct a lifestyle on a scale worthy of the productions he was doing. He was surrounded by a court of advisers, assistants, hangers-on, and indigent relatives whom he had put on the payroll; he had a series of women; he dressed with fastidious elegance and ate only in the best restaurants; when he travelled he did it in the style of a prince on the Grand Tour. What all this cost he had not the slightest idea – his money was managed for him by his chamberlain, his depressive brother Edmund, whom he had rescued from suicide (and who Helene Thimig thought was the greatest love of his life). He was, it was often said, a baroque figure. It was the opportunity of acquiring a baroque palace at a knock-down price in the great inflation after the First World War that brought him back to Salzburg, where he had begun his theatrical career a quarter of a century earlier with a single suitcase in a single room.

Le style est l'homme même, said the Comte de Buffon, and it is surely true that in any human being it is difficult to make a distinction between the man himself and his outward expression in deeds and way of being. In Reinhardt's case, though, the inner source of all that energy, achievement, and display seems particularly elusive. 'Rarely,' said Heinz Herald, one of his associates over many years, 'has a human being remained so anonymous to those close to him, or has been revealed so totally in his work, as Reinhardt.' Another of his associates, the Austrian playwright Hermann Bahr, wrote: 'Paradoxically one could say of Reinhardt that the real charm of his personality consisted of his having none.' He had, said his son Gottfried, 'a reticence touching on the pathological . . . His paralysing reaction to direct contact with people, his inability to communicate with them freely, is indicative of the dark pockets in his soul.'

He often seemed to inhabit his vast carapace as thinly as a night-watchman in an empty warehouse. He was a legendary host (particularly at Leopoldskron), and, according to Helene Thimig, 'he loved big gatherings – but only to look at. He was mad to have people around him – but he was desperate at being alone with individual people.' He was charismatic, persuasive, and articulate when he was dealing with actors, writers, and people whose support he needed. But outside his professional life it was different. Thimig said 'he found it extremely unpleasant to talk tête-à-tête, particularly in a separate space cut off from the company. He never knew what to say.' Reinhardt said of himself that he found it difficult to breathe except in 'the true unreality of the theatre'.

It is impossible to know whether he consciously recognised any parallel between himself and Everyman, the eponymous protagonist of the play to which he now found himself yoked. I can find no record of his saying anything to this effect. So far as I know he had not intended to revisit the piece after its outing in Berlin, where it had had a poor reception from the critics (though a warm one from the public). For the opening of the first Salzburg Festival, in 1920, he had commissioned a young Austrian writer, Max Mell, to provide him with a modern mystery play about his future heroine the Virgin Mary, in Salzburg dialect. But it was not ready in time, and he fell back on the nearest equivalent to hand, the *Everyman* that he had done in Berlin nine years earlier. Would a play in Salzburgerisch rather than High German have caught on as *Everyman* now did? Many other plays were performed in the Festival seasons that followed (some of them, including a suitably gigantic *Faust*, directed by Reinhardt himself). But it was *Everyman* that became its emblem. Reinhardt revived it every summer (apart from a couple of years in the twenties) until the Nazis came to power in 1938, and drove both him and the play into exile. It resumed its career and its emblematic status at Salzburg after the

Nazis (and Reinhardt) had gone, and has now outlived him by over sixty years.

The play is by Hugo von Hofmannsthal, whose long collaboration with Reinhardt had begun with his version of *Oedipus*. Hofmannsthal derived it from an English mystery play of the fifteenth century, *The Summoning of Everyman*, and it has a simple plot. God, outraged by the indifference and ingratitude of mankind, sends Death to summon Everyman to judgement. Everyman, suitably terrified, repents of his past failings, abandons his worldly possessions, proclaims his faith, and is welcomed into heaven, apparently redeemed.

How God, or Death, selects the individual who is to serve as an exemplar of humankind at large is not clear. The victim they hit upon between them, well-suited as he is to be a popular target for retribution, is no more an average citizen than Reinhardt was. Like Reinhardt he is wealthy and rejoices in it. He lives in a grand house, and receives his unexpected summons during the course of a sumptuous banquet he is giving for his mistress and troops of friends. (He even seems to have some of Reinhardt's social inhibitions – his mistress has to urge him to join his guests.) At this point in the play, however, and at the point in Reinhardt's career when he first produced it, their paths diverge. As soon as they discover the identity of Everyman's visitor, and the nature of the journey he has been summoned to make, his mistress, friends, and servants all desert him, and he can derive neither help nor comfort from his wealth. Reinhardt had another eighteen years to enjoy his worldly substance and the company of his associates.

The English original now seems archaic and inaccessible. One of its modern editors says that it 'was written in the interests of the established faith; to uphold the papal authority; to emphasise the claims of the priesthood; to insist on the efficacy of the sacraments.' Another editor detects the hand of a priest in its construction, and the dramatic focus is plainly on Everyman's redemption. Hofmannsthal, a real dramatist (probably best known outside Germany or his native Austria as the author of most of Richard Strauss's libretti, beginning with the magnificent *Rosenkavalier* – the first production of which, at Dresden in 1911, Reinhardt directed), has made it dramatically viable. One of the many things he has modified is the play's theology. The original is presumably among other things a contribution to the long-running debate about the relative importance of faith and works, and Good Works is the only one of the various personified virtues and faculties around Everyman who stands by him, and who single-handedly makes his redemption possible. Hofmannsthal has introduced the figure of Faith, and given her an equal role in Everyman's salvation.

Even in Hofmannsthal's version this aspect of the play is difficult for the non-believer to take much interest in – or to make much sense of. A faith hastily rediscovered under sentence of death and threat of eternal hellfire is surely as dubious as a confession obtained by torture. Good Works (or, as Hofmannsthal calls her, simply Works) is an even more curious figure. When we first meet her she is in a bad way as a result of Everyman's lifelong neglect – 'cold in the ground' in the original, 'pitifully weak' in Hofmannsthal – and unable to stir. How she regains her strength retrospectively, when she enters the story too late for Everyman to undertake any addition to his achievements in life, or any modification of them, it's difficult to understand. The moral would seem to be that there's no need to bother with behaving well, because you can always rewrite the record afterwards.

The strength of the piece now is its dramatisation of the unpredictability and inexorability of the end that waits for all of us, believers and non-believers alike. Any doubts I had about whether Hofmannsthal's handling of this could still be effective were abruptly shattered by seeing a DVD of Christian Stückl's production of the play at the 2004 Festival, with Peter Simonischek as a big, powerful, likeable, immensely human Everyman, caught in the rich fullness of his life by Jenz Harzer as a naked, grey-fleshed, burning-eyed Death. Even on the small screen it is an unforgettable experience.

In spite of the play's enduring power, and the success it had in Salzburg, the audience it found was not the one that Reinhardt had been aiming at. Ordinary local citizens didn't much like it, and in any case they couldn't afford the ticket prices. The customers (as always) turned out to be the rich and the tourists. Franz Rehrl, the Provincial Governor, was a strong supporter of the Festival – but for purely hard-headed reasons. 'Culture,' he said, 'equals business.' Not even the business, though, reconciled the intensely conservative citizens of Salzburg to the influx of the outsiders who brought it to them. One of these outsiders, of course, was Reinhardt himself. 'Philistines in Salzburg,' wrote Hofmannsthal to Richard Strauss in 1923, 'will never accept Reinhardt as president [of the Festival]. They hate him as a Jew, as a Lord of the Manor, as an artist and as a solitary human being whom they cannot fathom.' The tinge of anti-Semitism in local resentment was strong, and the most outspoken opponents of the Festival were the local forerunners of the Nazis. Already contemptuous of Catholicism as practised by Catholics, they were even more virulent about the 'hypocritical profit-Catholicism of Jews', among whom they included not only Reinhardt but Hofmannsthal, the Catholic grandson of a Jewish convert. Reinhardt was also a permanent target for the Viennese satirist Karl Kraus, still widely admired in *bien-pensant* circles today, who described him, with a wonderful combination of racial and social disdain, as 'an upstart from the Slovak working-class'.

Leopoldskron, too, turned out not to be the quiet artistic and intellectual cloister that Reinhardt had envisaged. It became inevitable, said Thimig later, to invite politicians and money as well. 'Particularly unpleasant,' she says, 'I found the representatives of the so-called "entertainment aristocracy".' Money (as always) came to dominate the Festival, like Mammon springing out of Everyman's trunk. At first everyone involved in the play worked for nothing. But as the seasons went by the well-known actors who came to Salzburg began to demand the kind of fees they could command elsewhere. The Festival accumulated a considerable deficit, and not even high ticket prices could keep it afloat. It seems to have been rescued by a millionaire, Camillo Castiglioni, who had amassed a fortune building planes during the First World War and speculating in the great inflation that followed it (and another Jew, like so many of the philanthropists who keep the arts going).

So poor Everyman had to be preserved by the very wealth that had failed to sustain him in the play, and redeemed at the expense of patrons who did not believe in Christian redemption. It sounds more and more like the situation in the British (and the German) theatre today, which struggles piously to present plays about poverty and degradation to an audience not very closely acquainted with either – and which has to be subsidised by the charitable efforts of people on even more remote terms with them.

Well, perhaps they learn a few things that they didn't know, and are persuaded to go out and give all they have to the poor. Perhaps the audience of *Everyman* were moved to make some early improvements to the Good Works section of their CVs. It certainly seems to have spoken to the Prince Archbishop of Salzburg. Gusti Adler, in her biography of Reinhardt, reports that at the first performance quiet tears rolled down his cheeks, and that when he pressed Reinhardt's hand afterwards he said that the production was better than a sermon. But then, according to Reinhardt, he was a saint anyway.

It's difficult to know about the rest of the audience. Reinhardt himself certainly didn't change his life-style. Is that a criticism of the play? Of the production? Of Reinhardt? He may of course have felt that if the Deutsches Theater and *Everyman* counted for anything, his record of Works was strong enough to counterbalance quite a lot of champagne and cigars. And Hofmannsthal was certainly right about the terrifying unpredictability of death. In 1929 his elder son shot himself, and Hofmannsthal himself died of a heart attack as he dressed for the funeral. Three days later the same unannounced visitor came for Reinhardt's beloved brother Edmund.

My play, like two earlier ones of mine, *Copenhagen* and *Democracy*, is based on the historical record, but perhaps rather more freely than they were.

Reinhardt himself, elusive and unforthcoming as his associates often found him, was in his letters and other writings immensely articulate, eloquent, sophisticated, and prolific. Most of the ideas that he expresses in the play are drawn from what he wrote, but I have not even begun to do justice to the depth of his intelligence or the breadth of his culture. The external events of his life – his difficulties with local philistines and anti-Semites, the attacks on his house (and on the Prince Archbishop's), his expropriation and exile – are drawn from the record. And from the terrace of Leopoldskron you can indeed see

Obersalzberg, above Berchtesgaden on the other side of the German frontier, where Hitler and other Nazi leaders had their villas.

Reinhardt's recollections of his childhood in Vienna, and of his first arrival in Salzburg, come mostly from his autobiographical notes. His working methods are described not only here but in the recollections of many professional colleagues, and also in three full-length memoirs – by his second wife Helene Thimig, by his personal assistant Gusti Adler, and by his younger son Gottfried. These are also the source for most of the details of his personal life – his relations with his brother Edmund, his efforts to support the rest of his extended family, the difficulties with his first wife, his princely travel arrangements, and his accommodation in Berlin and Vienna; for his distaste for handling or thinking about money, and his financial difficulties in exile, including his emergency cash arrangements (though he did have one success during his bleak American exile – *Rosalinda*, an adaptation of *Die Fledermaus* – which was produced in New York in 1942, and which just about kept him afloat); for his legendary parties; for his deferential consultation with Rothschild and other patrons; for his unfulfilled projects to commission a play from Shaw about the life of Christ and to film *Paradise Lost*.

Gottfried's memoirs (which he wrote in English) are particularly revealing, if somewhat overblown in style. His love for his father, reverence for his talent, and encylopedic knowledge of his affairs (in every sense) do not impede him from casting a coolly observant eye upon his manifold weaknesses. Reinhardt, he says, was 'a precocious, hypersensitive, fantasy-possessed, play-mad, cruel-tender child to whom tenderness from others was as necessary as food and drink . . . an enthusiast and a skeptic, courageous and quickly intimidated, a gambler and an evader of decision, at one time trusting providence, at another taking refuge in procrastination, immune to fatal catastrophe, but an easy prey to the most banal mishap . . .'

The character of Rudolf Kommer, Reinhardt's man of business and master of ceremonies, is also very fully documented by Gottfried, including his division of the human race into the imposters and the feeble-minded. Gottfried says he 'played confidant, counselor, caretaker, father confessor, procurer, arbiter, entertainer, to the interna-

tional upper crust'. He was a kind of eunuch, continuously but harm-
lessly in love with a harem of other people's wives and girlfriends
whom he entertained and consoled, and who all called him Kätchen in
affectionate gratitude. The guests at one of Reinhardt's great parties,
says Gottfried, would find themselves

> staring in surprise at a person who happened to be in their midst
> as if by accident and who chatted nonchalantly and without ever
> stopping. He chatted with the virtuoso brilliance of a pianist,
> eliciting complicated cadences from the keys without seeming to
> touch them. He would turn from one to the other, called most
> by their first names and acted with such ease that one would
> think this centrifugal mass of people, alien and feeling alienated,
> were the oldest acquaintances and had simply run into one
> another again, and that he was continuing a conversation long
> since begun . . .
>
> There was no spoilsport who did not start to grin at the sight
> of him. He was the heart of the whole company and pumped
> blood even into its stiffest and most congealed members. He
> entertained and found entertainment in everybody. He formed
> friendship upon friendship and quarreled with some to the
> point of physical violence, without, however, extinguishing his
> cigarette or his wit. He spiced the fat life of the rich with sharp
> truths, gave away boxes of candy, flowers and books, lunched,
> dined, supped (sometimes in repetition with first and second
> understudies), he debated, talked politics, criticized without
> surcease and, when he failed to incur enough contradictions, he
> started contradicting himself. He arranged divorces for
> excitable men, married off women, played with their children,
> concluded agreements between producers, poets, directors,
> musicians . . .
>
> At night, in the bar, he could make Jews yodel, Nazis *jüdeln*
> [talk with a Jewish inflection] . . . Without the slightest condes-
> cension, he could make every servant his friend and disarm
> every enemy with the perfect gallantry of a born aristocrat . . .

At the end of their long collaboration Reinhardt and Kommer became estranged from each other, though it's difficult to establish exactly how and why. According to Gottfried, Kommer wrote a long letter to Reinhardt 'enumerating, in Kommer's opinion, every error my father had ever committed and complaining about my father's ingratitude for his services'. Reinhardt responded with a farewell letter fifty-six pages long in which he gave a brilliant and generous account of Kommer's career and character, largely in the third person.

The originals of the other characters are somewhat less well documented. Gusti Adler was the niece of Victor Adler, the founder of the Austrian Social Democratic Party, and an old school-friend of Thimig's. She had started out in life studying art, and then become a cultural journalist. She worked round the clock for Reinhardt, says Thimig, and did everything for him, including buying rare books and antiques, and rare animals and exotic birds for the garden; the only thing she couldn't fix was the Salzburg weather. From her own book she emerges as devoted and totally uncritical.

Thimig, on the evidence of *her* memoir, was a little more detached. She came from a famous Viennese acting family, and had a successful stage career of her own. She fully shared Reinhardt's passion for restoring and furnishing Leopoldskron, but never, she says, a double bedroom, except in the bug-ridden hotel on the Mexican border where they were establishing their immigration into the United States as a preliminary to his getting a divorce in Reno from his first wife. Even on their train journeys between New York and Los Angeles they had a drawing-room suite with separate bedrooms. She is frank about the jealousy that she felt for some of the women who were drawn to Reinhardt – particularly Lady Diana Cooper, his Nun and Virgin, and Eleonora von Mendelssohn, the wealthy, beautiful (and drug-addicted) socialite who was closer to Reinhardt than she was to herself in the last painful weeks of his life. She is (fairly) frank, too, about the triangle that developed when she herself fell for the actor she was working with in a romantic comedy.

The Prince Archbishop of Salzburg, Dr Ignatius Rieder, seems to have been admired and loved by everyone (except by the Nazis, and perhaps by the droves of people who were leaving the church at that time to join them). He was profoundly conservative in demeanour and outlook, and maintained contacts with the imperial family even after the dissolution of the Dual Monarchy in 1918. Thimig describes him as having a peasant's face capped by snow-white hair, and always wearing a peasant's heavy boots. She found him particularly noble and good; Reinhardt described him as a saint, and as 'the angelic archbishop'. The Archbishop reciprocated. 'A good Jew like Reinhardt,' he said, 'is dearer to me than a bad Christian' – a sentiment that would perhaps sound platitudinous in a churchman now, but that was not to be taken quite so much for granted in Salzburg at the time. He was one of the relatively few people in Salzburg who were enthusiastic about the festival, and he gave Reinhardt permission to perform *Everyman* in front of the cathedral. (Reinhardt put his request in a letter; the reading of the play in support of the application is my expansion of this.) The two men developed a warm personal relationship. Thimig says that the Archbishop discreetly blessed Leopoldskron for them, in spite of its being a Jewish home, and she describes how he would sometimes tenderly stroke Reinhardt's arm and call him 'my son'.

Franz, Reinhardt's valet, has a slightly more oblique relationship to reality. The real Franz had, like mine, previously been valet to Luziwuzi, the transvestite Archduke Ludwig Viktor, who had caused much embarrassment to his brother the Emperor. (Franz's job description in his earlier post was not only valet but *Vorleser* – reader-aloud – though what he read I have been unable to discover.) But at some point, I think in the 1930s, Death came for Franz and he was replaced by Paul. Reinhardt retained Paul's services throughout the bleak years of American exile, even though he was often unable to pay him, which Paul seems to have been rather less sanguine about than my character. I have elided Paul with Franz.

Friedrich Müller is a degree more fictitious. He is based on a man called Friedrich Rainer, who shared with my character many of the political and racist views that were common at the time in Salzburg, as elsewhere in Austria, and who, like Müller, joined the Nazi party and went into local politics. I changed his name partly because 'Rainer' sounds confusingly like 'Reinhardt', but also because Rainer grew up not in Salzburg but in Sankt Veit, and because it was not Rainer who conveyed to Reinhardt Hitler's bizarre offer of rebirth as an honorary Aryan.

This is an event doubted by some but confirmed by both Thimig and Adler, who agree that the messenger was Death himself. Or, at any rate, Werner Krauss, the actor who played the part for many years in *Everyman*, and who was also an outspoken Nazi supporter. Reinhardt was particularly fond of him. He had made his name in 1920, in *The Cabinet of Dr Caligari*, but during the thirties he specialised in playing Jews in Nazi propaganda films. In 1933 Reinhardt cast him as Mephistopheles in his Salzburg *Faust* after he had agreed to sack the original casting, Max Pallenberg, because he was Jewish.

Müller's history, however, coincides closely with Rainer's after the Anschluss in 1938, when Hitler appointed Rainer Gauleiter of Salzburg. Up to then Rainer had called for the unconditional destruction of everything Catholic and Jewish in Salzburg. He now decided to preserve all the decadent baroque Catholic trappings of Leopoldskron – and to move into the house himself. During the war he continued his rise through the ranks of the Nazi administration, and ended up in charge of Friuli, the Italian province on the Yugoslav border. After the war he appeared as a witness at Nuremberg before being handed over to the Yugoslavs and hanged in Ljubljana in 1947 (though rumours persisted, as with other executed war-criminals, that he had somehow survived).

My translations of the extracts from Hofmannsthal's text are fairly free, but I hope reflect something of the dramatic quality of the original. I have been pretty cavalier in my selection, taking only what suits my purposes, occasionally slightly changing the order of events, and skipping completely the sections dealing with Everyman's redemption. Hofmannsthal's text is written mostly in iambic tetrameters, but with occasionally longer or shorter lines, and rhymed mostly as couplets, though he often varies this, so far as I can see randomly. Since I was using only short extracts which needed to be clearly distinguished from their prose background I thought that I should stick strictly to regular tetrameters and regular couplets.

I feel uneasy about taking such liberties with a writer as good as

Hofmannsthal. I can only say in justification that Hofmannsthal himself has made very free with his sources. The English text on which he has drawn, which may itself be taken from a Dutch original, is written in verse so irregular that its prosody is almost unfollowable. He has also heavily recast it, cutting among other characters Strength, Discretion, Five-wits, Beauty, Knowledge, and Confession, and adding some dozen new ones. He has reshaped the action and made it genuinely dramatic, and changed the whole theological basis of the play by introducing the character of Faith. His German editor Heinz Rölleke identifies material imported from completely different sources, some of them highly anachronistic – a rhymed prayer of Dürer's, songs from the Minnesingers, and scenes from Calderon and Maeterlinck. He has also, says Rölleke, drawn on Burton's *The Anatomy of Melancholy* for Everyman's character and on the nineteenth-century German sociologist Georg Simmel for Everyman's and Mammon's philosophy of money (both of which I have quoted at length).

I have taken further liberties with names and titles. Actors often called Reinhardt 'Max', but this was a collegial informality, and Thimig says that she always referred to him as 'Reinhardt'. Even this was a wifely intimacy, though, and to most people he was 'Professor Reinhardt', an honorary designation bestowed upon him by the Duke of Saxonia-Coburg-Gotha; Austrians are notoriously meticulous about titles ('Doktor Doktor', for example, if you have two doctorates) – and open-handed about creating fictitious ones for citizens unfortunate enough not to possess real titles. Aristocratic ranks were abolished in 1918, but the old titles that went with them often continue to be used, and waiters in Viennese coffee houses are said to call any unfamiliar customer 'Herr Baron' or 'Herr Direktor'. One of the reasons that Thimig was so anxious to get married to Reinhardt, says his son acidly, was to be addressed as 'Frau Professor'. In America he apparently became 'Doctor', but in English these usages applied to a theatre director sound – to my ears, at any rate – so odd and egregious that I have left him as plain Herr Reinhardt.

He usually referred to Thimig, she says, as '*die Leni*' – a characteristically Germanic usage that suggests both familiarity and respect, and that has no equivalent in English. To other people at that time, before her marriage to Reinhardt, she and Adler would have been 'gnädiges Fräulein' – gracious Miss – but a simple 'Fräulein' is the nearest approximation that sounds reasonable in English. Most of the references I have found to Dr Rieder, both at the time and since, call him *Fürsterzbischof*, Prince Archbishop, and when Reinhardt wrote to him he began his letter '*Eurer fürstlichen Gnaden*' – Your Princely Grace. This is really another 'Herr Baron'. The last real Prince Archbishop of Salzburg was Hieronymus von Colloredo, whose tenure ended in 1812, by which time the office had been secularised, so that all Colloredo's successors have been plain ordinary archbishops. Until the 1940s, though, they were still addressed as princes.

Real death is rarely the tidy and dignified event suggested by the mythic representation of it that forms the basis of Hofmannsthal's play. It wasn't for Hofmannsthal himself, who died still struggling to put on his top hat for his son's funeral. It wasn't for Rudolf Kommer, when he collapsed and died in 1943 in the lobby of his hotel room in New York, where the body had to be left until the coroner could be located – so that all the crowds of acquaintances who came to pay their respects had to step over him to do so.

Nor was it for Reinhardt when it came, slowly, over the course of three weeks and a series of strokes, in another New York hotel room seven months later, apparently after he had been bitten by a dog. Money ruled over his death-bed, as it had over so much of his life; Gottfried hushed up his condition for fear that it would frighten off the investors in the production he was trying to set up (an adaptation of Offenbach's *La Belle Hélène*, intended to follow up the success of *Rosalinda*).

Gusti Adler and Helene Thimig, however, both lived happily ever after – or at any rate for many more years after Reinhardt's death. Adler, who had followed him into exile in 1939, and worked for him unpaid in the evenings while she earned a living from her day job in the archive at Warner Brothers, continued at the studio until she was in her eighties, and lived on into her nineties. Thimig struggled back to Austria in 1946 to play her old role as Faith in *Everyman* at Salzburg, then went on to resume her distinguished stage career in Vienna. For twenty-five years she lived happily with the Austrian actor Anton Edthofer, and died in 1974 at the age of eighty-five.

Reinhardt's renunciation of Leopoldskron, I discovered as my researches continued, was not quite as simple as it seemed in the letter he wrote to his wife in 1942 that was quoted in the brochure. He continued to be profoundly anguished by his loss, and he never gave up the hope of recovering the house. In July the following year, three months before his death, he wrote another letter to his wife, twenty-eight pages long, laying out what seems to be a deposition to an Austrian exile organisation preparing for the post-war restitution of property stolen by the Nazis, in which he attempts to catalogue the contents of the house, to list the improvements and additions that he and his wife have made, together with all the services he has rendered to the Austrian nation, and all the honours and recognition he has received for his work. It is rather like Everyman's account of his estate – but offered after he has lost it, in the hope that Death might relent, and return it to him. Death did not oblige, any more than it did for Everyman.

It was, however, after endless legal difficulties and battles, returned to his heirs – his wife and sons, who sold it to the American academic organisation that runs it today. And there it still stands, in all its lofty baroque elegance. The great impresario has gone, and so have the princes and financiers who were his guests, together with the actors and musicians who entertained them, and the thieves and murderers who followed them. Now the guests drifting elegantly about the marble hall and the terrace are a new privileged class – the conference-goers of the world. You can rent its facilities yourself when the Seminar is not in session.

And in its afterlife it has achieved a certain celebrity through its artistic associations – even become a place of pilgrimage that attracts coach parties from all over Europe. Not because of Max Reinhardt, but because it served as a location in the film version of *The Sound of Music*.

SOURCES

BIOGRAPHY
Leonhard M. Fiedler, *Max Reinhardt* (1975)

PERSONAL MEMOIRS
Helene Thimig-Reinhardt, *Wie Max Reinhardt Lebte* (1973)
Gusti Adler, . . . *aber vergessen Sie nicht die chinesischen Nachtigallen* (1980,
    but expanded from *Max Reinhardt – sein Leben*, 1964). The title of the 1980
    edition refers to Reinhardt's reminder to Adler, as she left Leopoldskron to
    meet Lilian Gish off the boat from New York at Cuxhaven. She was to stop
    off on the way at Hagenbeck, the animal-dealers near Hamburg, to buy
    flamingos, pelicans, herons, and exotic ducks. 'But don't forget the Chinese
    nightingales!' he called after her.
Gottfried Reinhardt, *The Genius, a Memoir of Max Reinhardt* (1979). In
    English.

REINHARDT'S OWN WRITINGS:
Max Reinhardt, *Manuskripte, Briefe, Dokumente* (1998). The catalogue of a
    collection made by Dr Jürgen Stein, but with many quoted extracts.
Max Reinhardt, *Ich bin nichts als ein Theatermann* (1974 in the DDR, 1989 in
    the BRD). A collection of his letters about theatrical matters, together with
    brief memoirs by some of his associates.

THE STORY OF THE HOUSE AND THE FESTIVAL
Johannes Hofinger, *Die Akte Leopoldskron* (2005)
Stephen Gallup: *A History of the Salzburg Festival* (1987). In English.

ESSAYS AND DOCUMENTS
Ambivalenzen: Max Reinhardt und Österreich (2004). A collection of press-
    cuttings, other documents, and photographs.
Roland Koberg, Bernd Stegemann, Henrike Thomsen, editors, *Max Reinhardt
    und das Deutsche Theater* (2005). Essays, including a particularly interesting
    one by Christopher Balme, *Die Marke Reinhardt*, on Reinhardt's theatre con-
    sidered as a business enterprise.

(2008)

TRANSLATIONS AND ADAPTATIONS

Chekhov: Collected Plays

Chekhov's reputation now rests chiefly upon the four oblique and haunting plays he wrote in the last ten years of his life. In fact he was not really a natural dramatist. The page, not the stage, was his element. The skits and spoofs with which he began his literary career while he was still a medical student matured seamlessly into stories of the most exquisite restraint and insight, and his reputation no less seamlessly with them; even if he had never written a single line for the theatre he would still be one of the most marvellous writers ever to have lived. His sporadic parallel career as a playwright followed a quite different pattern. For the greater part of his life it remained a source of frustration, anguish, and self-doubt. Again and again he renounced it; again and again he discovered that he was 'absolutely not a dramatist'. He went through bouts of defensive cynicism, when he announced that the theatre bored him, that it was 'the venereal disease of the cities', and when at last he had a little success in the commercial theatre he made it clear to his friends that he was only doing it for the money. But then the transition he was trying to make, from page to stage, is one that remarkably few major writers in the whole history of literature have managed at all. And his struggles to understand and master the recalcitrant medium of the theatre changed forever its nature and possibilities.

The two careers were oddly out of step with each other from the very beginning. While he was still only starting out as a humorist in the comic journals he was already writing a serious and substantial work for the theatre – the huge untitled drama most usually known as

Platonov (and as *Wild Honey* in my adaptation of it). This was followed in 1885 by a long one-act play, based on one of his stories, entitled *On the Highroad*, which is melodramatic in tone, but which attempts a striking picture of society's lower depths. Neither of these was performed during his lifetime. The former was supposedly torn up after its rejection by the actress to whom Chekhov offered it, and did not resurface until sixteen years after his death, while the latter he seems to have abandoned after it was forbidden by the censor as being 'too gloomy and sordid', and also, to judge by the underlining in the censor's report, because it showed a member of the landowning classes in a drunken and destitute condition. His first seriously intended work of any length to come before the public (leaving aside his detective novel, *The Shooting Party*, which, for all its delicious brilliance, was written as a pot-boiler) was also a play – *Ivanov*, in 1887. It was written (in ten days, according to Chekhov) at the suggestion of the theatre manager Fyodor Korsh. Korsh specialised in light comedy, and Chekhov's sister Masha said he threw out his proposal – rather casually, during a conversation in the foyer of the theatre – because of Chekhov's reputation as a humorist. The play is not a humorous work, however – in fact it is possibly the most lowering thing that Chekhov ever wrote. Korsh apparently did not blench when he received the script; though Chekhov did when he saw Korsh's production of it. There were four rehearsals instead of the promised ten, and on the opening night only two of the cast knew their parts; the rest got through, said Chekhov, 'by prompter and inner conviction'. The reviews were decidedly mixed. So were the reactions of the first-night audience, with clapping, hissing, whistling, stamping, and 'absolute carnage' up in the gallery.

In the following year, 1888, Chekhov began the long and well-documented struggle (which we will examine when we come to look at each of the plays in detail later) with the material that was to become first *The Wood Demon* and then *Uncle Vanya*. But by this time his two careers had undergone a curious reversal. With the publication in that year of his long story *The Steppe* the successful boulevard journalist became accepted as a writer of serious fiction – while with Korsh's production of first *Swan Song* and then *The Bear* in the same year the unsuccessful serious dramatist emerged as a writer of popular boulevard comedies. In fact a number of his early comic pieces had been in dialogue form, so that one-act 'vaudevilles' were a more natural bridge into the theatre than four-act dramas. It still took him a long time to break out of the bridgehead he had established. When he attempted to relaunch his career as a serious dramatist with *The Seagull* eight years later it was an even worse disaster than *Ivanov* – such a disaster that he swore off playwriting once again. It was not until 1897, and the second production of the play at the Moscow Arts Theatre, that he finally managed to get his two careers in step.

What finally enabled Chekhov to succeed, where so many other writers have failed, in working both these apparently similar but fundamentally different modes, is something that goes very deep in his character: his elusiveness. It is the loss of their authorial voice that so often bewilders writers who turn from books to plays. How many government ministers, on permanent display to the public, could adapt to being civil servants, operating out of sight? Chekhov's strength was that he had no authorial voice to lose. Various critics have remarked upon the 'colourlessness' of his language. It is colourless in the same way that glass is colourless; we look straight through it without ever noticing it. We find ourselves seeing not Chekhov's world, but the world of his characters. We inhabit them, as they inhabit themselves, completely and without surprise. We find ourselves inside peasants – inside an old peasant woman, in one amazing story, to live shut up in her hut with her all the long winter among a family of peasants; inside a little boy, in the story that first made his literary reputation, as he travels across the hot summer steppe on his way to start school, moving with him out of his childhood into a huge world that stretches away to the horizon and beyond. We find ourselves inside doctors, certainly – but never one who bears much resemblance to Chekhov himself. One of his short stories, 'Ariadna', is told in the first person, and the narrator and his writings seem to be familiar to everyone he meets, as Chekhov and his writings were; but he remains uncharacterised, a listening ear for someone else's tale. In Chekhov's works, in fact, we find ourselves inside everyone except Chekhov. And yet we remain at the same time somehow detached from these people. Chekhov's other extraordinary power – which also helps to make his characters playable by actors – is to show us these new selves from outside even as we live inside them, with entirely unsentimental coolness and irony. It's like the experience one has in dreams, where one is both taking part in the action and looking down upon oneself as a dispassionate observer.

Chekhov's absence from his work, and his extreme detachment from his characters, must be fully grasped if we are to understand these plays. This has proved as difficult in the past as it has to accept the absence and inscrutability of God, and the plays have become obscured by the authorial intentions which people have read into them. Chekhov, like God, is sometimes seen as full of lovingkindness towards his characters, the only expression of which seems to be his supposedly wistful and elegiac view of the world. An impression lingers that the plays are about impoverished gentry with nothing to do all day but watch their fortunes decline; 'Chekhovian' is a synonym for a sort of genteel, decaying, straw-hatted ineffectualness. There are such characters, it's true – Gayev and his sister in *The Cherry Orchard*, and Telegin, the ruined neighbour who is living on Uncle Vanya's charity – but they are few in number. What we forget, when we are not face to face with them, is that most of the people in these plays are not members of the leisured class at all. They have to earn their living, and earn it through hard professional work. We catch them at moments of leisure, because this is when they can stand back and look at their lives, but their thoughts are with their jobs. The memory that remains with us from *The Seagull* is of people sitting in a garden and enjoying their 'sweet country boredom'. Who are these idle folk? They are two actresses, two writers, a doctor, a teacher, a civil servant, and a hard-pressed estate manager. Some of them have time to sit down because they are only at the beginning of their careers, some because they are at the end; the others are simply on holiday. The idleness of Masha and Andrey, in *Three Sisters*, is remarkable because it is in such contrast to the drudgery of Masha's husband and her other two sisters; the idleness of the fading landowners in *The Cherry Orchard* is being swept aside by the industrious energy of the new entrepreneurs and activists. At the centre of *Uncle Vanya* is a woman so drugged with idleness that she can't walk straight; but the corrupting effects of this are felt in the lives around her, and they are lives of hitherto unceasing toil – whether the pedantic labours of her husband, or the agricultural stewardship of Vanya and Sonya, or the sleepless rural medicine of Astrov. At the end of the play Astrov departs to his practice, and Vanya and his niece resume their drudgery on stage, in front of our eyes. This is surely remarkable. It's not the first time that work has been shown on stage. In *The Weavers*, first produced in Berlin three years earlier, Hauptmann had shown his characters labouring at their looms. For that matter we see the gravediggers briefly at work in *Hamlet*, and we have seen plenty of servants serving, soldiers soldiering, and actors rehearsing. But this is surely the first great theatrical classic where we see the principals set about the ordinary, humdrum business of their lives. Why is it the feckless Gayevs and the dozing Sorin who spring to so many people's minds first? A bizarre combination of nostalgia and condescension, perhaps – nostalgia for a lost world of servants and rural leisure, easy condescension from the moral superiority of our own busy lives. In fact work is one of the central themes in these harsh plays. Work as the longed-for panacea for all the ills of idleness; work as obsession and drudgery and the destruction of life; work as life, simply. What Sonya looks forward to in heaven for herself and her uncle at the end of *Vanya* is not finding peace, as some translations have it; what she says, five times over, in plain everyday Russian, is that they will *rest*.

A very different view of the plays has gained ground more recently – the idea that, far from being gentle expressions of regret for a vanishing world, they are declarations of faith in progress. It's not surprising that Soviet producers and critics should have wanted to claim Chekhov as a herald of the Revolution. But the somewhat similar views of the late David Magarshack, one of the most distinguished of Chekhov's translators, have had a good deal of influence upon English directors. Magarshack concedes, in his book *The Real Chekhov*, that the playwright 'was never impressed by the facile optimism of the revolutionaries who believed that by sweeping away the old order they would establish peace and harmony on earth'. But he argues that 'in all his plays Chekhov gives expression to his own social and political views by putting them into the mouths of his characters. He was very conscious that a writer's duty was to show an active interest in the social and political problems of his day'.

The only evidence that Magarshack offers for this assertion (apart from the interest shown by Astrov, in *Uncle Vanya*, in the destruction of the environment) is that he makes Trigorin say in *The Seagull*: 'As a writer I must speak of the common people, of their sufferings, of their future.' But even the most cursory glance at the passage in question makes it plain that, far from announcing a manifesto, what Trigorin is doing is complaining about the *miseries* of being a writer. Indeed, he concludes that in spite of this feeling that he ought to be dealing with the social questions of the day, all he can really write is descriptions of landscape, and that 'in everything else I'm false – false to the marrow of my bones'.

Trigorin, plainly, is labouring under the obligation he felt to do what was expected of the professional writer in Russia at the time. It was an obligation that Chekhov himself resisted. He gave an immense amount of his time and energy to practical work for others (free medical treatment for the local peasantry, organising against famine and cholera, building schools, reporting on the penal colony on Sakhalin), but he notoriously failed to be a progressive. As Simon Karlinsky shows, in the admirably combative glosses he offers in his edition of Chekhov's letters, the one section of Russian society that Chekhov consistently failed to please was the powerful progressive critical establishment; he lacked an ideology, he lacked social relevance. Chekhov himself put the matter beyond all reasonable doubt, because he did in fact issue what amounted to a manifesto of his beliefs; and it is very different from Trigorin's. It comes in a letter he wrote to the poet Alexei Pleshcheyev (and can scarcely have been intended to flatter Pleshcheyev's prejudices, since he most certainly *was* a progressive, and had in fact spent ten years in Siberia for his political activities). 'The people I fear', wrote Chekhov, 'are those who seek to read tendencies into what one writes, and who want to see me as straightforwardly liberal or conservative. I am not a liberal – not a conservative – not a gradualist – not a monk – not an indifferentist. I should like to be a free artist, and nothing else, and I regret that God has not given me the power to be one. I hate lies and violence in all their forms . . . Pharisaism, stupidity, and arbitrariness reign not only in jails and merchants' houses; I see them in science, in literature, and among young people . . . That's why I nourish no particular predilection for security policemen or butchers or scholars or writers or young people. Signs and labels I account mere prejudice. My holy of holies is the human body, health, intelligence, talent, inspiration, love, and the most absolute freedom, freedom from force and lies, in whatever form these last two might be expressed. That is the programme to which I should adhere were I a major artist.'

What makes this absolute detachment so difficult to accept is the eloquence and passion with which various characters in each of these last four plays present their own beliefs. Magarshack, as we have seen, implausibly picks Trigorin in *The Seagull* as Chekhov's mouthpiece. In *Three Sisters* he plumps for Vershinin, with his vision of the 'astonishingly, unimaginably beautiful life' that will be lived in two or three hundred years' time. He could equally well have chosen Tusenbach, in the same play, who also has his eyes fixed on the future. He is predicting (with some accuracy, as it turned out) a 'great healthy storm' that will blow society clean of idleness and boredom in twenty or thirty years' time. But he is also saying precisely the opposite to Vershinin, insisting that human life will *never* fundamentally change, because it follows its own laws. Trofimov, in *The Cherry Orchard*, believes that mankind is marching towards 'a higher happiness', to which he is showing others the way, even if he never sees it himself; but once again it's a different belief, because this 'march' is for him plainly a process of political struggle, not of natural evolution. There is a remark in Chekhov's notebooks, it's true, which faintly echoes the optimism of Vershinin and Trofimov – 'Man will become better when we have shown him to himself as he is' – and the writer Vladimir Tikhonov remembered him as saying that once people had seen themselves as they were 'they will surely by themselves create a different and better life. I shall not see it, but I know that everything will be changed, that nothing will be like our present existence.' It is difficult, though, to evaluate a remark which has been filtered through someone else's recollections. In the written record of the notebooks there is another entry that distances Chekhov from Vershinin and Trofimov almost as sharply as the Pleshcheyev letter does from Trigorin: 'We struggle to change life so that those who come after us might be happy, but those who come after us will say as usual: it was better before, life now is worse than it used to be.'

The most impassioned and moving visions of the future in these plays, however, are both expressed by women – by Olga at the end of *Three Sisters*, and by Sonya at the end of *Uncle Vanya*. These two heartbreaking speeches are quite different from Trofimov's second-hand rhetoric and Vershinin's obsessive 'philosophising'. They come from characters of such integrity, and are so powerfully placed, that we cannot help wondering, once again, whether they reflect some deep beliefs of this nature in Chekhov himself. But, once again, the beliefs are not consistent with each other. The forms of redemption that the two women expect are as different as the futures foreseen by Vershinin and Tusenbach; Olga, like Vershinin, expects the sufferings of the present to purchase happiness in this world – but a happiness which will be experienced only 'by those who live after us'. Sonya looks forward to some kind of personal recompense to herself and her uncle, but one which will be paid only in the next world. If Chekhov's views about the possibilities of happiness on earth are hedged by a faint ambiguity, his views on its likelihood in the next world are not. In a letter to the writer Shcheglov he states categorically that he had no religion.

On a number of occasions, in fact, Chekhov specifically dissociated himself from the ideas of his characters. 'If you're served coffee,' he says in a letter to Suvorin, his closest friend, 'then don't try looking for beer in it. If I present you with a professor's thoughts, then trust me and don't look for Chekhov's thoughts in them.' For him as author, he says in the same letter, his characters' ideas 'have no value for their content. It's not a question of their content; that's changeable and it's not new. The whole point is the nature of these opinions, their dependence upon external influences and so on. They must be examined like objects, like symptoms, entirely objectively, not attempting either to agree with them or to dispute them. If I described St Vitus' dance you wouldn't look at it from the point of view of a choreographer, would you? No? Then don't do it with opinions.' In another letter to Suvorin he took up the latter's complaint that one of his stories had not resolved the question of pessimism. 'I think that it's not for novelists to resolve such questions as God, pessimism, etc. The novelist's job is to show merely who, how, and in what circumstances people were talking or thinking about God or pessimism. The artist must be not the judge of his characters and what they are talking about, but merely an impartial witness. I heard a confused conversation, resolving nothing, between two Russian people about pessimism, and I have to pass on this conversation in the same form in which I heard it, but it will be evaluated by the jury, i.e. the readers. My job is merely to be talented, i.e. to be able to distinguish important phenomena from unimportant, to be able to illuminate characters and speak with their tongue.' The truth is that living characters in living fiction rarely parrot their author's opinions; nor do they speak nonsense. They speak for themselves, and their opinions are likely to have the same oblique and complex relationship to their author's opinions as their emotions do to his emotions, and their actions to his actions.

This same detachment of Chekhov's has led to another difficulty in understanding the plays which is much harder to resolve, and which is indeed likely to go on puzzling directors and actors, not to mention translators, as long as they are performed: whether or not they are to be taken as comedies. He designates the first of them, *The Seagull*, as a comedy; and so, on the whole, it is, for all its cool ambiguity. The difficulties really begin with the second, *Uncle Vanya*, where he refused to commit himself either way on the title-page – he describes it merely as 'Scenes from country life'. It is an overwhelmingly painful play. And yet there is plainly something ridiculous about Vanya himself – particularly in his effort to murder Serebryakov, and his failure to hit him at point-blank range. Are we to laugh or are we to cry? Both, no doubt. But this is easier to achieve in theory than in practice, and on the page than on the stage. An audience is a large, corporate creature with large, corporate emotions. It can stand close to the sufferer and feel his pain, or it can hold him at arm's length and see the absurdity of his helplessness; it finds it very difficult to be in both places at once. The ambiguity of the text gives the people who have to perform it genuine practical difficulties, and they must always be tempted to resolve them by pushing the tone in one direction or the other.

With the next play, *Three Sisters*, Chekhov joined in the debate himself. On the title page he called it a drama, and it must surely be one of the most heartbreaking plays ever written. But Stanislavsky in his memoirs recalls Chekhov at the first read-through of the play as being 'certain he had written a light-hearted comedy', and as being convinced, when the cast wept, that the play was incomprehensible and destined to fail. Nemirovich-Danchenko remembers him at the same occasion as struggling with a sense of embarrassment and repeating several times that he had written a 'vaudeville'. These protestations should perhaps be taken with some caution. Allowance must probably be made for the awkwardness of this first reading. Olga Knipper, who played Masha and was soon to become Chekhov's wife, recalls the cast not as weeping but as muttering discontentedly that it wasn't a play, that it was unactable, that there were no parts, while the author 'was smiling in embarrassment and walking about amongst us, coughing tensely'. Stanislavsky evidently conceded a little to Chekhov's view in the end. After the production had been running for three years, he wrote later, the audience 'began to laugh and grow quiet where the author wanted'.

The problem is most acute with the last play, *The Cherry Orchard*, where the tone is more ambiguous. Chekhov and Stanislavsky came to open disagreement about it. Chekhov not only described it on the title-page as a comedy; he insisted from first to last, as we shall see, that it was humorous. In his letters he called it a 'vaudeville'. He said it was 'not a drama but a comedy, in places even a farce . . . The whole play will be cheerful and frivolous . . .' He was not using these terms in some arcane private sense; the short plays are after all quite unambiguously cheerful and frivolous, quite straightforwardly comedies, farces, and vaudevilles. Stanislavsky's reaction to all this was to tell Chekhov bluntly that he was wrong. 'It's not a comedy, it's not a farce, as you wrote,' he informed him, after everyone had wept in the last act during the read-through at the Moscow Arts, 'it's a tragedy . . . I wept like a woman. I tried to stop myself, but I couldn't. I can hear you saying, "Excuse me, but it is in fact a farce . . ." No, for the plain man it is a tragedy.'

In the past most directors seem to have agreed with Stanislavsky. More recently the pendulum has swung the opposite way, and it has become fashionable to establish the comic nature of all these four plays by presenting the characters as ludicrously self-obsessed grotesques, and by supplying sight-gags that the author overlooked. This may be another example of Magarshack's eccentric influence. In his book *Chekhov the Dramatist* he urges the view that *The Cherry Orchard* is simply a funny play in its entirety. He even manages to find the last scene funny, where Firs is left locked into the empty house for the winter. He argues that the stage-direction says merely that Firs is lying motionless, not dying, and that someone will shortly realise what has happened, and come back and release him. This seems to me frankly preposterous. No doubt Firs is not clinically dead at the fall of the curtain, but anyone who believes he has a serious chance of emerging from that room alive has clearly never considered the practicalities of playwriting, let alone the effects of extreme cold upon extreme old age. In the course of the last act Chekhov establishes not once but three times, in a brilliantly escalating confirmation of misunderstanding, that the family believes Firs to have been taken off to hospital already; not once but four times that the house is to be closed up for the winter; and even twice that the temperature is already three degrees below zero. If you can believe that after all this there remained in Chekhov's mind some unexpressed hope that Gayev, say, might get the next train back from town, or that Yepikhodov might for some reason suddenly take it into his head to unlock the house again and inspect its contents, then you can believe that Wagner hoped the local Boy Scouts might put out the fire at the end of *Götterdämmerung* and give Siegfried and Brunnhilde artificial respiration.

Nor will the text as a whole support Magarshack's view. It is truly not possible to read the play in Russian without being moved, as Stanislavsky and his company were, to tears as well as to laughter. Some of Chekhov's references to the play's comicality have a characteristically teasing or self-mocking air – he was deeply shocked when Stanislavsky was said to be thinking of producing one of his actual vaudevilles at the Arts Theatre. He was also engaged in a running battle with Stanislavsky over the ponderousness of his staging. The trouble began from the very first moment of their first production together. This was how Act One of Stanislavsky's *Seagull* started, according to his prompt copy: 'Glimmer of lantern, distant singing of drunk, distant howling of dog, croaking of frogs, cry of corncrake, intermittent strokes of distant church bell . . . summer lightning, barely audible far-off thunder . . .' All this before the first two characters had even got on stage. Chekhov, grateful as he was for the success which Stanislavsky had at last given him with a serious play, was ungratefully cool about the production. He greatly disliked the slowness of Stanislavsky's tempo, and according to Nemirovich-Danchenko he threatened to put a stage-direction in his next play saying: 'The action takes place in a country where there are no mosquitoes or crickets or other insects that interfere with people's conversations.' Nothing about Stanislavsky's productions of the next two plays reconciled him. All the notes he gave about *Vanya*, when he finally saw it, were directed against the overtness of the action. With *The Cherry Orchard* he evidently feared the worst from the very beginning. 'I should very much like to be around at rehearsals to have a look,' he wrote anxiously to Nemirovich-Danchenko. 'I am afraid that Anya might have a tearful tone of voice (you for some reason find her similar to Irina) . . . Not once in my text does Anya weep, and nowhere does she speak in a tearful voice. In the second act she has tears in her eyes, but her tone of voice is cheerful and lively. Why in your telegram do you talk about there being a lot of people weeping in the play? Where are they? The only one is Varya, but that's because Varya is a crybaby by nature, and her tears are not supposed to elicit a feeling of gloom in the audience. In my text it often says "on the verge of tears", but that indicates merely the characters' mood, not tears. There is no cemetery in the second act.'

But even these quite specific comments can't be taken too literally, because they are at variance with Chekhov's own text. According to the stage-directions, Gayev is 'wiping away his tears' in Act Three. Ranyevskaya, at the end of the act, is 'weeping bitterly'. Both of them, at the end of the last act, 'sob quietly'. Part of what Chekhov wanted when he insisted on the comedy in his plays was surely a different style of playing; he was looking for lightness, speed, indifference, and irony; something that suggested not the inexorable tolling of fate but the absurdity of human intentions and the meaninglessness of events.

There are a number of common themes that weave their way in and out of these four last plays. One of them, as we have seen, is work. A more obscure one is the unacknowledged and unmentioned mysteries at the heart of all these families. In *The Seagull* there is an entirely unexplained and unremarked discrepancy between Arkadina's surname and her son's. It suddenly becomes clear, too, without a word being said, that it is Dorn, not Shamrayev, who is Masha's father. There is another suggestion of a similar relationship (first pointed out, I think, by Ronald Bryden) in *Three Sisters*, where Chebutykin – the doctor again – cherishes an intense attachment to Irina, whom he remembers carrying in his arms as a baby, and whose mother had been the love of his life. In *Uncle Vanya* the old nurse recalls – again without comment or explanation – that Serebryakov's first wife, who had loved him with all her heart, 'couldn't sleep at night for grieving . . . did nothing but weep'. This had been when their daughter, Sonya, was still little, and 'didn't understand'. And why, in *The Cherry Orchard*, has Ranyevskaya adopted Varya? There is no mention of her background or parentage. Is she known (to everyone but us) to be the illegitimate daughter of Ranyevskaya's drunken late husband?

In all the plays, too, something is being lost. All attempts at forward motion – all the brave forays into the world of work and endeavour – are counterbalanced by the undertow of regret; there is some loss that will never be made good, even if all the bright prophecies of the optimists were to come true tomorrow. In *The Seagull* it is the innocence and hopes of Konstantin and Nina. In *Vanya* it is Vanya's life – sacrificed, as he comes to realise, to a worthless object, wasted through his own timidity and diffidence. In *Three Sisters* it is the lives of all three women that drain away in front of our eyes. In *The Cherry Orchard* the trees that begin in blossom and end beneath the axe are everything that can ever be lost by mortal man – childhood, happiness, purpose, love, and all the brightness of life.

But Chekhov's technique and ideas develop over the course of the four plays. Although *The Seagull* (as I shall argue later) represents something entirely new in the history of the theatre, there are still one or two elements which Chekhov has not completely succeeded in accommodating to his new aesthetic. Konstantin's account in the last act of what has happened to Nina over the past two years is awkwardly and belatedly expository, dramatically inert, and curiously old-fashioned in tone – though it might be argued that it is only natural for him, as a writer of the time, to talk like a nineteenth-century short story. The soliloquies, too, have the air of survivals from an earlier convention. Elsewhere in the play we are left, as we are in life, to work out for ourselves what people are thinking and feeling from what they actually choose or happen to say to each other. It jars when we are suddenly given direct access to Dorn's thoughts about Konstantin's play, or to Konstantin's assessment of his own stories. Arkadina, after she believes she has broken Trigorin's will to leave her, even gives us an aside ('Now he's mine'); though again it could be argued that, since she is an actress, it may be she rather than Chekhov who has imported the line from the theatre. He is still relying heavily upon soliloquy in *Uncle Vanya*, but by the time he came to write the last two plays he has abandoned it. Andrey, in *Three Sisters*, delivers his disquisitions unheard to the deaf Ferapont. Firs, locked into the house alone at the end of *The Cherry Orchard*, is an old man talking to himself, as he has earlier even in other people's presence.

The abandonment of soliloquy is part of Chekhov's developing naturalism. In *The Cherry Orchard*, however, he was plainly beginning to move on again. It is more dependent upon mood and symbolism than the first three plays, and some of the symbols – notably the breaking string – remain unexplained and oblique in their significance. He may have been planning to go further in this direction with the extraordinary new departure he was contemplating at the time of his death – a play about Arctic exploration.

There is another, even more fundamental, development over the course of the plays, and that is in the way they are resolved. All Chekhov's previous full-length plays culminate in the shooting of the central character. Platonov, in the untitled play, is shot by his rejected mistress. Ivanov, in the play that bears his name, and Voynitzky, in

The Wood Demon, shoot themselves. The technique survives into *The Seagull*, where there is no one central character, but where it is still the suicide of a principal that brings the play to a close. But in *Vanya* Chekhov finally thought his way past this tidy convention. Two more characters will die, it is true. Tusenbach's death in *Three Sisters*, though, is the result of a meaningless quarrel. It is shown not as *his* tragedy – the imminence of it gives him his first real awareness of the world and his first real pleasure in it – but as one more of the losses which empty the sisters' future of meaning. Firs is left dying at the end of *The Cherry Orchard*, but the sale of the estate, which finally destroys any hopes the Gayevs have had in life, has already occurred at the end of Act Three, so that the last act is left once again to show life continuing. The tragedy in these last plays is not death but the continuation of life; the pain of losing the past, with all the happiness and wealth of possibilities it contained, will always be compounded by the pain of facing the future in all its emptiness. 'The ability to endure' had already been identified by Nina at the end of *The Seagull* as the most important quality in life. In *Uncle Vanya* Sonya takes it up as her watchword – 'Endure, uncle! Endure!' – as she coaxes Vanya through his despair at the prospect of living for another dozen years, and as the future dwindles to a 'long, long succession of days and endless evenings' unilluminated by either any sense of purpose or any prospect of alteration. The three sisters, after all their hopes have gone, understand that they 'have to live'.

The courage to endure which is called upon at the end of *Vanya* and *Three Sisters* is connected by both Sonya and Olga with the passionate hopes they express for some remote future in this world or the next. These hopes, as we have seen, do not imply any similar faith on Chekhov's part. This makes them no less moving; nor does our own unbelief. Indeed it is surely the very impossibility of their visions, of Sonya's sky all dressed in diamonds and Olga's peace and happiness on earth, that makes the speeches so poignant. And yet the force and insistence of the idea, in the two successive plays, is very striking. I suspect that for once we do get some insight into Chekhov himself here – not into his beliefs or opinions, certainly, but into some much deeper and less coherent feeling, some similarly poignant yearning for a future whose unattainability he was just beginning to grasp. It is a common experience for people in early middle age, which is where Chekhov was when he wrote these plays, to come over the brow of the hill, as it were, and to see for the first time that their life will have an end. But the end with which Chekhov came face to face in mid-life was suddenly much closer still. It was not until six months after he had finished *Vanya* that he had his first major haemorrhage, and that his tuberculosis was finally diagnosed. But he had been spitting blood for a long time. He insists over and over again in his letters that this is the most normal thing in the world; but the more he insists the more one wonders. As Ronald Hingley puts it in his biography: 'Can Anton really have been unaware, still, that he suffered from tuberculosis? It seems incredible that a practising doctor could continue to ignore symptoms of which the possible purport might have struck any layman. On the other hand, as Chekhov's own works richly illustrate, human beings have an almost infinite capacity for self-deception. Did the man who deluded others about the desperate condition of his health also delude himself? Or did he hover between self-deception and self-knowledge?'

It was at some point in that final year before the diagnosis was made that he was writing *Vanya* and giving up the idea of death as a dramatic resolution. Perhaps somewhere inside himself he had begun to recognise what was happening to him. Perhaps, now that he was suddenly so close to it, death seemed a little less neat, a little less of an answer to the equation; perhaps it began to seem more like something you could look as far as, or beyond, but not at. And even if Chekhov hadn't yet seen the truth about his condition, perhaps Sonya and the others had in a sense seen it for him. A writer's characters, particularly when they are not forced to represent his conscious thoughts, can be appallingly well informed about his unconscious ones. It is ironical. Chekhov most sedulously absented himself from his works. Sonya's passionate invocation of an afterlife in which he did not believe may be one of our rare glimpses of him – and of an aspect of him that he couldn't even see himself.

One-Act Plays

The first four plays in this collection (*The Evils of Tobacco*, *Swan Song*, *The Bear*, and *The Proposal*) are a selection from the one-acters with which Chekhov first made his reputation in the theatre. They are in a different mode from the four great dramas that follow; offered not as art but as entertainment. *The Evils of Tobacco*, in 1885, was his first attempt at the form. He intended it, he said, 'in the secrecy of his heart', for performance, but in the event it was published in a collection of his stories, and seems not to have been performed until fifteen years later. It was the next one, *Swan Song*, that gave him his first small success in the theatre. He adapted it from one of his stories ('Calchas'), and it was produced at Korsh's in 1888, just after the debacle with *Ivanov*. It was merely part of a mixed bill, but it was a vastly more suitable piece for the house, and it was well enough received for proposals to be made for remounting it at the Maly, one of the imperial theatres. It must have seemed clear where his future in the theatre lay, and in the same month he was already writing *The Bear*. This was an original, not an adaptation. He subtitled it 'a joke in one act', and it is indeed a comedy pure and simple, with none of the pathos of *Swan Song*. Chekhov complained that he and his sister could have acted better than the cast at Korsh's, but it made the audience laugh non-stop, and by the following year another commercial management, Abramova's, was fighting Korsh for the rights. It went on to cause a 'furore' at the Alexandrinsky, the imperial theatre in St Petersburg, and then to take the provinces by storm. Chekhov found it being played in several of the Siberian towns he passed through on his way to Sakhalin in 1890. It became such a favourite of amateur dramatic groups that Chekhov was complaining a decade later that 'practically every lady I meet begins her acquaintance with me by saying: "I've acted in your *Bear*!"' And Tolstoy, who thought all Chekhov's later plays were even worse than Shakespeare's, was reported by Olga Knipper to have laughed until he could laugh no more.

Chekhov followed this up the same year with another one-act 'joke' in much the same vein, *The Proposal*. He expressed some doubts about this one. In a letter to the writer Shcheglov he said that he had 'knocked it together specifically for the provinces'. It would pass muster there, he thought, but he did not propose to put it on in the capital. It was in fact successfully performed in Moscow at the Maly, and given in St Petersburg before the Tsar, who was moved to send the author his compliments.

There are four more short plays, not included here, that Chekhov wrote over the next few years. The most interesting of them, to my mind, is *Tatyana Repina*, a parody of a drama by his wealthy publisher friend Suvorin. It seems to have been intended purely for Suvorin's amusement, and it makes insufficient sense without a knowledge of Suvorin's original. It is nevertheless striking in the way it counterpoints an endless Orthodox marriage service with the scandalised comments of the congregation when they realise that the bridegroom's abandoned mistress, who has supposedly poisoned herself, is present in the church. There is also a good comic character in the sceptical old watchman at the church, who dismisses the whole idea of weddings. 'Every day they go marrying and christening and burying, and there's no sense in any of it . . . They sing, they burn incense, they read, and God never listens. Forty years I've worked here, and not once did God ever listen . . . And where this God is I don't know . . . There's no point in any of it . . .'

The other three one-act plays from this period, *The Reluctant Tragedian*, *The Wedding*, and *The Anniversary* (together with a fourth, *The Night before the Trial*, which he left unfinished), were all adapted from his old stories. They seem to me notably weaker than the earlier plays, and they had a less striking success at the time. Even so, *The Wedding* made Tolstoy 'collapse with laughter' (as reported by Olga Knipper, at any rate), and *The Anniversary*, when it was finally performed in St Peterburg over a decade later, to mixed notices, still had the audience, according to one critic, 'not so much laughing as simply rolling with laughter'. Chekhov designated most of the one-act comedies on their title-pages as 'jokes', and consistently disparages them all in his letters. *The Proposal*, he said, was 'a mangy little vaudeville'. *The Bear* was 'a piffling little Frenchified vaudeville' which he had written because he had nothing better to do, having used up so much 'sap and energy' on his novella *The Steppe* that he was incapable of doing anything serious for a long time afterwards. When, in later years, Olga Knipper reported that Stanislavsky was interested in the rewritten version of *The Evils of Tobacco*, Chekhov was so appalled at the idea of 'doing a vaudeville at the Arts Theatre' that he wrote back to her saying she had gone mad, and adding three exclamation marks. He claimed to have dashed these wretched 'vaudevilles' off at odd moments. He had ruined *The Evils of Tobacco*, he said, because he had only two and a half hours to write it in. *Swan Song* he claimed to have written in one hour and five minutes. The work on the latter, of course, involved mostly just transcription from an existing story, but even so it at least challenges the record playwriting speeds credited to Noel Coward and Alan Ayckbourn, each of whom is said to have written a full-length original play in three days. If Chekhov could have maintained his claimed rate with original material over the full course he would have completed *Hay Fever* or *Absurd Person Singular* inside a single working day.

Still, at the time he wrote most of these plays he was going through a phase of hating the theatre altogether. It was in his letter to Shcheglov about *The Proposal*, urging him to give up his love-affair with the stage, that he diagnosed the modern theatre as 'the venereal disease of the cities'. In fact a letter to another writer, Bezhetzky, suggests that he regarded 'vaudevilles' as a slightly less pathological manifestation than other types of play. 'I don't like the theatre,' he told him, 'I quickly get bored – but I do like watching vaudevilles.' With characteristic self-mocking jauntiness he said he also believed in vaudevilles as an author, and that 'anyone possessing fifty acres and ten tolerable vaudevilles I reckon to be a made man – his widow will never die of hunger.' If a vaudeville turned out badly, he urged Bezhetsky, 'don't be bashful – just stick a pen-name on it. The provinces will swallow anything. Just try to see there are good parts. The simpler the setting and the smaller the cast, the more often the vaudeville will be done.' The cynical tone is no doubt all part of the flippant pose, but the content is hard-headed, practical advice (as true now, of course, as it was then) that he was following himself. It was offered only a month before urging Shcheglov to flee the theatrical pox; and only a month after *that* he was telling Suvorin that he was going to turn to vaudevilles when he had written himself out in other directions. 'I think I could write them at the rate of a hundred a year. Ideas for vaudevilles pour out of me like oil from the Baku wells.' He even wondered whether he shouldn't donate his 'stake in the oilfield' to Shcheglov.

Chekhov may well have taken his vaudevilles more seriously than his offhandedness about them suggests. He was notably flippant about *The Seagull*, too. And the four in this collection, at any rate, have solid theatrical virtues. *The Evils of Tobacco* and *Swan Song* both touch upon some deeper desolation than boulevard plays normally care to show; the old actor gazing forlornly into the blackness of the empty theatre, and the wretched lecturer who is not so much hen-pecked as hen-eaten and left as droppings, have something in common with Gogol's Poprishchin and Akaky Akakiyevich. And *The Bear* and *The Proposal* are classics of the comic theatre, full of energy, invention, and actors' opportunities. They are larger than life, certainly, but splendid in their magnification.

Chekhov's designation for them both, 'joke', is usually translated into English as 'farce'. The term is of course a capacious one, but there is a considerable difference between these plays and most French or English farces. As we know the form it usually depends upon panic, and the panic is usually generated by guilt and the prospect of some kind of social disgrace. The panic leads in its turn to deceit, which produces further and yet more alarming prospects of disgrace, from which grows ever greater panic, in a spiral known to scientists as positive feedback. There is no panic in *The Bear* or *The Proposal*, no deceit or threatened disgrace. What drives these characters is a sense of outrage – of anger at the failure of others to recognise their claims, whether to money or to land or to a certain status. In their anger they lose the ability to control their destinies or even to recognise their own best interests, just as the characters of traditional farce do in their panic. This is what these plays have in common with English and French farces – that their characters are reduced by their passions to the level of blind and inflexible machines. This reduction is precisely what Bergson thought was the defining factor in all comedy. But if the other four plays in this collection are in any sense comedies, as Chekhov claimed, Bergson's explanation will not do for them. When Vanya in his rage and despair shoots at Serebryakov he is comic, but he is not in any way like a machine. This is surely one of the distinctions between the vaudevilles and what is to come.

The Seagull

'A comedy – three f., six m., four acts, rural scenery (a view over a lake); much talk of literature, little action, five bushels of love.'

Chekhov's own synopsis of *The Seagull*, in a letter to Suvorin written a month before he finished it in 1895, is once again self-mocking and offhand. (His cast-list is even one f. short, unless he added the fourth woman only during that last month, or when he revised the play the following year.) He says in the same letter that he is cheating against the conventions of the theatre, but no one could have begun to guess from his flippant résumé how extraordinary an event was being prepared for the world. No doubt Chekhov took the play more seriously than the letter suggests, but even he can scarcely have realised quite what he had on his hands: a catastrophe so grotesque that it made him swear never to write for the theatre again; a triumph so spectacular that it established him as a kind of theatrical saint; and the first of the four masterpieces that would redraw forever the boundaries of drama.

He was thirty-five by this time, and had still had no real success as a serious playwright. For all his apparent casualness, as he finished *The Seagull* and read it through he had a moment of fundamental doubt. 'I am once again convinced', he wrote to Suvorin, 'that I am absolutely not a dramatist.' Then there were prolonged difficulties in getting the play past the theatrical censor (see A Note on the Translation, p. 210), which almost made him despair of the whole enterprise. But once this hurdle was behind him Chekhov's apparently offhand mood returned. The play was to be performed at the Alexandrinsky Theatre in St Petersburg, where *Ivanov* had been well received seven years earlier after its disputed opening in Moscow, and his letters in September 1896, as rehearsals approached, have the same cheerful flippancy as his original account of the play to Suvorin. They read with hindsight as ironically as the banter of some doomed statesman as he goes all unknowing towards his assassination. To his brother Georgi: 'My play will be done in the Alexandrinsky Theatre at a jubilee benefit [for the actress Levkeyeva]. It will be a resounding gala occasion. Do come!' To Shcheglov: 'Around the 6th [of October] the thirst for glory will draw me to the Palmyra of the north for the rehearsals of my *Seagull*.' To his brother Alexander: 'You are to meet me at the station, in full dress uniform (as laid down for a customs officer retd.) . . . On 17 Oct my new play is being done at the Alexandrinsky. I would tell you what it's called, only I'm afraid you'll go round boasting you wrote it.'

The 17th, when it came, was indeed a resounding gala occasion. 'I have been going to the theatre in St Petersburg for more than twenty years,' wrote a correspondent in a theatrical journal afterwards, 'and I have witnessed a great many "flops" . . . but I can remember nothing resembling what happened in the auditorium at Levkeyeva's twenty-fifth jubilee.' The trouble started within the first few minutes of Act One. Levkeyeva was a popular light comedy actress, and even though she had no part in the play the audience were minded to laugh. The first thing that struck them as funny was the sight of Masha offering a pinch of snuff to Medvedenko, and thereafter they laughed at everything. Konstantin's play – Konstantin with his head bandaged – it was all irresistible. By Act Two, according to the papers next day, the dialogue was beginning to be drowned by the noise and movement in the audience; by Act Three the hissing had become general and deafening. The reviewers struggled for superlatives to describe 'the grandiose scale' of the play's failure, the 'scandalous' and 'unprecedented' nature of 'such a dizzying flop, such a stunning fiasco'. The author, they reported, had fled from the theatre.

According to his own accounts of the evening Chekhov had escaped from the theatre only when the play ended, after sitting out two or three acts in Levkeyeva's dressing-room, had eaten supper at Romanov's 'in the proper way', then slept soundly and caught the train home to Melikhovo next day. Even Suvorin, though, accused him of cowardice in running away. All he had run away from, he protested in a letter to Suvorin's wife, was the intolerable sympathy of his friends. He told Suvorin: 'I behaved as reasonably and coolly as a man who has proposed and been refused, and who has no choice but to go away . . . Back in my own home I took a dose of castor oil, had a wash in cold water – and now I could sit down and write a new play.'

But Suvorin, with whom he was staying, recorded in his diary that Chekhov's first reaction had been to give up the theatre. He had not come back until two in the morning, when he told Suvorin that he had been walking about the streets, and that 'if I live another seven hundred years I shan't have a single play put on. Enough is enough. In this area I am a failure.' When he went home next day he left a note telling Suvorin to halt the printing of his plays, and saying that he would never forget the previous evening. He claimed to have slept well, and to be leaving 'in an absolutely tolerable frame of mind'; but he managed nevertheless to leave his dressing-gown and other belongings on the train, and the accounts he subsequently gave of the evening in various letters to friends and relations make it clear how painful the experience had been. 'The moral of all this', he wrote to his sister Masha, 'is that one shouldn't write plays.'

Things at the Alexandrinsky improved somewhat after the first night. 'A total and unanimous success,' wrote Komissarzhevskaya, who was playing Nina, in a letter to Chekhov after the second performance, 'such as it ought to be and could not but be.' There were encouraging reports from other friends, too, but Chekhov remained sceptical. 'I couldn't help reflecting', he replied to one sympathiser, 'that if kind people find it necessary to comfort me then things must be in a bad way.' In fact the play was withdrawn after five performances, and was subsequently attacked by reviewers even when it appeared in published form, clear of the shortcomings of the production. Still, within a month or so his theatrical hopes had revived again, and he was telling Suvorin of the existence of a new play 'not known to anyone in the world' – *Uncle Vanya*. And two years later, in a stunning reversal of fortune of the kind that occurs in plays (though never in

Chekhov's own), *The Seagull* triumphed in Moscow as noisily as it had failed in Petersburg.

In fact the event went rather beyond anything one might find in a play; it was more like something out of a backstage musical – particularly as recounted by Stanislavsky (who was both directing and playing Trigorin) in his memoir of Chekhov. For a start the fate of the newly founded Moscow Arts Theatre depended upon it. The other opening productions had mostly either failed or been banned by the Metropolitan of Moscow, and all hopes were now riding aboard this one salvaged wreck. There was a suitable love interest depending upon the outcome of the evening – the leading lady (Olga Knipper, playing Arkadina) and the author had just met, and were to marry two plays later – provided there *were* two more plays to allow their acquaintance to develop. Moreover, the author had now been diagnosed as consumptive and exiled to Yalta. The dress rehearsal was of course a disaster. At the end of it Chekhov's sister Masha arrived to express her horror at the prospect of what another failure like the one in Petersburg would do to her sick brother, and they considered abandoning the production and closing the theatre.

When the curtain finally went up on the first night the audience was sparse, and the cast all reeked of the valerian drops they had taken to tranquillise themselves. As they reach the end of Act One Stanislavsky's paragraphs become shorter and shorter:

> We had evidently flopped. The curtain came down in the silence of the tomb. The actors huddled fearfully together and listened to the audience.
>
> It was as quiet as the grave.
>
> Heads emerged from the wings as the stage staff listened as well.
>
> Silence.
>
> Someone started to cry. Knipper was holding back hysterical sobs. We went offstage in silence.
>
> At that moment the audience gave a kind of moan and burst into applause. We rushed to take a curtain.
>
> People say that we were standing on stage with our backs half-turned to the audience, that we had terror on our faces, that

none of us thought to bow and that someone was even sitting down. We had evidently not taken in what had happened.

In the house the success was colossal; on stage it was like a second Easter. Everyone kissed everyone else, not excluding strangers who came bursting backstage. Someone went into hysterics. Many people, myself among them, danced a wild dance for joy and excitement.

The only person who remained completely calm seems to have been Chekhov himself, since he was eight hundred miles away in the Crimea, exiled by his consumption. But when after Act Three the audience began to shout 'Author! Author!', as audiences do in this kind of script, and Nemirovich-Danchenko explained to them that the author was not present, they shouted, 'Send a telegram!' In the event he was informed of his triumph not only by telegram, but in shoals of letters from everyone present. Judging by how rarely he referred to it either beforehand or afterwards in his own letters from Yalta, however, he had kept this production at a distance emotionally as well as geographically, and the Moscow success was considerably more remote from him than the Petersburg failure.

There were of course external reasons for the play's extraordinarily different reception in the two capitals. The choice of Levkeyeva's benefit night in St Petersburg, on the one hand, and the fact that it had been produced there at nine days' notice; the thorough preparation in Moscow on the other hand, with twelve weeks' rehearsal. But the play would almost certainly have elicited a passionate response of one kind or another. Its influence has been so widespread and pervasive since that it is difficult now to realise what a departure it was. The traditional function of literature in general, and of drama in particular, has always been to simplify and formalise the confused world of our experience; to isolate particular emotions and states of mind from the flux of feeling in which we live; to make our conflicts coherent; to illustrate values and to impose a moral (and therefore human) order upon a non-moral and inhuman universe; to make intention visible, and to suggest the process by which it takes effect. *The Seagull* is a critical survey of this function. For a start two of the characters are writers. One of them is using the traditional techniques without questioning them, the other is searching for some even more formalised means of expression; and what interests Chekhov is how life eludes the efforts of both of them. Konstantin cannot even begin to capture it, for all the seriousness of his intentions; Trigorin feels that in the end all he has ever managed to do without falsity is landscapes, while his obsessive need to write drains his experience of all meaning apart from its literary possibilities. The extraordinary trick of the play is that all around the two writers we see the very life that they are failing to capture. What Chekhov is doing, in fact, is something formally impossible – to look behind the simplification and formalisation by which the world is represented in art and to show the raw, confused flux of the world itself, where nothing has its moral value written upon it, or for that matter its cause or its effect, or even its boundaries or its identity.

The most obvious characteristic of this approach is the play's ambiguity of tone. Chekhov calls it a comedy, but does not give us any of the stylistic indications that are customary when events are to be seen as comic. Indeed, what we are watching has not even been clearly organised into *events*; a lot of it bears a striking resemblance to the non-events out of which the greater part of our life consists. Then again, the play is to a quite astonishing extent morally neutral. It displays no moral conflict and takes up no moral attitude to its characters. Even now, after all these years, some people still find this difficult to accept. They talk as if Arkadina and Trigorin, at any rate, were monsters, and as if the point of the play were to expose her egotism and his spinelessness. It is indeed impossible not to be appalled by Arkadina's insensitivity towards her son, or by the ruthlessness with which she attempts to keep Trigorin attached to her; moral neutrality is not moral blindness. But Konstantin continues to find good in her, for all his jealousy and irritation, and she remains capable of inspiring the love of those around her. Konstantin's assessment is just as valid as ours; the devotion of Dorn and Shamrayev is just as real and just as important as our outrage. There is moral irony, too, in her manipulation of Trigorin; had she succeeded more completely in blackmailing him to remain with her she might have saved Nina from the misery that engulfs her. It is hard to respect Trigorin as we see him crumble in Arkadina's hands, harder still to like him when we know how he has treated Nina. But Masha likes and respects him, and for good reason – because he listens to her and takes her seriously; no grounds are offered for discounting her judgement. And when Trigorin wanders back in the last act, makes his peace with Konstantin, and settles down to lotto with the others, he is once again neither good nor bad in their eyes, in spite of what he has done; he is at that moment just a man who always seems to come out on top, whether in lotto or in love. We are perfectly entitled to find against him, of course – but that is our own verdict; there has been no direction to the jury in the judge's summing-up; indeed, no summing-up and no judge.

But then nothing is fixed. Everything is open to interpretation. Are we, for instance, to take Konstantin seriously as a writer? Impossible, after Nina's complaint that there are no living creatures in his work. But then it turns out that Dorn likes it, and he is a man of robust good sense (though not good enough to prevent his ruining Polina's life). And in Act Four we discover that Konstantin is at any rate talented enough to be able to make a career as a professional writer. But even then Trigorin's judgement remains the same as Nina's, and Konstantin comes round to much the same view himself.

No one is valued for us; nothing is firmly located or fully explained. Why is Arkadina called Arkadina? She is Sorina by birth and Trepleva by marriage. It could be a stage-name, of course, or she could have married more than once. The people around her presumably know. They do not trouble to tell us. Has Dorn had an affair with Arkadina in the past? Is this why Polina is so relentlessly jealous of her? Is it what Arkadina is referring to when she talks about how irresistible he had once been? (In an earlier draft Polina begins to weep quietly at this point; but that may of course be for the lost early days of her own love.) In an astonishing moment at the end of Act One we do in fact stumble across one of the unexplained secrets of this world, when Dorn snatches Masha's snuff-box away from her, admonishes her for her 'filthy habit', and flings it into the bushes. From that one gesture of licensed impatience we understand why Masha feels nothing for her father, why she sees herself as being 'of dubious descent', and why she feels so close to Dorn; because Dorn is her father, not Shamrayev. But who knows this, apart from us and Dorn? Not Masha herself, apparently. Does Shamrayev? Arkadina? Medvedenko? We are not told; the clouds that have parted for a moment close in again.

But then which of them knows about Dorn's relationship with Masha's mother in the first place? Perhaps everyone; or perhaps no one. We can only speculate. In any case it is characteristic of the relationships in the play; overt or covert, they are all one-sided, unsatisfactory, anomalous, and unlikely ever to be resolved. Medvedenko loves Masha who loves Konstantin who loves Nina who loves Trigorin who is supposed to love Arkadina, but who doesn't really love anyone, not even himself. No one's life can be contained in the forms that marriage and family offer. Konstantin's dissatisfaction with the existing dramatic forms is only a special case of this general condition. Plainly Chekhov is not advocating new social forms, in the way that Konstantin is calling for new literary ones. In the end even Konstantin comes to think that it is not a question of forms, old or new – the important thing is to write from the heart; nor are there any social forms suggested in the play which could ever contain the great flux of life itself. Is there any trace of Chekhov himself for once in either of the two professional writers in the play? Konstantin is scarcely likely to be a self-portrait, overwhelmed as he is by an artistic family, obsessed by questions of literary theory, and unable to create a living character; Chekhov's parents, after all, ran a provincial grocery, he displayed no interest in theory, and life is the very quality in which his stories and plays abound. But Trigorin is another matter. He is a celebrated and successful author, in much the same way that Chekhov was. His passion is fishing; so was Chekhov's. His modest estimate of his place in Russian letters is very much the kind of thing that Chekhov might have said mockingly about himself. More importantly, it seems at any rate plausible that his painful memories of beginning his career reflect something of Chekhov's own experience, and the terrible compulsion to write which is eating his life certainly closely echoes what Chekhov said about himself in a letter to Lika Mizinova – 'Not for one moment am I free of the thought that I must, am obliged to write. Write, write and write' – particularly since the only palliative for his obsession is the fishing. The passage in Trigorin's works to which Nina's inscription on the medallion refers ('If ever you have need of my life, then come and take it') is a line from one of his own stories. Then again, the little tricks of style that Konstantin identifies in Trigorin's stories, as he despairingly compares them with his own in Act Four – the short cuts that he believes make things easy for Trigorin – are Chekhov's own. The two details he quotes that Trigorin uses to set up his moonlit night – 'the neck of a broken bottle glittering on the bank of the millpool and the shadow of the water-wheel black beside it' – are almost precisely the ones that Chekhov had used a decade earlier, with similar economy, to establish the moonlit night in a story called *The Wolf*. It is a compelling piece, full of the life that evaded Trigorin, and Chekhov can scarcely have been mocking his own technique, because a month or two after he wrote it he gave his brother Alexander a lesson by post in short-story writing in which he quoted variants of the same two details to illustrate how to breathe life into descriptions of nature by the use of specific concrete details.

There would be something characteristically self-mocking, of course, in choosing a second-rate author to represent himself, but the parallel breaks down soon enough. When Trigorin confesses to Nina that all he can write is landscapes we realise that the picture which has been built up deliberately excludes the very essence of Chekhov's literary identity. Nor do any of the other biographical details fit. Arkadina is indeed based in part upon an actress, Yavorskaya, who seems from her letters to have been very briefly his mistress. But Chekhov, unlike Trigorin, had no difficulty in disentangling himself from her, and in keeping women at arm's length generally. One of the women who were in love with Chekhov, Lika Mizinova, he kept at bay so successfully that she provided a model for not one but two of the characters in *The Seagull*: first Masha, with her life ruined by the unquenchable but unreciprocated love she has for Konstantin, and then Nina. To forget the Masha-like feelings she had for Chekhov, Lika threw herself into a disastrous affair with a friend of his, the Ukrainian writer Potapenko, who left his wife and went off to Paris with her, where he made her pregnant and then abandoned her. Potapenko, ironically, having provided Chekhov with a model for the more dubious aspects of Trigorin, was then called upon by him, after the play was finished, to undertake on his behalf all the endless negotiations with the censor.

Nina was also contributed to by another of Chekhov's admirers, the writer Lidia Avilova, whom he treated even more high-handedly. She gave him a charm for his watch-chain with a page reference inscribed upon it, exactly as Nina does Trigorin with the medallion, and referring to the same passage. Meeting her later at a masked ball, Chekhov promised to give her the answer to this from the stage in his new play. Ronald Hingley, in his biography of Chekhov, recounts how she went to the catastrophic first night in St Petersburg and struggled to hear the promised answer through the uproar all around her. She noted the page reference given by Nina, and when she got home looked up the same page and line in a volume of her own stories. It read: 'Young ladies should not attend masked balls.' By this time, anyway, says Hingley, Chekhov had passed Avilova's fervently inscribed charm on to Komissarzhevskaya, the actress playing Nina, and it was being used on stage as a prop. If Chekhov had modelled Trigorin's behaviour with women on his own the play would have ended after Act Two.

There are, as I have argued earlier, some slightly awkward survivals in *The Seagull* from the existing dramatic conventions of the day. The other complaints which are sometimes made against the play, however, seem to me to stem from misunderstandings. The symbolism, for instance, is occasionaly disparaged as a portentous device to be outgrown by Chekhov in the three later and even greater plays. In fact there is rather less symbolism in *The Seagull* than in the others. The only symbol is the seagull itself, and this is set up not by Chekhov but by Konstantin, as Nina immediately recognises when he lays the bird accusingly at her feet. It is part of the portentousness and inertness of Konstantin's art, not of Chekhov's – and it is then taken up by Trigorin and absorbed into the machinery of *his*, when he discovers the dead bird and outlines his story of the girl who is destroyed with the same wilfulness and casualness. Between them they burden Nina with an image for herself and her fate that comes to obsess her. One of the themes of the play, as I have argued, is the way in which art warps and destroys the life that it draws upon. The message of the seagull, as it stands there stuffed and forgotten at the end of the play, is precisely of the deadness of the symbolic process.

Many people, too, have had difficulty in the past with the scene in the last act between Nina and Konstantin. The difficulty has arisen because it has often been regarded, and played, as a version of the traditional mad scene, where the pathos of the heroine who has lost or been rejected by her love is demonstrated by her retreat from reality into a world of illusion. This is plainly not the case with Nina for the greater part of the scene; she gives an entirely clear, calm, and sane account of her experiences. The problem comes when she says, as she does in all the English translations of the play that I have come across, 'I am a seagull.' The poor girl thinks she is a bird; her mind is plainly going. Now, there is a much more reasonable construction to place upon her words here, but it is obscured by a difficulty in the translation of the Russian which may at first sight seem quibblingly small. In the Russian language there is no such thing as an article, either definite or indefinite. No distinction can be made, in speech or thought, between what English-speakers are forced to regard as two separable concepts – 'a seagull' and 'the seagull'. So when Nina signs her letters 'Chaika' (Seagull), it is perfectly open to Konstantin to regard this as a sign of distraction, of the sort suffered by the grief-stricken miller in Pushkin's *The Water Sprite*, who tells people he is a raven. But what Nina herself means, surely, when the distinction has to be made in English, is not that she is *a* seagull but that she is *the* seagull. In other words, she is not identifying with the bird but with the girl in Trigorin's story, who is the Seagull in the same way that Jenny Lind was the Swedish Nightingale, or Shakespeare was the Swan of Avon. This is the idea that has seized hold of her – not that she has white wings and a yellow beak – but that she has been reduced to the status of a manipulated character in Trigorin's fiction – a character whose fate can be summed up in a single image. This is an obsessive thought, and she makes repeated efforts to throw it off, but it is not in any sense a deluded one. She *has* been manipulated; she is another victim of the distorting and deadening process of art. One can't help wondering if Avilova and Lika Mizinova ever came to feel that they had this in common with Nina, as well as everything else.

If her picture of herself as being the seagull of Trigorin's projected story is sane and sober, so is her claim to have found her way at last as an actress. We have no way of judging whether her hopes are well-founded; but her feeling that she is on the right path at last is an entirely rational one. Konstantin takes it seriously, anyway – seriously enough to realise that he by comparison is still lost, and to shoot himself in despair as a result. Faced with that testimony to the seriousness of his judgement we are scarcely in a position to dissent.

And this in fact is the final irony of the play – that in the end the Seagull herself escapes, wounded but still flying. It is the shooter who is shot, the writer who is written to death. Konstantin, not Nina, turns out to be the real victim of Trigorin's story, the true Seagull; Konstantin, who first brought the creature down to earth and declared it to be a symbol, is the one who ends up symbolised, lying as inert and irrelevant in the next room as the poor stuffed bird is in this. Perhaps Mizinova and the others found some symbolic comfort in that.

Uncle Vanya

No one knows exactly when *Uncle Vanya* took its present form. It was most probably in the summer of 1896, between the completion of *The Seagull* and its disastrous premiere in St Petersburg. It was first produced in the following year, as the second of the four last plays. But in its origins it goes back to a much earlier period than *The Seagull*. It is substantially a reworking of *The Wood Demon*, which was conceived nearly a decade before, at the time when Chekhov was still only just emerging as a serious writer. Its development can be followed with unusual closeness, partly because of the existence of this earlier version, and partly because it started out, bizarrely, as a collaboration with Suvorin, the early stages of which are recorded in their correspondence. Its progress towards its final form was tortuous and painful, and it is the story of Chekhov's own development as a dramatist. It was many times nearly abandoned; so was Chekhov's new career. At an early point both play and career nearly took off in a startlingly different direction, when Chekhov proposed changing the subject to the story in the Apocrypha of Holofernes and his decapitation by Judith, or else Solomon, or alternatively Napoleon on Elba, or

Napoleon III and Eugénie. The possibilities are as extraordinary to consider as Vanya's own missed alternative career as a Schopenhauer or a Dostoyevsky.

The first work on the proposed collaboration seems in fact to have been done by Suvorin rather than Chekhov. Suvorin, Chekhov's closest friend, was a publisher by trade, and a man of great wealth, but he had literary ambitions of his own – he wrote *Tatyana Repina*, the play which Chekhov parodied, and stories which he submitted to Chekhov's practical and often devastating criticism. The earliest reference to their joint venture is in a letter Chekhov wrote to him in November 1888, where he acknowledges receipt of 'the beginning of the play', and congratulates Suvorin on the creation of one of the principal characters – Blagosvetlov, who was to become Serebryakov in the final version. 'You've done him well: he's tiresome and irritating from the very first words, and if the audience listens to him for 3–5 minutes at a stretch, precisely the right impression will be produced. The spectator will think: "Oh, dry up, do!" This person, i.e. Blagosvetlov, should have the effect on the spectator of both a clever, gouty, old grouser and a dull musical comedy which is going on for too long.' It was a little ironical that this tedious character was Suvorin's contribution to the enterprise, because some people thought later that Chekhov had *based* him on Suvorin.

In the same letter Chekhov goes on to remind Suvorin of 'the bill of our play' – a list of eleven characters, with a description of each of them. Of these eleven, four can be recognised as the precursors of characters in the final version of *Uncle Vanya*. One of them, Blagosvetlov's daughter, bears little resemblance to the plain, hardworking Sonya she eventually became, and is more like Yelena, her lethargic and beautiful stepmother. But the other three are already the substantial originals of Serebryakov, Astrov, and Vanya himself. Blagosvetlov is a retired government official, not an academic, but he is 'of clerical origins, and was educated in a seminary. The position he has occupied was achieved through his own efforts . . . Suffers from gout, rheumatism, insomnia, and tinnitus. His landed property he got as a dowry . . . Can't abide mystics, visionaries, holy fools, poets, or pious Peters, doesn't believe in God, and is accustomed to regard the entire world from the standpoint of practical affairs. Practical affairs first, last, and foremost, and everything else – nonsense or humbug.' Astrov, at this stage, is still a landowner rather than a doctor. But he already has his amazingly prescient concern for ecology (and is already nicknamed the Wood Demon because of it). He already believes that 'The forests create the climate, the climate influences the character of the people, etc. etc. There is neither civilisation nor happiness if the forests are ringing under the axe, if the climate is harsh and cruel, if people are harsh and cruel as well . . .' Blagosvetlov's daughter is attracted to him, as Yelena is in *Vanya*, 'not for his ideas, which are alien to her, but for his talent, for his passion, for his wide horizons . . . She likes the way his brain has swept over the whole of Russia and over ten centuries ahead . . .'

His account of the proto-Vanya is brief, and contains characteristics which were later discarded ('Drinks Vichy water and grouses away. Behaves arrogantly. Stresses that he is not frightened of generals. Shouts.') But in outline Uncle Vanya is already there – and in describing him Chekhov is also laying down the first outline of the plot: 'The brother of Blagosvetlov's late wife. Manages Blagosvetlov's estate (his own he has long since run through). Regrets he has not stolen. He had not foreseen that his Petersburg relations would have such a poor appreciation of his services. They don't understand him – they don't want to understand him – and he regrets he has not stolen.'

Chekhov says in his letter he will sketch out the rest of Act One himself and send it to Suvorin. He undertakes not to touch Blagosvetlov, and suggests sharing the work on Blagosvetlov's daughter, because 'I'll never be able to manage her on my own.' The great arborealist will be Chekhov's up to Act Four, then Suvorin's up to a certain scene where Chekhov will take over because Suvorin will never manage to catch the right tone of voice. Then he will leave Suvorin to start Act Two, as he did Act One.

It is difficult to believe that this strange two-headed beast would have been any substitute for the *Vanya* it would presumably have displaced. Fortunately, perhaps, Suvorin seems to have backed down, and left Blagosvetlov as his sole contribution, because a month later Chekhov was writing to ask him why he was refusing to collaborate on *The Wood Demon* (as it was by this time called), and offering to find a new subject altogether if Suvorin would prefer it. This was when he proposed switching to Holofernes or Solomon, or one of the two Napoleons. (Chekhov himself did in fact start on the Solomon project; a fragment of a monologue for the king was found among his papers – see A Note on the Translation, p. 215.) But not even the attractions of a biblical or historical subject could tempt the literary-minded magnate back into harness, and the following spring Chekhov reluctantly began to struggle with the material on his own.

There were some moments of elation in the weeks that followed, judging at any rate from the bulletins to Suvorin. 'Act III is so scandalous that when you see it you'll say: "This was written by a cunning and pitiless man" . . .'; 'The play is terribly strange, and I'm surprised that such strange things are emerging from my pen.' There were also more or less simultaneous moments of discouragement, when he informed other correspondents that he was not going to write plays, and that he was not attracted by the idea of fame as a dramatist. By the end of May, with only two acts written, he had given up, and in September he had to start all over again from the beginning.

Then, when it was at last finished, the play was rejected out of hand by both the Alexandrinsky Theatre in St Petersburg, which had just successfully staged *Ivanov*, and by the Maly in Moscow. An unofficial meeting of the Petersburg section of the Theatrical–Literary Committee, which vetted all plays submitted for production in the imperial theatres, judged it 'a fine dramatised story, but not a drama'. Lensky, the actor for whose benefit performance the play had been offered to the Maly, returned the manuscript to Chekhov with a particularly crushing dismissal. 'I will say only one thing: write a story. You are too contemptuous of the stage and of the dramatic form, you have too little respect for them, to write drama. This form is harder than that of the story, and you – forgive me – are too spoiled by success to study as it were the basic ABC of the dramatic form, and to learn to love it.' Even Nemirovich-Danchenko, another member of the committee, who was later to be a co-founder with Stanislavsky of the Moscow Arts Theatre and one of Chekhov's most important patrons, thought that Lensky was right in diagnosing ignorance of the demands of the stage (though he thought Chekhov could easily master them). 'Say what you like,' he wrote, 'clear, lifelike characters, an interesting conflict, and the proper development of the plot – these are the best guarantee of success on the stage. A play cannot succeed without a plot, but the most serious fault is lack of clarity, when the audience can't possibly grasp the essence of the plot. This is more important than any stage tricks or effects.' Chekhov swore again – not for the last time – to give up playwriting. But in the end he rewrote once more, and did a completely new version of the last act, with which he had been having difficulties from the beginning. The play was then produced, in December 1889, by Abramova, one of the Moscow commercial managements. It was dismissed by the critics not only as untheatrical, but also as 'a blind transcription of everyday reality', and was taken off after three performances.

With hindsight, the most remarkable thing about *The Wood Demon* is how much of *Uncle Vanya* is already there – often word for word. All the essential material of Act One, including most of the big speeches; almost the whole of Act Two; and in Act Three the entire scene in which Serebryakov proposes to sell the estate. It seems amazing that this wealth of brilliant scenes was not enough to alert even the most sluggish producer and the most jaded critic to Chekhov's powers in the theatre. But it is true that they fail to make the impact they should because he had not yet overcome certain faults recognisable from his two earlier full-length plays, *Ivanov* and the play without a title. The characters are too simple; too noble and Tolstoyan in the case of the Wood Demon himself, too coarsely comic in the case of Orlovsky, the debauched son of a local landowner. The setting of the first and last acts has wandered in pursuit of the picturesque; and there is something unsettling about the tone of the whole. It may have seemed offensively naturalistic to contemporary critics, but to the modern reader it veers more towards the facetiousness of Chekhov's early comic journalism, and towards a certain bucolic jollity, which sit oddly with the story that is beginning to emerge. At the end of Act Three all resemblance to the later version ceases. Vanya attempts to shoot not Serebryakov but himself, and succeeds. So the last act is left without a Vanya, and instead proceeds by way of a sunset picnic alongside an old watermill to a happy ending, with the Serebryakovs more or less reconciled, the Wood Demon and Sonya paired off, and even the debauched Orlovsky settling down with a nice girl. Nemirovich-Danchenko's assessment of the play is shrewd; the story is not clear. And the reason is that Chekhov has not yet recognised the story he is trying to tell.

After its failure in Moscow the play was abandoned again, and might well have remained so for good. It seems to have been Prince Urusov, a jurist and well-known literary figure, who provoked Chekhov into starting work on it again – somewhat ironically, because Urusov admired the earlier version so much that he persisted to the end in believing that Chekhov had ruined it by turning it into *Uncle Vanya*. It was Urusov's request for permission to reprint the text of *The Wood Demon*, in fact, that made Chekhov re-read it. He evidently did not like what he saw (years later he was still telling the loyal Urusov: 'I hate that play and I try to forget about it') and it was presumably this reawakened dissatisfaction that made him set to work on it again. The internal evidence, at any rate – the dates of the diaries and notebooks which were the provenance of some of the material in the new version – suggests that the reworking was done the following year, in 1896. The letter that he wrote to Suvorin that December, a month after the debacle with *The Seagull*, seems to refer to *Vanya* as a finished text. If this dating is correct then the project was probably only just completed in time, since his experience with *The Seagull* had made him swear off playwriting once again.

The play in its new form still faced one final rebuff. The Maly Theatre asked for it, which gave the Theatrical–Literary Committee the chance to produce an even more magisterial rejection and scheme of improvement than before. Its report identified a number of 'unevennesses or lacunae' in the play, and complained of 'longueurs', such as 'the extended eulogy of forests, shared between Sonya and Astrov, and the explanation of Astrov's theory of arboriculture'. The committee was worried about the distressing frequency with which it believed Vanya and Astrov were shown suffering from hangovers, and the unfortunate effect that would be produced if this were thought to be the cause of Vanya's attempt to shoot Serebryakov. It felt that Vanya

and Astrov 'as it were merge into a single type of failure, of superfluous man', and it complained that 'nothing prepares us for the powerful outburst of passion which occurs during the conversation with
Yelena'. It reserved its greatest concern, though, for Vanya's treatment
of Serebryakov. 'That Vanya could take a dislike to the professor as
Yelena's husband is understandable,' it conceded; 'that his sermonis-
ing and moralising cause irritation is also natural, but the disillusion-
ment with Serebryakov's academic stature, and indeed more precisely
with him as an art historian, is somewhat strange . . . nor is it a reason
for his being pursued with pistol shots, for his being hunted down by
someone who is no longer responsible for his actions.' The unfairness
of shooting professors because you have a low opinion of their academic achievements seems to have spoken deeply to the committee's
learned members.

This time, however, Chekhov declined all suggestions for rewriting.
By now, in any case, the play had been successfully produced in a number of provincial theatres, and it was finally established in Moscow by
being produced at the Arts Theatre – though its reception there was
initially more muted than the hysterical success which *The Seagull* had
just enjoyed. With hindsight we can see that Chekhov's reworking of
the material from *The Wood Demon*, whenever it was done, has shifted it across the crucial divide that separates the four last plays from all
his earlier ones, and indeed from all the earlier ones in the world.

Some of the changes he has made are straightforward improvements
in dramatic technique. He has concentrated the setting of the play on
the place where the real events of the story actually happen – the
Serebryakovs' estate – and he has stripped out the superfluous characters. But in the course of doing this he has had an idea of genius. He
has elided the debauched young neighbour, Orlovsky, with the Wood
Demon. The most upright and selfless character in the original play is
now the one who also indulges in periodic drinking bouts; instead of
being in love with Sonya he is now, like Orlovsky, first coarsely knowing about Vanya's relations with Yelena, and then ready to propose a
passing liaison with her himself; he has become Astrov in all his dark,
self-contained complexity. And Yelena, a figure of uncompromised
virtue in the original version, has become fascinated by him, so that,

engaged as she is to advance poor Sonya's cause with him, she has become touched by the same characteristic ambiguity. With these changes the whole tone of the play has been modified. The mood has changed from one of comfortable idleness to one of uncomfortably interrupted work. The bucolic geniality and the facetiousness have gone, and left exposed the sense of wasted life at the heart of the story.

Chekhov's second masterstroke in the rewriting, even more fundamental and consequential than the new ambiguity of the characters, is his alteration to the aim of Vanya's revolver. All his full-length plays up to this point, as we have seen, have resolved with the death of one of the central characters. Now, instead of letting Vanya likewise tidy himself away after his confrontation with Serebryakov, he has had the idea of making him turn murderer instead of suicide – and of failing.

In the first place this is simply a more interesting development. For the pacific and long-suffering Vanya to have been driven to attempt murder tells us much more about the intensity of his anger and of his sense of betrayal; and his missing the target is something he at once recognises as bitterly characteristic. This is slightly obscured by the traditional translation of his line. 'Missed again!' sounds as if it refers only to the two shots. The word he uses in Russian, however, refers not only to a missed shot but to any kind of mistake (see p. 213). What he is thinking of is surely all the missed opportunities in his life, and in particular his failure to have made advances to Yelena when she was still free. Then again, the fact that he misses at point-blank range opens up a whole series of questions about the nature of these mistakes. Perhaps they are not serious attempts at all; even as he pulls the trigger he *says* 'bang!' like a child with a toy revolver. And even if he sees them as seriously intended, are they examples of what a modern psychiatrist would call self-sabotage? And if they are, is the unconscious objective to protect himself from the consequences of success? Not only from being tried for murder, but from being tested as lover and husband, from having the chance (as he at one moment believes he could have done if only he had lived 'normally') to become a Schopenhauer or a Dostoyevsky – and *then* failing, with no possibility of concealing his own responsibility for it?

In the second place, the failure of this dramatic gesture to have dramatic consequences destroys the drama; or rather it destroys the neatness with which the slow and confused changes of the world we inhabit are concentrated theatrically in simple and decisive events. The world of *Vanya* is the ambiguous and unresolved world of *The Seagull* – stripped of even the final note of resolution suggested by Konstantin's suicide. Most of the relatively few notes Chekhov gave to the director and actors were to do with this dislocation and diffusion. Exiled in Yalta, he missed the Moscow production, but when he saw it on a tour the Arts Theatre made to the Crimea in 1900, one of the actresses in the company remembered his telling them afterwards that Sonya shouldn't kneel and kiss her father's hand on the line 'You must be merciful, father' at the end of Act Three, because 'after all that wasn't the drama. All the sense and all the drama of a person is on the inside, and not in external appearances. There was drama in Sonya's life up to this moment, there will be drama afterwards – but this is simply something that happens, a continuation of the shot. And the shot, in fact, is not drama – just something that happens.'* In a similar spirit he deprecated Stanislavsky's direction that Astrov should make his pass at Yelena, in Act Four, 'like a drowning man clutching at a straw'. By then, says Chekhov in a letter to Knipper, who was playing Yelena, Astrov knows that nothing is going to come of his attraction to her, 'and he talks to her in this scene in the same tone of voice as he does about the heat in Africa, and kisses her in the most ordinary way, quite idly'. Stanislavsky remembered him as saying, after the performance in the Crimea, '"He kisses her like that, though." – And here he planted a brief kiss on his own hand. – "Astrov has no respect for Yelena. In fact when he leaves the house afterwards he's whistling."'

More important even than the nature of the failed murder are the consequences it has for the last act. Chekhov, as we have seen, had already tried various versions of this. What had caused the problem

* There is something askew – and perhaps this is in keeping with the obliqueness of the play – about either Chekhov's note or the actress's memory of it, because his own stage-direction calls for Sonya to kneel, if not to kiss her father's hand, while the line can hardly be construed as a 'continuation of the shot' because it occurs before it.

was his odd insistence, in all the variants of *The Wood Demon*, on placing Vanya's suicide at the end of Act Three, so that this traditional dramatic resolution still left everything unresolved for everyone else. But he had been feeling his way towards *something* with this arrangement, and now that Vanya remains alive it becomes clear what it is: precisely that – remaining alive. He has given dramatic expression to the theme first broached by Nina in *The Seagull*, which dominates all the last three plays – survival itself, the tragedy not of death, but of continuing to live after life has been robbed of hope and meaning.

Three Sisters

Chekhov does not name the town where the Prozorov family lives in *Three Sisters*, but we discover its spiritual identity soon enough; its name is Exile.

Like so many others for so many reasons in Russian life and literature, they find themselves in a place which they see not as *here* but as *there*. In their hearts they inhabit Moscow, where the spring comes early and there is love and fame. In the flesh they find themselves resident in some dull town in the north of Russia, where the winter lingers and no one has ever been heard of. In a letter to Maxim Gorky, Chekhov said it was a town like Perm, which gives some geographical scale to their plight. Perm is seven hundred miles from Moscow, in the northern Urals, and at that time there was no direct railway line to Moscow. The 1914 Baedeker lists a twice-weekly express to St Petersburg, taking about two days, while the ordinary train to the next nearest town of any size along the line, Yekaterinburg (where the imperial family were shortly to be murdered), took twenty-three and a half hours. The great Russian distances dominate the Prozorovs' lives. They watch the cranes flying overhead on their huge autumn journeys to the south. They welcome the other birds of passage in the play, the soldiers, as they arrive from the ends of the Empire with their baggage of new ideas and old quarrels and boredom and desperate wives; and they watch them depart again, bound maybe for the Chita garrison in

Siberia, two thousand miles to the east, or for the kingdom of Poland, fourteen hundred miles to the west, to live in yet more lodgings with 'two chairs and one sofa, and stoves that always smoke'; permanent exiles. The play was written in exile, too – in Yalta, where Chekhov had been banished by his doctors, thirteen hundred miles away to the south-west. In his letters he refers to Yalta as his prison. He complains about the cold, the heat, the cruel wind. He longs for Moscow – and, like the Prozorovs, puts off his planned visit from week to week, and day to day, while he finishes the play. When he finally took it to Moscow to copy it out, in October 1900, he must have felt he was escaping from his own text.

The characters in the play – the Prozorovs and the soldiers alike – are exiles in time as well as in place. The sisters look wistfully back towards their Moscow childhood, longingly forward to their Moscow future. Tusenbach is waiting for the 'great healthy storm' that will blow society clean of idleness and boredom in twenty or thirty years' time. Vershinin has his eyes fixed on the 'astonishingly, unimaginably beautiful' life that will be lived in another two or three hundred years. Solyony lives in the past; he identifies himself with Lermontov, who died fifty years before. Chebutykin wonders if he has ceased to exist entirely. The only time that none of them regards as home is the one they actually inhabit, somewhere in the last decade of the nineteenth century. Tusenbach finds his way back to the present briefly in the last act, when he notices the beauty of the world around him as if for the first time in his life. But then he is on his way to be killed; he has no future to distract him.

This sense of the difficulty that human beings have of living in the present lies at the very heart of the play. It has been much misunderstood. The play was written, it is true, at the beginning of a new and hopeful century, when belief in progress was high, and when the pressures upon the archaic despotism of imperial Russia were plainly becoming irresistible. Many people shared with Vershinin and Tusenbach the vision of a future in which everything would in one way or another be totally changed. Some influential commentators have argued that Chekhov was one of them. (Magarshack, for instance: ' . . . He makes the idealist Vershinin his mouthpiece on the future of mankind, taking, as usual, great care that the expression of his views should be strictly in character.') But he made it abundantly clear in his letters, as I have shown earlier, that the characters in his plays express their own views, not his. And even if we knew nothing of Chekhov's general attitude, it is obvious from the internal evidence of the play that Vershinin and Tusenbach are not the author's spokes-men. For a start they disagree totally with each other about the nature of the changes they expect. Then again all hopes for the future – par-ticularly the utopian ones of Vershinin – are parodied by the fatuous optimism of Andrey in Act Four, after he has comprehensively denounced the town's sordid record up to now: 'The present is loath-some, but then when I think about the future – well, that's another story. It all becomes so easy and spacious; and in the distance there's a gleam of light – I can see freedom, I can see me and my children being freed from idleness, from roast goose and cabbage, from little naps after dinner, from ignoble sponging off others . . .'

And really the whole structure of the play is designed to undercut Vershinin. He insists that life is already becoming 'steadily easier and brighter'. But more than three years go by in the course of the play, and *nothing changes* – not at any rate for the better – nothing even begins to change. Vershinin philosophises on regardless – obsessively, never interested in anyone else's views, plainly seeking some rational-isation for the unhappiness of his own life. He is a bore on the subject. What's marvellous, though, in Chekhov's understanding of him – and of his hearers – is that, although he threatens boredom each time he returns to the question, he never does in fact bore – he rides boredom down, he becomes eloquent, he captures the imagination. Olga, at the end of the play, is even more compelling when she justifies her courage in facing life, after the destruction of all the sisters' hopes, by a rather similar appeal to the future: 'We shall be forgotten – our faces, our voices, even how many of us there were. But our sufferings will turn to joy for those who live after us. Peace and happiness will dwell on earth, and people living now will be blessed and spoken well of.' I have shown earlier why I think that this last speech of Olga's, like the apparently similar speech by Sonya at the end of *Uncle Vanya*, is no more a direct expression of Chekhov's own hopes or beliefs than the visions of Vershinin or Tusenbach. It is also immediately undercut by Chebutykin. From the very beginning of the play, as David Magarshack notes in his book *The Real Chekhov*, the separate upstage conversations of Chebutykin and the other officers are used as an ironic counterpoint to what is being said downstage. And there at the end of the play sits Chebutykin, upstage and alone, the last remaining member of this chorus. 'Anyway, it doesn't matter,' he says to himself after Olga's speech, 'it doesn't matter.' Not that his view is any more authoritative. He sees life one way, because he's Chebutykin, and he's given up, and she sees it another way, because she's Olga, and she hasn't. And if it's Chekhov speaking through Olga, then it's equally Chekhov replying to himself through Chebutykin; the drama is within Chekhov exactly as it is within all of us.

Chebutykin's comment is an apt one, too. Because whatever happens to future generations, even if some benefit accrues to them from the sufferings of the three sisters – and there is no suggestion as to how this might happen – it still won't matter as far as *these* people are concerned, and *they* are the ones whose fates we have been invited to examine. Drama makes the generalities of the human condition specific in particular men and women; the fate of those who remain offstage is beyond representation or consideration.

'It doesn't matter.' The phrase is on everyone's lips throughout the play. Masha tries to hush Vershinin's declaration of love, then concedes that it doesn't matter. It doesn't matter to Andrey whether the mummers come or not. Even Vershinin, dejected at the anomie of military and civilians alike, uses it. Indifference is the mode of the play, not optimism; indifference to a world that offers only indifference in return.

With hindsight, we might possibly think that Tusenbach has proved the best of the three prophets, not only because the storm he was predicting did in fact occur – and in almost exactly the twenty years he estimated – but because of his suggestion that the time they live in might be remembered with respect. His assertion that there were no executions then is not quite right – there were no civil executions in Russia then, but, according to the 1900 Brockhaus, general cases could still be transferred to the military courts for disposal by military law. All the same, a Russian in years to come might look back, if not with respect, then at least with affection, as Andrey does, to evenings out at the Grand Hotel on Resurrection Square, or at Testov's on the corner of Theatre Square. Anyone who knew Moscow in Soviet times might feel a pang for the incorporation of Resurrection Square itself into the great barren plain known as the Square of the Fiftieth Anniversary of the October Revolution. And if you happened to be walking along the Sadovoye Ring, and you came to a street turning off it to the north-east that started out as Karl Marx Street and ended up as Bakunin Street, you might have felt something more than a pang to realise that this was Old Basmannaya Street, where the sisters lived their happy days as children. (They couldn't have lived in a more Muscovite-sounding street; *basman* was a kind of bread, and *basman-nik* was a colloquial name for an inhabitant of the city.) Perm has in fact gone back to being Perm, after leaping to the unfortunate conclusion that it was really called Molotov. And what happened to the Prozorovs when Tusenbach's good healthy storm broke? They would all have been in their forties by then; so would Tusenbach himself. Did they survive their good healthy wetting? Did they flee to Paris or New York, into yet deeper exile? Or did they remain, to be scattered at some point in the next few decades into camps still further north, still further east? And did they, as they laboured there, recall Tusenbach's other successful prediction, that in twenty or thirty years' time every-one would be working?

If the play is about one thing then it is not about the hopes held out by Vershinin, or by Olga, or by any of them. It is about the irony of those hopes – about the way life mocks them. Irina's hopes of redemp-tion by work are betrayed by the the actual experience of it; Andrey's hopes of academic glory are betrayed by Andrey himself; the sisters' hopes of Moscow are deferred and deferred and then shelved for ever. Even, conversely, Anfisa's fear of being put out into the street is vain – she finds herself better housed and better off than she has ever been before. The only character whose hopes seem likely to be realised is Natasha, and then because her hopes are so small and concrete and piecemeal – another baby, another room of the house to put it in, another little triumph. This is the future as it's actually going to be –

not an unimaginable beauty on earth, but Protopopov in the sitting-room.

But the irony goes deeper than this. It wouldn't make any difference even if their hopes *were* realised. As Vershinin says, if the sisters actually did live in Moscow they would cease to notice it. Perhaps in their hearts they understand this. Even Irina. She has no ties – she could leave for Moscow at any time. But she doesn't. And Vershinin's objection is valid against not only the sisters' hopes but his own as well. 'Happiness', as he says, 'is not for us and never can be. All we can do is long for it.'

Even more ironically, one of the things that destroys their chance of happiness is their hope of achieving it, which alienates them from the life they actually lead. And the final irony of the play is its demonstration that we cannot live without the hopes that cut us off from life. We are both poisoned and nourished by the act of hope itself. And when all hopes for ourselves have been destroyed – as the sisters' have been at the end of the play – then we summon whatever dogged courage we can muster to confront the rest of our lives – and we start to tell the old consoling story once again; only this time not about ourselves, but about another people, living under quite different laws, on the far side of the storms.

The Cherry Orchard

By the time Chekhov came to write *The Cherry Orchard*, in 1903, he was dying. This final play gave him one of the hardest struggles he had ever had. For a start he was increasingly exhausted by his illness, while his waning strength was further eroded by the discomfort of his life in Yalta, and by travelling back and forth to Moscow because of disagreement between his doctors about which climate would suit him best. There was tension in the household, too, between his sister Masha and his new wife, Olga Knipper; while the short hours of his working day were wasted by the perpetual stream of visitors that his fame attracted. In the end the play was a triumph, and at the first performance, on 17 January 1904, his forty-fourth birthday, he was brought up on stage between Acts Three and Four for lengthy speeches and presentations. But by this time he was visibly failing; he had only another four months to live.

It was the play itself that presented the greatest problems. He had been thinking about it for two years before he began to write, and it had been conceived from the very first as a comedy. 'The next play that I write', he said in a letter to Knipper in March 1901, 'will definitely be a funny one, a very funny one, at any rate in conception.' In another letter he described it as 'a four-act vaudeville', and in the autumn of that year, according to Stanislavsky, he gave the actors at the Moscow Arts a kind of oral trailer for what he had in mind. Three of the four disconnected details he produced were essentially comic: a servant who went fishing; a cheerful billiards enthusiast with a loud voice and only one arm; and the owner (male or female) of a country estate who kept borrowing money off the servant. This list may have been more in the nature of a whimsical camouflage for his intentions than a serious exposition of them – it would have been very much his style. He may even have been joking when he included as the fourth item an even smaller and more disconnected detail: 'a branch of cherry blossom sticking out of the garden straight into the room through an open window'.

From this one tiny visual flourish, however, came the real play – and all his difficulties with accommodating it to his original comic conception. During the course of the next two years he must have traced that branch back out of the window – back to the orchard in which the tree was rooted, back to the social history and economic forces which explained why that orchard had been planted and why it was now about to be felled. The trail took him not only outwards through Russian society and across the Russian landscape, but backwards in time through his own writing and his own life. From where he now stood, on the brink of his last work, and at the end of his life, he found himself returning to themes he had touched upon in his stories over his entire professional career, and going back further still, to his childhood. As a schoolboy in Taganrog he had heard stories told by the mother of one of his friends about her life as a landowner before the

Emancipation (on an estate where there was an ancient serf like Firs) in Poltava province, which was famous for its cherry orchards. He had spent summer holidays as a child on a rural estate out in the steppe to the north of Taganrog, where his grandfather (a manumitted serf himself) was steward. He had heard the distant sound of a breaking cable in the mines while he was staying with a boyhood friend on another property in the steppe. His own modest family home had been sold off to pay his father's debts – and bought by the wealthy friend who had promised to save it. By the time he began to write the play, that single branch at the window had led him to a world which was remarkably difficult to accommodate in a 'four-act vaudeville'.

In fact *The Cherry Orchard* is the most elusive and difficult of all these four last plays. It is noticeably less naturalistic than the first three, and more dependent upon mood and symbolism. It is also even less directly dramatic. The conflict from which the play springs is intense; the Gayev family is being broken apart by powerful forces – forces rooted deep in history and in the society around them. But in the whole course of the play only one dramatic event is thrown up by this conflict – the crisis itself, the announcement by Lopakhin that he has bought the estate. There is a curious air of detachment about some of the episodes. Charlotta Ivanovna's musing about her past, and the irruption of the Passer-by, seem like side-eddies at the edge of the main river. For the whole of this second act, in fact, the narrative comes to a halt. Life hangs suspended for a while in the old mode before everything finally changes, like water scarcely moving in the depths of the millpool before it plunges down the race to the wheel.

Chekhov confessed to Knipper that he had been 'scared' himself by the 'lack of movement' in Act Two. So was Stanislavsky when he saw it in rehearsal. 'For a long time the play was not working,' he wrote later. 'Particularly the second act. It contains no action, in the theatrical sense, and at rehearsals seemed very monotonous. It was essential to show the boredom of doing nothing in a way that was interesting.' He asked for cuts. Chekhov did more than cut; he rearranged and rewrote. (The material that came out can be found in A Note on the Translation, pp. 220–22.) The cuts were restored in Mike Alfreds's 1986 production of the play at the National Theatre, London, but this seems to me quite wrong. The alterations went into the original pro-duction only a month after it had opened, when it was already an established success. It is difficult to believe that Chekhov would have made them at that stage if he had not fully concurred in them himself. But they shed a little more light on several of the characters. Charlotta Ivanovna has a good line about Ranyevskaya – 'She's perpetually mis-laying things. She's mislaid her life, even.' And Firs is more plainly seen as what he is – a peasant, an ex-serf, rather than a kind of Russian Jeeves.

Two other characters have in the past been much misunderstood by directors. Natural sympathy for the Gayev family and their feckless charm has sometimes obscured the qualities of Lopakhin and Trofimov, the representatives of economic and political progress who are in their different ways pushing them to the margins of life. ('Suddenly no one needs us any more,' as Gayev sadly discovers in Act Four, when the money has gone.) They both feel genuine love for their unintended victims, and Chekhov's letters make it clear that he took a characteristically objective view of both of them. 'Lopakhin is a busi-nessman, it's true,' he wrote to Stanislavsky, conscious of the way in which progressive prejudice was likely to work, 'but he is in every sense a decent person. He must behave with complete decorum and propriety, without pettiness or trickery . . . In casting this part it must be kept in mind that Lopakhin has been loved by Varya, a serious and religious young lady; she wouldn't have fallen in love with some grasp-ing peasant.'

Trofimov has suffered in different ways. In the past he has some-times been portrayed in English productions as an inadequate and immature personality who is afraid to emerge from university and face the real word. This view has been given currency by the translation which has become traditional for his ironic description of himself – 'the eternal student', a phrase that suggests in English not only the cor-rect primary meaning of remaining a student forever, but also (as in 'the eternal schoolboy' or 'the eternal triangle') the idea of his being the unchanging student *type*. The Russian phrase, *vyechniy studyent*, has quite a different overtone; it is a variant of *vyechniy zhid*, literally 'the eternal Jew', but in English the Wandering Jew, who was condemned to wander the earth for all eternity without shelter. Chekhov makes the implication of this clear in the same letter to Knipper in which he admits to his worries about Act Two. His other anxiety, he says, is '. . . the somewhat unfinished state of the student, Trofimov. The point is that Trofimov is perpetually being exiled, perpetually being thrown out of the university – and how do you show things like this?' Exiled, of course, for his political activities; and the difficulty of showing things like this being the censor (who, even as it was, cut two passages from Trofimov's speeches – about the condition of the workers and about the effect that the ownership of serfs has had upon the Gayev family). Chekhov plainly takes Trofimov seriously as a man who holds sane and genuine convictions for which he is prepared to suffer. But then to go to the opposite extreme, as was done in Trevor Griffiths's adaptation of the play, and to turn him into a 'positive hero' in the Socialist Realist sense, is also an absurdity. Even if we had not discovered by now that Chekhov's characters are never puppets, Trofimov and his beliefs, like Vershinin and his, are obviously being held at some slight ironic distance. He is plainly ridiculous when he claims to be 'above such things as love'. Even his sincerest speeches topple into rhetoric about mankind marching towards higher truth and higher happiness. (His excited outburst to Anya at the end of Act Two – 'On, on, on! We are going to that bright star that blazes from afar there, and no one can hold us back! On, on, on! In step together, friends!' – echoes a famous revolutionary ode by Pleshcheyev, the writer to whom Chekhov addressed his disclaimer of all political and religious enthusiasm – 'On, on, with neither fear nor doubting/ To great and valorous feats, my friends . . . !/ And like a guiding star on high/ Let blaze for us the sacred truth . . .'). He complains about people doing nothing but talk even as he stands there doing nothing but talk. Lopakhin and Trofimov, in fact, like all Chekhov's characters, speak out boldly and sincerely in their own voices. Each rises to his heights of magnanimity and understanding, and each comes up against his own particular limitations.

The greatest problem, though, in playing and understanding *The Cherry Orchard* is the one discussed in more general terms earlier – the question of whether it is a comedy. It is even more acute here than in the earlier plays. Chekhov was from the very first markedly more insistent than before that the play was funny, and even after the material had changed out of all recognition in the writing he remained firm on this point. He designates it a comedy on the title-page, as he had *The Seagull*. He wrote to Stanislavsky's wife: 'What has emerged in my play is not a drama but a comedy, in places even a farce . . .' (He used the French term, not the words 'joke' or 'vaudeville' which he applied to his one-act plays.) To Knipper: 'The last act will be cheerful – in fact the whole play will be cheerful and frivolous . . .'

It does in fact seem to me to be a comedy in some sense that the other plays are not, and I think it is possible to grasp this aspect of it without losing sight of its painfulness; indeed, to see the suffering of the characters as being expressed through the comic inappropriateness of their reactions. The slothful reluctance of the Gayevs to face what is happening to them, their inability to save the ship by jettisoning the cargo, is undoubtedly comic. And Chekhov is right about the last act: it is predominantly cheerful. The crisis has occurred at the end of Act Three, as it does in *Uncle Vanya*. What it calls forth in the characters, however, is not a spirit of endurance, as it does in the earlier play, but the absurd lightening of the spirits that occurs, as Chekhov has observed with the most wonderful ironic shrewdness, after a decision has been taken, however terrible, and the worst has actually happened. It is notable that in this last play, with his own death only months away, Chekhov is struck not so much by the inexorable nature of terrible events as by their survivability, by their way of slipping out of the mind, once they have occurred, and of disappearing in the endless wash of further events.

But the cheerfulness is deeply poignant. The worst *has* happened, and it is a bad worst. The Gayevs' happiness has been irretrievably lost, as both brother and sister for one moment realise before they leave the house; and their future will be even bleaker than Nina's on her tours of second-rate provincial theatres, or Vanya's and Sonya's at the account-books of their provincial estate, or the Prozorov sisters' in their grim northern exile. A few months' work at the bank for Gayev; a few months with her hopeless lover in Paris for Ranyevskaya. Then resolution and love and the last of the money will all run out. They will have neither home nor occupation; nothing. There is something absurd about their prospects, though, because the Gayevs remain too feckless to understand them; they lack the tragic dignity that Sonya and her uncle and the Prozorov sisters all muster in the end. This is why, finally, the play is a comedy. It is the comedy of inertia and help-lessness in the face of truly desolating loss. There is no simple formula for playing it, or for responding to it; the problem it sets us is the prob-lem of life itself.

A Note on the Translation

This is not a complete collection of Chekhov's plays. I thought it inap-propriate to include *Wild Honey*, my version of his first, untitled play, because I extensively reshaped and rewrote the original text, whereas the translations in this volume are all entirely straight – as close to the original as I can make them. They are also intended for production, and if you are asking actors and directors to commit themselves to a text you must first be committed to it yourself. I have therefore includ-ed only those plays which I felt I could translate up to this standard. I have omitted the weaker one-act plays. (In a separate volume, entitled *The Sneeze*, I have supplemented the four one-act plays included here with adaptations of some of Chekhov's stories to make up a complete evening.) I have also omitted *The Wood Demon*, which is of great interest academically as an early version of *Uncle Vanya*, but of little theatrically since all the best material in it appears to vastly greater effect in the latter play.

I hesitated for much longer over *Ivanov*. This is a play which has been quite frequently produced, and found to be of dramatic interest. It has notable champions. Ronald Hingley believes it to be not only an improvement upon its predecessor, the untitled play, but finer than *The Seagull*, which he thinks has been 'overrated in general esteem'. The late Dr Simon Behrman, a physician with a close interest in Chekhov, wrote to me urging its value, more plausibly, as a classic account of depression, and as a symptom of Chekhov's own depressed state of mind. It does indeed have a characteristically depressive lack of energy and action. When we first meet the wretched Ivanov in Act One he is already in low spirits and wracked by guilt, and he continues so to the end of the play, when he shoots himself. At no point does he undergo any development or even variation of mood, except at the end of Act Two, when Sasha declares her love for him. At this he 'gives a peal of happy laughter' and has a vision of a new life starting. But this altered state lasts for only some twenty-five seconds, by my calculation, before he realises with horror that they are being watched by his wife, and relapses into guilt and inertia, never to re-emerge.

It is impossible not to compare him as a character with Platonov, in the earlier, untitled play, who also betrays his wife, and who also falls victim to guilt and melancholy. But Platonov goes through a hundred moods. His spirits soar as well as plummet. He has moments of ridiculous hope, is self-deceiving as well as self-knowing, has impossible ideals, feels love and malice and friendship as well as despair and emptiness; and is, above all, *changed* by the events of the play. The characters around Ivanov make a poor contrast, too, with the figures around Platonov. Ivanov's wife has an interesting history – she has renounced her Jewish faith to marry him and been rejected by her family in consequence – but remains dramatically a helpless victim, unlike Platonov's wife, who suffers a similar marital humiliation, but who refuses to be patronised by her repenting but unreforming husband. Ivanov's new love, Sasha, is a pale figure beside the two women who pursue Platonov. All the other characters are dismissed, with an impatience and high-handedness that come oddly from Chekhov, as grasping, dishonest, philistine, drunken, slothful, or priggish. I may be as blind as it seems to me Hingley is to the virtues of the untitled play and *The Seagull*, but, however many times I re-read the original, I do not see how to make a translation of this material which I can expound to a director and defend to a cast.

(I have to say, however, that my confidence in my judgement of the play has been severely shaken since the earlier editions of this collection by the immensely effective production that Jonathan Kent did of it at the Almeida Theatre, in David Hare's excellent version. I was mortified that Hare had been able to perceive virtues in it that I couldn't, and make them manifest, even though he can't read Russian.)

Any translator of Chekhov must be painfully aware of the very large number of other versions of these plays which have been made over the years, and also of Chekhov's own hostility to the whole idea of being translated – 'I can't stop them, can I? So let them translate away; no sense will come of it in any case.' All the earlier English versions, so far as I know, have been made either by people who could read the original but who had no experience in writing plays, or by English dramatists who knew the original only through the literal version of a collaborator, or through earlier published editions, combined often with a mysterious inner certainty about what Chekhov was saying, or what he ought to have been saying if only he had been more like themselves. My only qualification for trying again is that I happen both to know Russian and to write plays. Translating a play is rather like writing one. The first principle, surely, is that each line should be what that particular character would have said at that particular moment if he had been a native English-speaker. This involves inhabiting that character, or trying to, as intimately as if he were one's own. The second basic principle, it seems to me, is that every line must be as immediately comprehensible as it was in the original; there are no footnotes in the theatre, and no turning back to a previous page.

Practical difficulties arise in applying these principles, particularly with familiar references to matters that are unfamiliar to a modern English audience. I have expanded some of these, and cut others. The hardest problems are caused by the many literary allusions. They are all explained in the detailed notes on the individual plays that follow. I have dealt with them in various ways in the text. Some of them are inessential, and would in any case be obscure to a modern Russian audience, and these I have felt free to cut. But most of them are both essential to the sense and, to a Russian, current coin, burnished with use. I have done my best with these, but there is no way of catching that well-worn familiar shine.

The other general problem is that of names. Russians address each other and refer to each other sometimes by their surnames (Voynitzky, say), sometimes by a combination of given name and patronymic

(Ivan Petrovich, to take the same familiar character), just occasionally by the patronymic alone, and often by a diminutive of the given name (in this case Vanya), or by any one of a bewildering range of its variants (Ivasha, Isha, Ishuta, Iva, Vanyukha, Vanyusha, Vanyura, Vanyuta, to name but a few allotropes of this same single name), or even, among the educated classes before the Revolution, by its French equivalent (Vanya's mother calls him Jean). English-speaking actors have great difficulties with these shifting clouds of unpronounceable syllables. So do English-speaking audiences, who neither understand the implication of the different combinations nor remember which characters they belong to. To transliterate them blindly would clearly be a breach of my second principle (immediate comprehensibility) – and also, I think, of my first. These characters must all become native English-speakers, and native English-speakers do not attempt foreign words and names. I have therefore simplified ruthlessly. This changes the feel of some relationships, particularly between servants and their masters.

The transliteration itself is another problem. Where mine is inconsistent, or departs from usual practice, it is because I have simplified it to make it easier for actors to get a reasonable approximation to the original sound. Rigidity can in any case produce nonsense. The surname of the Baron in *Three Sisters*, for example, was clearly transliterated into the Cyrillic from a German original, 'Tusenbach'. Elisaveta Fen recovers it into English in her translation as 'Toozenbakh', which is like the translating machine that is supposed to have put 'Out of sight, out of mind' into Japanese and recovered it into English as 'Invisible, insane'. Other translators go to the opposite extreme, and put given names into English. Never 'Vanya', for some reason – I know of no translation entitled *Uncle Jack* – but in the same play Ronald Hingley gives 'Helen Serebryakov' and 'Michael Astrov'. Why not Tony Chekhov, in that case? And why should Russians be the only people to enjoy the advantage of anglicisation? Why not Charles Marx and Henry Ibsen? John-James Rousseau and Leonard from Vinci? Nor do I see any reason for imposing male surnames on the women. Why should Ranyevskaya and Serebryakova have to become Mrs Ranyevsky and Mrs Serebryakov any more than Mrs Warren and

Mrs Tanqueray should have to be introduced to Russian audiences as Warrena and Tanqueraya? I am also baffled by the habit that some critics have of referring to *Madame* Ranyevskaya and *Madame* Arkadina. They are not Frenchwomen, and are nowhere in the original given French honorifics.

I have used the new and authoritative thirty-volume *Complete Collected Works and Letters* throughout. I had already translated *Three Sisters* and *The Cherry Orchard* before I could lay my hands on Volumes 12 and 13, which contain the plays, and I have revised my versions of these with the help of the very copious and thorough notes in this edition, upon which I have drawn extensively throughout. I have also made a number of changes in these last two plays as a result of the experience gained in translating the earlier ones. It took me a long time, for example, to work out the state an English-speaker would be in when he was speaking *skvoz' slyozy* – literally 'through tears' – in view of Chekhov's insistence that the people who do this are not crying. It took me even longer to find out that when a watchman can be heard 'knocking' in the garden at night he is doing it (to warn off intruders) with a *kolotushka* – a kind of mallet – against a piece of wood.

I should like to thank the National Theatre, which commissioned the first of these translations, *The Cherry Orchard*, and so started me off on the whole enterprise. I am also grateful to the various producers who first commissioned the other three translations, even though the original productions were all aborted. I had valuable help and advice from Nelya Yevdokimova in Moscow, Zoya Anderson in London, and Dr Anthony Stokes in Oxford, and was saved from a number of blunders and misreadings by looking at various earlier published translations. Dr Donald Rayfield, Professor of Russian and Georgian at Queen Mary and Westfield College, and one of the world's most distinguished and original Chekhov scholars, very generously made a considerable number of suggestions for corrections and improvements to the first two editions of this book, and they are incorporated here. If anyone were to make a line-by-line comparison he would discover that Professor Rayfield has extracted me from at least half a dozen small but shameful errors.

Since the third edition of these translations Professor Rayfield's massive and definitive biography of Chekhov has appeared. It contains a great deal of new material prudishly suppressed under the Soviet regime, or tactfully ignored by scholars, and he has a magisterial command of all the evidence, old as well as new, and of all the background to the period. His work entails quite considerable modification to our received ideas of Chekhov, and I have also used it to correct or supplement various minor points in the Introduction and in these notes.

I hope that, with the help of all this and in spite of all that, these versions have something of the feel of the original. The naturalness and simplicity of Chekhov's style have been noted before. His characters' speech often has another elusive quality, too – a certain glancing eloquence which seems to catch very precisely the truth in their hearts. Translations sometimes fail to convey this transparency, this sense of looking straight through the words into the people who utter them. The intense pleasure of translating these plays is that it brings one close both to their strong and subtle construction and to the people who inhabit them – closer, I suspect, than any performance in the theatre ever will. It's only Chekhov himself who eludes one still.

The vaudevilles present relatively few difficulties. I have taken some liberties, though, with *The Evils of Tobacco*. However quickly and cynically Chekhov claimed to have written his short plays, he took considerable care over correcting and improving them in the various published editions through which they subsequently went. He lavished particular care upon *Tobacco*. Even if he spent only two and a half hours, as he claimed, on the original version, he must have spent many times more than that on the later ones. Over the years the piece went through six major revisions. The last of them was almost at the end of his life, in 1902, when he was planning *The Cherry Orchard*. This was so radical that he claimed the result as an entirely new play, and indeed the whole tone of the piece, if not the substance, has certainly changed considerably by this time. By the sixth edition the comedy has largely drained away, and left the hapless Nyukhin without the snuff-taking that presumably first gave him his name (Sniff), but with a confession of despair now as stark and unconcealed in its way as Uncle Vanya's or Andrey Prozorov's. I have restored some of the humour of the earlier versions. Although I have used the final edition of 1902 as the basis, and Nyukhin still reaches his direct confession of despair at the end, we are obliged first of all, as we were in Chekhov's earlier versions, to perceive the man's wretchedness for ourselves through his efforts to conceal it.

I have also slightly truncated *Swan Song*. In the original the old actor performs not only the various extracts from Shakespeare given here, but also a speech from *Boris Godunov* and some lines from another work of Pushkin's, his great epic poem *Poltava*. The play goes on to conclude with Chatsky's bitter farewell to Moscow at the end of Griboyedov's *Woe from Wit*. Once again the play was subject to rewriting, and in earlier editions ended with all or part of the *Othello* quotation; while in the original story from which the play was taken the old actor is led miserably off to his dressing-room at the end without ever demonstrating his vanished greatness at all. I have reverted to the *Othello* ending. The Shakespeare on its own seems a perfectly adequate demonstration of Svetlovidov's past glories, and while the Pushkin and the Griboyedov would be as familiar to Russians as the Shakespeare is to us I can see no way of making them even recognisable to an English audience. Chekhov plainly felt that the Shakespeare (in translation) would present no difficulty to Russians. Whether this disparity is a testimony to the universality of English drama or to the parochialism of English audiences I do not know.

The Seagull begins with a literary allusion. The famous opening lines – 'Why do you always wear black?' – 'I'm in mourning for my life' – are a quotation from Maupassant's *Bel-Ami*. Most of the literary allusions in the play, however – fortunately from a translator's point of view – are to Shakespeare again, and clearly identified as such by the characters who make them. I have in fact added an extra line of Shakespeare. In the original, Arkadina slips into playing the closet scene from *Hamlet* with Konstantin because in Russian Gertrude's speech begins 'My son'. I have made her start with a line of Gertrude's from the play scene as an alternative way in.

But there are one or two Russian allusions that should be mentioned. Sorin, in Act Three, goes into town to get away for a little from what he calls, in the original, 'this gudgeon's life'. I have slightly reorganised this to make it at any rate clear to non-anglers that gudgeons live in the mud on the river-bottom. But I can find no way to suggest the literary background of the allusion, which is to the fish in Saltykov-Shchedrin's chilling fable *The Wise Gudgeon*. Saltykov's gudgeon, terrified of being eaten by a pike or crushed by a crab, digs a hole in the mud and hides himself in it, only to emerge to snatch his food when everything else is asleep and then to rush back in terror, unable ever to fulfil his natural function in life by marrying and having children. 'And in this way,' says Saltykov, 'the wise gudgeon lived a hundred years and more. And all the time he trembled and he trembled. Neither friends nor relations did he have; he neither went to see anyone nor did anyone come to see him. He never played cards, nor drank strong drink, nor smoked tobacco, nor chased after pretty girls – only trembled and thought the one same thought: "God be praised, I seem to be alive!"' This is the picture of Sorin's life that the original would suggest to a Russian audience. The danger that terrifies the poor gudgeon most, incidentally, is the prospect of being caught by an angler and turned into fish-soup – a fate which Sorin avoided but which one might think Nina did not.

Konstantin, in Act Four, refers to the mad miller in *The Water Sprite*. This is the fragment of a verse-drama by Pushkin about a miller's daughter who is made pregnant and abandoned by a prince. She throws herself into the millstream, whereupon her father becomes demented with grief, and declares that he is the raven of the locality. The drowned girl herself becomes a water sprite, and seems to be on the point of getting her revenge when the fragment ends. The parallel with Nina and Trigorin is obvious.

There is another quotation, or what appears to be a quotation, that I have not been able to identify. Arkadina's line in Act One, given here as 'Come, then, away, ill-starred old man,' appears in Russian to be metrical in form and poetic in vocabulary and word-order. I assume it is a line from some part which Arkadina has played, and indeed in an earlier draft of the act she goes on to add: 'In some play or other it says: "Come to your senses, old man!"' Arkadina's line in Act Two, given here as 'I am troubled in my soul', also looks suspiciously poetic in the original. I have consulted a number of sources and a number of Russian friends without success. The lines may well be from forgotten plays, or even entirely fictitious. On the other hand there may be a little more meaning to be gleaned here.

Chekhov gives precise references for all the songs that Sorin and Dorn sing to themselves. I have retained the titles of only the two which may still be familiar. The others, which have disappeared into the mists of time and would be entirely unfamiliar even if disinterred from the archives, I have reduced to unspecified humming.* On the other hand I have slightly expanded Dorn's reference to Jupiter's anger in Act One to reconstruct the classical saying to which it alludes.

I have followed the new edition referred to above in restoring the cuts and changes demanded by the censor. Potapenko, the friend who was ironically (see p. 179) charged with shepherding the text through the process of censorship, reported to Chekhov that there were unexpected difficulties. 'Your Decadent looks with indifference upon his mother's love-affairs, which is not allowed by the censor's rules.' The censor himself later wrote to Chekhov direct to remove all doubt about what he wanted done. 'I have marked a number of places in blue pencil,' he explained, 'in addition to which I think I should make clear that I had in mind not so much the expressions themselves as the general sense of the relations established by these expressions. The point is not the cohabitation of the actress and the writer, but the calm view taken of this state of affairs by her son and her brother.'

The censor also required the excision of a line in Polina's anguished private conversation with Dorn in Act Two, after '. . . to stop lying': 'For twenty years I was your wife, I was your friend.' This clearly reinforces the implication that Dorn is Masha's father, but it has not been restored in the new edition for some reason, and I have not restored it here.

---

* The songs both in *The Seagull* and in the other plays now *have* been disinterred by Donald Rayfield, in a paper he presented to the 1987 Chekhov Colloquium in Cambridge. Dr Rayfield makes it clear that they all ironically underline and counterpoint the text, but there is no way I can see of giving this practical effect in production.

Negotiations dragged on throughout the summer of 1896, with Chekhov making some changes and Potapenko making others. After one suggested alteration, in a letter to Potapenko, Chekhov added in exasperation: 'Or whatever you like, even a text from the Talmud.' In the first printed version of the play, in journal form in December 1896, which was not subject to theatrical censorship, Chekhov reverted to his original text. It is true that in all the subsequent book editions he used the censored text; but these were published with the assurance on the title-page that the plays they contained had been 'passed unconditionally by the censorship for production'. The changes are small and of no very great significance, but there seems no possible reason now for not using the text that Chekhov himself plainly wanted.

There is a double irony, as things turned out, in Konstantin's allusion to the censorship in the first act – one intended by Konstantin and another added by circumstance. I have slightly expanded the reference, to make it comprehensible while leaving it oblique (Russian audiences, of course, have had more experience in reading between the lines). Konstantin explains his premature departure from university by likening himself to an item which has failed to appear in the press 'owing to circumstances beyond the editor's control'. Chekhov had the same difficulty with Trofimov in *The Cherry Orchard* – how to explain that someone had been expelled from university for his political activities. It was impossible to get a direct reference to this past the censor – but not, apparently, a reference to the process of censorship itself.

I have cut some of the French variants of personal names in *Uncle Vanya*. 'Hélène' is too remote from 'Yelena' for English ears to make the connection fast enough. I have, however, retained Maria Vasilyevna's 'Alexandre' for Alexander and 'Jean' for Vanya, which do seem in some way characteristic of her abstraction from the muddy realities of Russian rural life.

The Ostrovsky play that Astrov refers to in Act One, when he is looking for his cap to leave, is *The Girl without a Dowry*. Paratov, the reckless, dashing cad who has broken the heart of the girl in the title, and who is just about to break it again, introduces himself to

Karandyshev, her pusillanimous fiancé, in the words that Astrov quotes – 'a man with large moustaches and small abilities'. Astrov has presumably prompted himself to think of Ostrovsky by what he has muttered just before this, which is a quotation from a character in another of Ostrovsky's plays, *Wolves and Sheep*. In its original context it is an incoherent protestation of ignorance from a timid aunt when she is interrogated by the despotic local matriarch about whether her niece already has a suitor. The point of the line in its original context is its comical incoherence, but out of that context it is so elliptical as to be meaningless, and I have cut it. Astrov is quoting again in Act Two when he talks to Sonya about Yelena's beauty. The line comes from Pushkin's poem, *The Tale of the Dead Princess and the Seven Bogatyrs*. This is the same story as Snow White and the Seven Dwarfs (though the *bogatyrs* with whom Pushkin's princess finds refuge are not dwarfs but the warrior-heroes of Russian folk-tales), and the line is adapted from what the mirror says to the wicked stepmother after she has disposed of her rival. To make this clear I have modified it to refer to its more familiar equivalent in Grimm. There is plainly an ironical parallel between the mirror's telling the stepmother about the stepdaughter's beauty, and Astrov's telling the stepdaughter about the stepmother's.

There is another literary reference which I have cut, as having no point but its familiarity, and no familiarity in translation (probably none today even in Russian). When Vanya in Act One describes Serebryakov writing in his study from morning until far into the night he adds in the original a quotation from a satire upon odes by one I. I. Dmitrievich (1760–1837), which in translation would run roughly:

> We rack our brains and crease our brow,
> And scribble odes and more odes yet.
> But not the smallest hint of praise
> Do either odes or author get.

I have also, for similar reasons, cut the words of the song that Astrov sings in the middle of the night, in Act Two, and his reference, later in the same scene, to his Feldscher's idiosyncratic pronunciation. I have made a slight change in the wonderful scene in the same act where Yelena and Sonya are reconciled. What they do in the original is drink *Brüderschaft*, and what they thereby resolve to be to each in future, of course, is *ty*, the second person singular. I have made another small change in Act Four, when Telegin in the original describes Vanya's attempt to shoot Serebryakov as 'a subject worthy of Aivazovsky's brush'. Aivazovsky was a nineteenth-century painter who was most celebrated for his marine studies, though he also painted a number of battle scenes, and it may be these that Telegin has in mind. He turned out some six thousand works, but not even this impressive productivity will make his name meaningful to a modern English audience.

I regret any pain caused by the demolition of two landmarks familiar to generations of English audiences. 'Missed again!' or something like it is a funnier line than Chekhov's, but fails to capture an important part of the sense. What Vanya says in the original is 'A *promakh* again?!' A *promakh* is not just a miss; it is any kind of mistake or false move, and surely (see p. 189) refers to more than just the two shots. Then there is the question of Telegin's nickname. This is given in every translation I have come across as 'Waffles'. The Russian, *Vaflya*, does indeed mean a waffle, but Telegin is given the name, as he explains, because of his pockmarked appearance. I can find no grounds for believing that 'Waffles' in English suggests the after-effects of smallpox. It sounds comfortably like an English nickname, it is true, but its implications are surely all wrong. To modern English ears it might indicate a taste for meaningless verbiage; nearer the time, according to Partridge, a waffles ('low, 1904') was 'a loafer, a sauntering idler'. Telegin's speech becomes confused when he is upset, but he doesn't waffle. He is idle, certainly, but his idleness is not sauntering – it goes with his abnegation, humility, and saintly devotion to the ideals of love and marriage. I can think of no English nickname that suggests pockmarks. And even if a suitable English equivalent did exist, there would surely be something odd about applying it to a Russian. A lot of English nicknames sound embarrassing enough attached to Englishmen; applied to Russians, nursery locutions such as 'Waffles', 'Boofy', 'Bingo', etc. seem as bogus as spats and co-respondent shoes. The only possible proceeding with '*Vaflya*', it seemed to me in the end, was to leave it out. I have made do with the occasional diminutive, and shifted Telegin's reference to his pockmarks into his earlier remarks about his 'unprepossessing appearance'.

In the original, Serebryakov is planning to use the money left over from the sale of the estate to buy a modest dacha 'in Finland'. Finland was at the time a grand duchy of the Russian Empire, and it seems at first sight mysterious why Serebryakov should want to live in the countryside there if he can't stand the countryside anywhere else in Russia. Its attraction, though, as Ronald Hingley has grasped in his translation, was no doubt that the Finnish frontier was only twenty miles from St Petersburg, and I have stolen Hingley's solution.

I have left one line as opaque as it is in the original. It comes in the scene where Astrov is telling Sonya that there is no light in the distance for him because there is no one he loves. In describing his life he says that he is 'ceaselessly pummelled by fate'. He offers no details, and to English ears it sounds the kind of thing that Russians tend to say in plays. Sometimes, however, they say them with very specific meaning. The phrase recalls Ranyevskaya's complaint to Trofimov, the 'Wandering Student' in *The Cherry Orchard*, that 'you do nothing but get yourself tossed by fate from one place to the next', and, as we have seen, Trofimov's problem, like Konstantin's in *The Seagull*, was his political activity – while Chekhov's was getting any reference to this past the censor. Does Astrov have similar views and similar problems? I know of no external evidence to support this interpretation, but one has always to be prepared for the lines between the lines in Russian texts. In a play I translated by a Soviet writer (*Exchange*) a character said of his grandfather simply that he had 'recently returned to Moscow'. I remember how foolishly over-suspicious I felt when I asked the author if the absence of any reference to where he had returned *from* could possibly imply that it had been exile, or the camps. I also remember how naive I felt when I saw his surprise that I should have to ask, since it was already there in black and white, as he saw it, clearly stated in good plain Russian.

Chekhov did in fact start on the Solomon project which he at one stage discussed with Suvorin as an alternative to the early versions of *Vanya*, and the following fragment, found among his papers, suggests how different it would have been. The metaphysical anguish which the king expresses in this monologue appears to derive not from the figure of wealth and wisdom in Chronicles but from the author of Ecclesiastes. The ascription to Solomon in the first verse of Ecclesiastes ('The words of the Preacher, the son of David, king in Jerusalem') was once taken literally, but is now thought to be conventional. The book is now considered to be the work of a much later author, and its wonderful melancholy Epicurean charm more Hellenistic than Judaic.

SOLOMON: (*alone*) O, how dark life is! No night in all its blackness when I was a child struck such terror into me as does my unfathomed existence. My God, to my father David Thou gavest but the gift of bringing words and sounds together as one, of singing and praising Thee with plucked strings, of sweetly weeping, of wresting tears from the eyes of others and of finding favour with beauty; but to me why gavest Thou also a languishing spirit and unsleeping hungry thought? Like an insect born out of the dust I hide in darkness, and trembling, chilled, despairing, fearful, see and hear in all things a fathomless mystery. To what end does this light of morning serve? To what end does the sun rise from behind the Temple and gild the palm-tree? To what end is the beauty of women? Whither is yonder bird hastening, what is the meaning of its flight, if it and its fledglings and the place to which it hurries must like me come to dust? O, better I had never been born, or that I were a stone to which God had given neither eyes nor thoughts. To weary my body for the night I yesterday like a common workman dragged marble to the Temple; now the night is come, and I cannot sleep . . . I will go and lie down again . . . Phorses used to tell me that if one imagines a flock of sheep running and thinks hard about it then one's thoughts will dissolve and sleep. This will I do . . . (*Exit.*)

I have expanded a few references in *Three Sisters* which might otherwise have been unfamiliar – to Dobrolyubov and the Panama Affair, for example – and have tried to suggest the way in which Masha and Vershinin, at their parting, address each other for the first time (in our hearing, at any rate) by the intimate *ty*. But the real difficulties in this play are (once again and more than ever) the literary allusions. I have completed quotations where necessary to make internal sense, but cannot give them the air of familiarity they should have. The lines that Masha gets on the brain ('On a far sea shore an oak tree grows . . .') are the opening of the Prologue to Pushkin's *Ruslan and Ludmilla*; a magical invocation of the world of fairy-tales, introducing the story of Ruslan's attempts to recover his abducted bride. Solyony's lines, 'The peasant had no time to gasp/ Before he felt the bear's hard clasp,' are from Krylov's fable *The Peasant and the Workman*, about a peasant who is saved from a bear when a workman manages to hit it on the head with an axe, and who then complains that this has ruined the value of the bear's skin. Solyony returns to Krylov in Act Three with, 'We could spell out the moral of the piece/ But let us not provoke the geese,' which is the end of a fable about a flock of geese being driven to market who stand on their dignity because of their noble descent, from the sacred geese who saved the Capitol in Rome. 'Not teasing the geese' has become a Russian commonplace.

Solyony also quotes Chatsky, the hero of Gribyedov's *Woe from Wit* – 'I may be odd – but who's not odd,/ Save fools alike as peas in pod?' – then goes straight on with a reference to Aleko. Aleko is the hero of Pushkin's poem *The Gypsies*, a high-born youth who falls in love with a Gypsy girl, is accepted into her family, and then murders both her and her lover when she proves unfaithful. The relevance to Solyony's own nature is obvious, though the words he seems to be quoting do not actually occur in the original. Lermontov, Solyony's idol, so admired the poem that he used it as the basis of a libretto for an opera. The lines that Solyony quotes in the last act ('Rebelliously he seeks the storm,/ As if in storms there promised peace . . .') are from *The Sail*, probably Lermontov's most famous poem, and indeed one of the most celebrated evocations in any literature of the lonely defiance of the Romantic hero.

Masha quotes (or slightly misquotes) from two of Gogol's stories. 'Living in this world, my friends, is dull work,' is Gogol's reflection (though in the original he says nothing about living) as he leaves the little town of Mirgorod in the rain and mud of autumn at the end of

How Ivan Ivanovich Quarrelled with Ivan Nikiferovich, the story of how two former friends have grown old and grey in the lawsuit which has arisen after one of them called the other a gander. 'Silence . . . silence . . .' is from *The Memoirs of a Madman*. Or more precisely, 'Never mind, never mind . . . silence,' which is what the wretched government clerk in the story tells himself every time he thinks of the unattainable charms possessed by the daughter of the head of his department.

Chebutykin's lines in Act One ('For love and love alone/ Was man put in his earthly home') are the start of an aria in an old and forgotten comic opera, *The Werewolves*. In a letter to Stanislavsky, Chekhov says that the song from which Chebutykin sings a snatch as he goes off in Act Three ('Won't you deign to eat this date . . .') comes from an operetta whose title he has forgotten, and I have reduced it to unspecified humming. Donald Rayfield, in his paper on the songs in Chekhov's plays, suggests that operetta underlies the whole structure of *Three Sisters*. The plot, he says, mimics that of *The Geisha*, a popular operetta version, first produced in 1896, of the *Madam Butterfly* story.

In Act Four Chebutykin keeps singing the first two lines from the chorus of *Ta-ra-ra boom-de-ay*. In the American original the chorus consists simply of this same nonsense phrase repeated four times over, and until I read Dr Rayfield's paper I had supposed that Chebutykin's version ('*Tarara boombiya/ Sizhy na tumbe ya*,' where the second line means literally 'I sit on a kerbstone') was the doctor's own abstracted improvision, which led me to provide a no less offhand couplet to translate it. Dr Rayfield points out that Chebutykin is singing the standard Russian version of the song, which, instead of repeating the first line, turns to melancholy introspection. (It continues: '*I gor'ko plachu ya/ Chto malo znachu ya*' – 'And I weep bitterly/ That I'm of little significance.') I have reluctantly decided that the least obtrusive solution is to return to the original words.

Vershinin, in the same act, begins to sing 'To love must young and old surrender', the magnificent bass aria from the last act of *Eugene Onegin*, in which Prince Gremin tells Onegin that the tempests of love are beneficial both to the man in the flower of youth and to the 'grizzled, hardened warrior'. The parallel with Vershinin's own feelings is obvious; Gremin tells Onegin how dreary his life has been until

Tatyana appeared, 'and like a ray of sunlight in the midst of my unhappiness gave me life and youth, youth and happiness'. Tchaikovsky's libretto here is a curious reversal of Pushkin's original, where the unnamed prince who has married Tatyana makes no comment on the success of the match. In the passage that starts with the same line Pushkin is discussing not the prince's love for Tatyana but Onegin's – and his view of late love is very different from Tchaikovsky's. The effects of love upon the young, he says, are as beneficial as spring storms. But in late life it comes like the storms of autumn, that 'turn the meadows into marsh, and strip bare the woods around'.

One of the minor puzzles of the play is exactly what game Masha and Vershinin are playing with their little private conversation in Act Three that goes 'Trum-tum-tum . . . – Tum-tum . . . – Tra-ra-ra? – Tra-ta-ta.' It may (or may not) help elucidate it to know that it was apparently based on an incident that occurred in February 1896 in the restaurant of the Slavyansky Bazar in Moscow when, according to a pseudonymous eye-witness, an unnamed actress who later played Masha (and who may have been the Yavorskaya with whom Chekhov had already had an affair the year before) made her feelings plain to him as follows:

'Tra-ta-ta,' she said, laughing.
   'What's that?'
   'Tra-ta-ta!'
   'Are you in love?'
   She gave a loud laugh, shrugged her shoulders and shook them hard, then, raising her voice, declaimed:
   'Tra-ta-ta . . .'
   'Indeed! But how has he so captivated you?'
   She laughed even more, leaned over the back of the chair, and as if breathless with passion, her eyes narrowed and with a catch in her voice said almost quietly:
   'Tra-ta-ta . . .'

Chekhov laughed heartily, apparently, and promised to use it.
   Another considerable problem is finding consistent equivalents for

the many recurring words and phrases. The hardest – and most ubiquitous – is *vsyo ravno* and its variants, which I have rendered as 'It doesn't matter' (see p. 194). 'It's all the same' would be closer, but is less capable of being adapted to all the different situations in which it occurs. The effect of repetition must, I think, in a play where it is used so consciously, take precedence over exactitude.

In *The Cherry Orchard* I have teased out *vyechniy studyent* (see pp. 199–200), and attached a date to the emancipation of the serfs, which would have been as firmly located in Russian minds as (say) the Second World War in ours. I have cut Charlotta's commonplace to Simeonov-Pishchik in Act Three, when she queries his capacity for love, '*Guter Mensch aber schlechter Musikant*' ('A good man but a bad musician'), since I suspect that very few British theatregoers understand even that much German. I have supplied what Chekhov merely specifies in a stage-direction, the first few lines of Alexei Tolstoy's marvellously bad poem 'The Scarlet Woman', which is about a Judaean courtesan who boasts that she will subdue Jesus with one of her irresistible looks, and instead is herself subdued by John the Baptist with one of his.

Rather more hesitantly, I have supplied some of the lines to which the Passer-by alludes only cryptically in the original. The speech as written is merely: 'My brother, my suffering brother . . . go out to the Volga; whose groans . . .?' The first half is a misquotation from an indifferent poem by Nadson. The second comes from what seems to me a rather magnificent one by Nekrasov, *Reflections on the Gateway to a Great House*. It changes the nature of the scene to have the Passer-by recite several lines, but the two poems do parallel a lot of what Trofimov says, and it is clearly in breach of my second principle of translation (immediate comprehensibility) to have a man come on and say, 'Go out to the Volga; whose groans . . .?' It may also be relevant in understanding this scene that the word for 'Passer-by', *prokhozhy*, meant in Siberian usage at that time someone who was tramping the roads to escape from prison or exile. Chekhov must have come across this usage on his journey to Sakhalin, though whether he intended any part of that sense here I do not know.

Before Chekhov rewrote Act Two after the opening in Moscow (see p. 198) Charlotta did not appear in the scene at the beginning of the act, and Trofimov did not have his two speeches at the end, where he asks Anya to have faith in him, and sees happiness coming with the rising moon. Instead the act began with a scene between Trofimov and Anya:

> YASHA *and* DUNYASHA *are sitting on the bench.* YEPIKHODOV *is standing beside it.* TROFIMOV *and* ANYA *come along the path from the estate.*
> ANYA: Great-aunt is all alone in the world – she's very wealthy. She's no love for Mama. The first few days I was there I found it very hard – she didn't say much to me. Then she cheered up and started to laugh. She promised to send the money – she gave me and Charlotta some for the journey. Oh, but it's a horrible feeling, being the poor relation.
> TROFIMOV: It looks as if there's someone here already . . . Sitting on the bench. Let's go on, then.
> ANYA: I was away from home for three weeks. I started to pine most dreadfully.
> TROFIMOV *and* ANYA *go out.*

Then Dunyasha says, 'All the same, how lovely to spend some time abroad . . .' After Ranyevskaya's line, 'Perhaps we'll think of something,' the original text continued:

> VARYA *and* CHARLOTTA IVANOVNA *come along the path from the estate.* CHARLOTTA *is wearing a man's suit, and is carrying a gun.*
> VARYA: She's a sensible, well-brought-up girl, and nothing can happen, but all the same she shouldn't be left alone with a young man. Supper at nine o' clock. Make sure you're not late.
> CHARLOTTA: I'm not hungry. (*Hums quietly.*)
> VARYA: It doesn't matter. You must be there for appearances' sake. Look, they're sitting over there, on the bank.
> VARYA *and* CHARLOTTA IVANOVNA *go out.*

And at the end of the act, after Anya's line: 'You put it so beautifully!' the scene originally continued:

TROFIMOV: Sh . . . Someone's coming. It's that Varya again! (*Angrily*) It's outrageous!
ANYA: Come on – let's go down to the river. It's nice there.
TROFIMOV: Come on, then.
ANYA: The moon will be rising soon.

ANYA *and* TROFIMOV *go out.*

Enter FIRS, *then* CHARLOTTA IVANOVNA. FIRS *mutters away as he looks for something on the ground near the bench. He strikes a match.*

FIRS: Oh, you silly billy!
CHARLOTTA: (*sits down on the bench and takes off her peaked cap*) Is that you, Firs? What are you looking for?
FIRS: The mistress has lost her purse.
CHARLOTTA: (*searches*) Here's her fan. And here's her handkerchief – it smells of perfume. (*Pause.*) There isn't anything else. She's perpetually mislaying things. She's mislaid her life, even. (*Hums quietly.*) I haven't got proper papers – I don't know how old I am. So I think of myself as being young . . . (*Puts the cap on* FIRS, *who sits motionless.*) Oh, I love you, my dear sir! (*Laughs.*) *Ein, zwei, drei!* (*Takes the cap off* FIRS, *and puts it on herself.*) When I was a little girl, Mama and my father used to go round all the fairs . . .

And she gives what is now the opening speech of the act, down to 'I don't know anything.' Then:

FIRS: When I was twenty, twenty-five years old, I was going along one day with the deacon's son and the cook, Vasily, and just here, on this stone, there was a man sitting . . . a stranger – belonged to someone else – we didn't know him . . . For some reason I got scared, and I went off, and after I'd gone the other two set on him and killed him . . . He'd got money on him.
CHARLOTTA: So? *Weiter!* Go on!
FIRS: So then along came the law, and they started to question

us. They took the pair of them away . . . they took me, too. I was two years in jail . . . Then that was that, they let us go. It was a long while back. (*Pause.*) I can't remember it all.

CHARLOTTA: An old man like you – it's time for you to die. (*Eats the cucumber.*)

FIRS: Eh? (*Mutters to himself.*) So there they were, they all went along together, and there they stopped . . . Uncle jumped down from the cart . . . he picked up the sack . . . and inside that sack was another sack. And he looks, and there's something going twitch! twitch!

CHARLOTTA: (*laughs quietly*) Twitch, twitch! (*Eats the cucumber.*)

Someone can be heard walking quietly along the path and quietly playing the balalaika. The moon rises. Somewhere over by the poplars VARYA *is looking for* ANYA.

VARYA: (*calling, off*) Anya! Where are you?

Curtain.

(1988)

Wild Honey

In 1920, sixteen years after Chekhov's death, a new and unknown play by him came to light. The bulky manuscript, in Chekhov's own hand, was found inside a safe-deposit in a Moscow bank. The circumstances of the discovery are somewhat cloudy. But then there is an element of mystery about the play itself. The title-page of the manuscript was missing, and with it all record of the play's identity and origins. Since it was published by the Soviet Central State Literary Archive in 1923 it has become known under a variety of appellations. In England it is usually called by the name of its hero, Platonov; or rather, as English-speakers insist on pronouncing it, Plate On/Off. From the handwriting and the frequent provincial usages it was plainly written at the very beginning of Chekhov's career. In fact it is agreed by all authorities to be his first extant play. The puzzle is to know whether it is also the first full-length play that he ever wrote; and the question is not entirely academic.

It is a remarkable and tantalising work. Commentators seem to have been more struck by its youthful shortcomings than by its surprising strengths. Its defects are obvious enough. Its length, for a start; if it were staged uncut it would run, by my estimate, for something like six hours. In fact it is altogether too much. It has too many characters, too many disparate themes and aims, and too much action. It is trying to be simultaneously a sexual comedy, a moral tract, a melodrama, a state-of-Russia play, and a tragedy. The traces of Chekhov's early theatregoing as a schoolboy in Taganrog (often in disguise, to elude the school inspector – it was a forbidden vice) are too baldly obvious.

Platonov himself is that archetype of nineteenth-century Russian literature, the 'superfluous man'. He is also Hamlet, the hero crippled by conscience and indecision; and Chatsky (in Griboyedov's *Woe from Wit*), the hero incapacitated by chronic honesty. The play is also marred by a certain coarseness, particularly in the drawing of some of the minor characters; perhaps most particularly in the characterisation of Vengerovich, 'a wealthy Jew' (though his predictable vulgarity is somewhat counterbalanced by a streak of outspoken idealism in his son). Worse, for the workability of the play, is a rambling diffuseness of action and dialogue. Worse still, at any rate for the adaptor who is trying to find a practical solution to all these problems, is a defect that foreshadows one of the great glories of the later plays – a fundamental ambiguity of tone between comic and tragic, which will eventually be resolved into a characteristic Chekhovian mode, but which appears here mostly as an indeterminate wavering. All in all, it has been generally dismissed as unstageable. Ronald Hingley, in his biography, describes the play as a botched experiment which it is not surprising that Chekhov should have wished to bury in decent oblivion. What interests the commentators most is the way in which the later plays are here prefigured. Platonov is a sketch for Ivanov; Anna Petrovna, the widowed local landowner, foreshadows Ranyevskaya. There is the great theme of the lost estate, and the dispossession of the rural landowners by the new mercantile bourgeoisie, that will recur in *The Cherry Orchard*. There is the unhappy wife attempting to poison herself, as in *Three Sisters*. There is the drunken doctor, and the vain longing of idle people to lose themselves in work, and so on.

All this is true. More striking by far, however, to someone engaged in the actual practice of playwriting, are the play's precocious and inimitable virtues. Platonov himself, for a start. He may be a mixture of Hamlet and Chatsky and others; but overwhelmingly, wonderfully, appallingly he is Platonov. He is not really like anyone else at all; he is not even remotely like his author. He is like himself, and – even more to the point – he just is. So is Anna Petrovna. She is a most surprising character to find in a nineteenth-century play. There are plenty of heroines of the time who inspire erotic feeling in men (and who usually end up dead or disfigured for their pains). There are a few, like

Katerina Ismailovna in Leskov's *A Lady Macbeth of the Mtsensk District*, who are driven by some dark appetite of their own, and who pursue it to crime and degradation. But where else is there one who is permitted to express such shining physical desire, and to remain – though punished, it is true, by the loss of her estate – essentially unhumiliated? And where else would such a powerful charge of feeling have led, by an only too human process of contrariness and confusion, to the seduction of the wrong woman? David Magarshack, in *Chekhov the Dramatist*, sees Anna Petrovna as a figure out of a mediaeval morality play, the personification of lust. She is nothing of the kind. She is a living, breathing, changeable human being who has a warm friendship for Platonov as well as desire. She repeatedly surprises – in the sudden impatience provoked by Platonov's vacillation, for example, and the sudden mean contempt with which she turns not only upon Sofya, when she discovers her to be her successful rival, but upon Sofya's wretched husband for failing to be man enough to control his wife; and perhaps most of all in the despair she reveals to Platonov in their last great scene together.

In this play for the first time we see Chekhov demonstrating his uncanny ability to enter the lives of people both unlike himself and outside his own experience. He makes Platonov twenty-seven, but the desperation that the reappearance of Sofya releases in him is the desperation of middle age, when we realise that our youth and promise have gone, and that we shall do no better in life. He does not specify Anna Petrovna's age; she is simply 'a young widow'. But she, too, is driven by the same fear that life is passing her by. It is difficult to understand how Chekhov could have known at the age he was then what it was like inside the hearts and minds of people who see their lives already beginning to slip from their grasp.

But what age *was* he exactly? This is where we come to the mystery. The only known account of the play's origin comes from Chekhov's younger brother Mikhail. He referred several times in articles and memoirs written in the years after Chekhov's death, to an 'unwieldy' play which he later specifically identified with the one found in the safe-deposit. He says that his brother wrote it 'in the year after his arrival in Moscow', and 'in his second year at university' – both of which phrases fix the year as 1881, when Chekhov was twenty-one, and studying medicine at Moscow University. (Chekhov's sister, in a letter written in the 1920s, refers to the play as having been written in his first year at university, which is not significantly different.) Mikhail says that Chekhov 'dreamed of having [it] produced at the Maly Theatre in Moscow', and that he showed it to a well-known actress, M. N. Yermolova. In fact Mikhail says that he copied the play out for Chekhov, who took it round to Yermolova in person, in the hope that she would put it on for her benefit performance. And indeed on the first page of the manuscript from the safe-deposit (which is presumably the draft from which Mikhail worked when he copied it out) is a partly erased note in pencil, addressed to Marya Nikolayevna Yermolova, saying: 'I am sending you . . . Mar Nik. Have no fear. Half of it is cut. In many places . . . still needs . . . Yours respectfully, A Chekhov.' The actress was apparently not impressed. 'I do not know what answer Yermolova gave my brother,' wrote Mikhail later, 'but my efforts to make a legible copy of the drama went completely for nothing; the play was returned and was torn up by its author into little pieces.'

Now, this is puzzling enough. Chekhov, to judge by his other works, was not a precocious writer. At the age of twenty-one he had only just started out on his career as a humorous journalist, and the sketches and spoofs that he was producing then are short, facetious, and two-dimensional. They are often quite stylishly flippant, but they are within the range of a humorously inclined medical student. The sheer size of the play would be surprising enough in this context. Donald Rayfield, in *Chekhov: The Evolution of his Art*, advances a plausible textual reason for dating the play two years later (a bizarre reference to Sacher-Masoch, whose works Rayfield believes Chekhov came across only when he was preparing his dissertation in 1883). But even then Chekhov had only just begun to write real stories. It is difficult to believe that he could have written some of the scenes in the play at that stage of his career. One might be tempted to suspect a forgery – except that it is even more difficult to believe that anyone else wrote them, at any stage in any career.

But this is only the beginning of the puzzle. Because two years before he entered university, when he was eighteen and still at school in Taganrog, Chekhov had already written a full-length drama. It was called *Bezotzovshchina* and it was read both by his elder brother Alexander, who found in it two scenes of genius, but who dismissed the whole as unforgivable, and by Mikhail, who says he kept a copy of it until his brother arrived in Moscow to start university, when he asked for it back and tore it up into little pieces. This was the last anyone ever saw of it. Or was it? A play without a title, and a title without a play . . . Some scholars have always maintained that the two are in fact one.

On the face of it this is beyond belief. If it is difficult to imagine how Chekhov could have written the play when he was a medical student of twenty-one, it is clearly even more difficult to imagine how he could have done it when he was a schoolboy of eighteen. Besides, if Mikhail was familiar with the first play, why should he say (as he does) that the play he copied out for Yermolova to read (and of which he lists details that plainly identify it with the one from the safe-deposit) was another one? It is possible to imagine that only one text was torn up into little pieces, and that Mikhail has attached one single recollection to two different occasions. It is very difficult to believe, though, that he would have failed to remark upon the fact if the play he had copied out was the same as the one he had seen before – or even noticeably similar to it.

Still, this was a quarter of a century and more after the events, and memory can be deceptive. It may be significant that in the final edition of his memoirs, in 1933, Mikhail expunged all reference to the destruction of either manuscript. And in the authoritative thirty-volume *Complete Collected Works and Letters* of Chekhov which is now in the course of publication in Moscow, opinion has hardened in favour of the one-play theory. M. P. Gromov, in his exhaustive introduction to the play in this edition, bases his conclusions on the evidence of the handwriting and language; on the fact that none of the historical events referred to in the text occurred later than 1878; on the unlikelihood of Chekhov having in the course of four increasingly busy years written two major plays; on the provenance of the setting and some of the characters' names from the Taganrog area – there was for instance a General Platonov living next door to the school; and on the appropriateness of *Bezotzovshchina* as a title.

I am not competent to comment on the evidence of the handwriting and language, and respect the intensive research on which Gromov has drawn. All the same, I am not sure that I find his arguments convincing enough to close the case. There is some evidence that he overlooks. He notes the date when Sacher-Masoch's book was translated into Russian (1877), but does not consider Rayfield's argument that Chekhov came across it only in 1883. Nor does he consider the many snatches of medical Latin in the text, or the plausibility of the symptoms in Platonov's attack of DTs, all of which suggest the medical student rather than the schoolboy.

Then again, *Bezotzovshchina*, which means the general condition of fatherlessness, seems to me to have no particular applicability to the play. This is why the question of the play's identity has some practical importance; if its title really is *Bezotzovshchina* then this plainly affects our reading of the text. Gromov argues that 'a desperate quarrel is occurring in the play between fathers and children . . . The children are insecure and unhappy because they do not have fathers whom they can respect.' In the original text, it is true, Platonov speaks bitterly about his memories of his drunken father, and this may reflect the feelings that Chekhov had about his own father's bullying mediocrity. But it has no real bearing upon the action of the play, and the other examples that Gromov offers of a 'quarrel' between the generations seem to me either insignificant or misconstrued, and in any case irrelevant to the action. No doubt everyone in the play would behave better if he had been better brought up; but then so would most of the characters in most of the world's plays.

Any reader with an interest in this, or in any of the other academic questions posed by the play, will have to consult the original text, which can be found in Volume 11 of the complete edition referred to above, or in Volume 12 of the twenty-volume edition by Yegolin and Tikhonov, published in 1948. There is also an English translation of the complete text by Ronald Hingley in Volume 2 of the Oxford Chekhov. My version was commissioned by the National Theatre (at the suggestion of Christopher Morahan, who was the moving force behind this enterprise, and who first persuaded me to read the original). It is not intended as an academic contribution or as a pious tribute, but as a text for production. It is extensively reworked, and I have not been influenced by Gromov's reading. There is no more reference to fatherlessness than there is to plates being turned on and off.

It is not, of course, the first time that this 'unstageable' play has been staged. It was done in England as *Platonov* at the Royal Court in 1960, with Rex Harrison playing the name part, in a fine translation by Dmitri Makaroff (who was once, briefly, one of my instructors in Russian). I follow with hesitation in the steps of one of my own teachers. But Makaroff's translation was simply a condensation of the original, and it seemed to me that it needed a more radical approach than this. Chekhov's text is more like a rough draft than a finished play. It may never have been intended as anything else. If Mikhail is right, Chekhov tore up the fair copy. The manuscript from the safe-deposit is quite heavily corrected already, but the pencilled note to Yermolova suggests that there were more corrections to come. Not that mere corrections would have been enough. Any translator of the late Chekhov plays becomes aware how tightly and elegantly organised they are – how each apparently casual and autonomous word is in fact advancing the business of the play. The more one works on these plays, the more exactly one wishes to recreate each line in English. But the more closely one looks at the text we are considering here the more one's fingers itch to reshape it.

In fact the only way to proceed, it seemed to me, was to regard the play, if not the characters, as fatherless, and to adopt it – to treat it as if it were the rough draft of one of my own plays, and to do the best I could with it, whatever that involved. I have not sought to make it more like any of Chekhov's other plays. What I have tried to do is to recognise the story and characters that are beginning to emerge, and to give them more definite dramatic form. To this end I have felt free to reorganise the chronology of the play; to shift material from one place to another and one character to another; to write new lines and to rewrite old ones. I have cut out entire subplots. I have reduced the number of characters from twenty to sixteen, and brought on a couple more – two of the peasants who shoot Osip. I have tried to resolve the tone of the play by reducing the melodrama and the editorialising, and by moving from lighter comedy at the beginning, through farce, to the darker and more painful comedy of the final scenes. I should perhaps stress that the farcical element is not something that I have imposed upon the play. I have refocused it, but it was there in the original. So was the pervasive erotic atmosphere. So was the feminism. The emancipation of women was a topic of the time – Sofya refers to it in her first scene with Platonov. But the painful directness with which Anna Petrovna finally talks about her fate as an educated woman with nothing to do is something alive and felt – and it is there in the original, not added by me with hindsight as a nod to modern sensibilities.

Then there was the question of a title. The play has sometimes been called *Without Fathers*, from *Bezotzovshchina*, but I have explained my reasons for rejecting this. I am not enamoured of *Platonov* as a title, even if a national campaign could be launched to pronounce it correctly (Plat-*awn*-ov). It has also been called *That Worthless Fellow Platonov*; *Ce fou de Platonov*; and *Don Juan, in the Russian Manner*. They all suggest that the play centres exclusively around the one character, which is plainly not how Chekhov thought about it, or he would scarcely have offered it in the first place to an actress. The best title to date seems to me to be Alex Szogyi's *A Country Scandal*. But Chekhov himself has provided an even better one in the text. The play covers the period of the Voynitzevs' honeymoon (and its catastrophic end). Anna Petrovna refers to it in a phrase that seems to include all the various sexual intrigues – 'a month of wild honey' (in the original, 'a month smeared with wild honey'). This seems to me to evoke precisely both the wayward sweetness of forbidden sexual attraction, and the intense feeling of summer that pervades the play.

It is a presumptuous enterprise to rewrite someone else's work. I realise that by the very act of giving these characters and their story more definite form I have deprived them of the 'indefiniteness', the *neopredelyonnost'*, that Glagolyev in the original finds so pervasive in Russian society at the time, and of which he suggests Platonov as a hero; the very quality, so difficult to pin down precisely, that to a foreigner seems one of the most characteristically Russian at all times.

I was encouraged in my presumption, though, by a letter from

Chekhov to his brother Alexander in 1882, urging him to approach the translations he was then doing with more freedom. 'Either don't translate rubbish, or do – and polish it up as you go along. You can even cut and expand. The authors won't be offended, and you will acquire a reputation as a good translator.' The original in question here, of course, is far from being rubbish, and any virtues in this version must be credited towards Chekhov's account, not mine.

One final puzzle – the circumstances of the play's discovery. This is a minor footnote to literary history. It has no bearing on our understanding of the play, but it does perhaps tell us a little more about Russian 'indefiniteness', and its survival in Soviet form.

In his otherwise scrupulously thorough introduction to the text in the new thirty-volume Chekhov, Gromov becomes curiously evasive on the subject of the actual discovery. He merely quotes, without explanation, an account by N. F. Belchikov. Perhaps Nikolai Fyodorovich Belchikov, who died only recently, needs no introduction to Soviet readers. He was in fact the scholar who introduced and annotated the first edition of the play in 1923, after the fortunate discovery was made. He was thirty at the time, and he subsequently went on to a long and successful career as a Soviet literary specialist, joining the Party in 1948, at the height of Zhdanov's campaign against the arts, and ending up, in his late eighties, as head of the editorial board producing this same collected Chekhov in which Gromov is writing. Gromov quotes him thus: 'As N. F. Belchikov recounts, in the Moscow bank of the Russo-Azov Company were located the personal safes of its depositors. Here were preserved letters, documents, papers, little items of monetary or personal value, etc. Here among them was the safe of M. P. Chekhova. In it was discovered the manuscript of the play . . .'

Gromov does not say *where* Belchikov 'recounts' all this – an odd omission in such a scholarly edition. Perhaps it was over a glass of tea in the editorial offices. It was certainly not in Belchikov's own introduction to the first edition, where he says merely that the manuscript was among the Chekhov papers that 'were accessioned to the Central State Literary Archive in 1920' – a remarkably self-effacing formulation, because it is plain from Gromov's article that Belchikov was actually present when the great discovery was made. He says: 'N. F. Belchikov recalled, also lying in the same safe, an ancient stitched blue bead reticule that had possibly belonged to Y. Y. Chekhova [Chekhov's mother].' In fact there is an odd air about the whole account, as quoted by Gromov – a *neopredelyonnost'* that seems characteristic of certain Soviet accounts of awkward events. It is a series of impersonal constructions that beg all the obvious questions about who opened the safe and why.

Now, a lot of human discovery is only relative. Columbus's discovery of America was no discovery to the native peoples who lived there already. This discovery of the play, similarly, was scarcely a discovery to M. P. Chekhova, who had put the manuscript into her safe-deposit for the same reason that people usually put things into safe-deposits – precisely in order to stop them being 'discovered'. M. P. Chekhova was Chekhov's devoted sister Masha, who had inherited his house in Yalta, and all the papers inside it. From his death up to the time of the Revolution she had been hard at work sorting and publishing this material. In 1914, as Gromov himself mentions, she told the correspondent of the *Moscow Gazette* in Yalta: 'A long play without a title, written in the eighties, was recently found by me while sorting my brother's papers.'

So the discovery had already been discovered six years earlier. In a letter from Masha to Maxim Gorky written in 1918 she explains that she has moved all her brother's papers to Moscow for safekeeping – some of them to her flat in Dolgorukovskaya Street, 'the more precious' into a safe-deposit. Gromov does not mention this letter, written because Masha was desperately anxious about the fate of her brother's papers in Moscow during the period of the Revolution (she was unable to leave Yalta then because of her mother's illness) and wanted Gorky's help in having a guard put on both flat and safe-deposit until her arrival. But Gorky never received the letter, and in a note she appended later Masha recorded: 'And in the event A.P.'s literary and other valuables were removed from the safe in my absence.'

Nor, curiously, does Gromov mention either of the other letters written by Masha that make clear her feelings about the 'discovery'. In

1921, after being cut off from Moscow for three years by the Civil War, she wrote to Meyerhold asking for his help in getting protection for her brother's papers; she had now heard that her flat in Dolgorukovskaya Street had been 'wrecked'. And in a letter to Nemirovich-Danchenko at the Moscow Arts Theatre, written a year or more later (the date is uncertain), she was still hoping that her brother's manuscripts, 'seized from me out of the safe-deposit, will in time be returned to me by the State Literary Archive'.

There is no reference, either to the terrible journey that Masha undertook in 1921, as soon as it became possible to travel to Moscow, to find out what had happened to the papers. The Civil War had only just ended in the Crimea, and conditions were chaotic. The only place she could find in the overcrowded train was up in the luggage-rack, and she would have been put off *en route* as a class enemy if she had not happened to notice a boy reading one of Chekhov's stories in the compartment, and been able to identify herself as the writer's sister. She was fifty-eight years old at the time. The journey took three weeks.

There may of course have been good reason why corners were cut, which Gromov felt his editor would be too modest to want publicised. All those indefinite impersonal constructions may conceal only the most diligent attempts to contact Masha in the war zone, and the most high-minded impatience to extend our knowledge of Chekhov's work. Belchikov's career would no doubt have prospered even without this windfall. In any case, what does it matter? Masha's safe-deposit was a very small egg among all the eggs that were broken to make that enormous omelette. She survived. In fact she was appointed official guardian of her brother's old house in Yalta, and lived to be ninety-four. At the end of her life she wrote gratefully about how the new Soviet government had come to her aid in 1920. Perhaps there was a little tactful *neopredelyonnost'* here, too. It hadn't seemed quite like that at the time, to judge by her letters, when the flat in Moscow was wrecked; when she got back from sorting that out only to find that the house in Yalta had been shot up by 'hooligan-bandits' in her absence, and she wrote to Nemirovich-Danchenko: 'At night I am alone in the whole house, I scarcely sleep, of course, I'm afraid and I don't know how I shall go on living. The prospect is a gloomy one – hunger, robbery, and the lack of any means of existence . . . ! Please don't forget about me. Bear in mind that I am very afraid and that I am suffering. If there should happen to be any money to spare, please send me some – against royalties. I implore you!' Nor when she added a wistful note about Nemirovich's life in the relative cleanliness of the Moscow Arts Theatre, where 'it smells of old times'; nor when she wrote to him again, some time between 1922 and 1924, complaining about the seizure of her brother's manuscripts from the safe-deposit, saying that 'there is among them much that is still unpublished, even a play written by him when he was a first-year student, all his letters to me, and up to some hundred photographs. A lot has disappeared, of course, such as relics, for example – I don't even want to remember it . . . I ought to come to Moscow myself and see to a great many things, but I am living in the most unfavourable conditions. My situation is undefined, unexplained, hopeless, and lonely. Many promises are made, but so far nothing has been done.'

Old and irrelevant pain. But perhaps worth recovering from the haze of the indefinite for one moment in all its sharpness.

(1984)

The Fruits of Enlightenment

Tolstoy is probably better known in England for the boots he insisted on making, in one of his phases of social and spiritual self-mortification, than for his plays. But the drama was a form to which he returned over and over again during his career. He tended to see plays as vehicles for his didactic aspirations, and, it has to be said, most of them sank under their cargoes.

He was first taken by the theatre when he arrived in St Petersburg in 1855 at the age of twenty-seven, the young war-correspondent hero of Sevastopol. He sketched out two plays with a theme foreshadowing *The Fruits of Enlightenment* – the dissipation of upper-class life. One play was to show the form it took on the country estates of the rich, and the other in their town houses. But he was unable to decide which it was that needed exposing the more urgently, and neither piece was ever written. It was in the early sixties, just before he started on *War and Peace*, that he completed his first play – *The Contaminated Family* – and its subject was the great historical divide that Russia had just crossed in 1861, the emancipation of the serfs. The old serf-owner and his family of the title are 'contaminated' by contact with one of the New Men of the age – in the first draft a *déclassé* student like Bazarov in Turgenyev's *Fathers and Children*, in the second a money-grubbing tax official who has learnt to conceal his greed beneath the new vocabulary of progressive ideas. But by the time Tolstoy returned to drama in the 1880s, with both *War and Peace* and *Anna Karenina* behind him, his approach had changed; he had become interested in the movement for popular theatre. It seems to have started on one of his

235

walks around Moscow in the early eighties, when he saw the *balagany* on Virgin Field – simple popular farces played in fairground booths. The audience, he wrote in his diary, were 'wretched starveling factory folk. Teach me, Lord, how to serve them.' He decided to provide 'judicious diversion' for them by writing *balagan* shows of his own, and started with *The First Distiller*, a temperance tract of surprising feebleness. In the late nineties he returned to the problems of the landowning classes with an essay in dramatic autobiography, *And Light Shines in the Darkness*. The hero is a mouthpiece for Tolstoy's own disgust with the idleness of upper-class life, and his desire to give away his estate to his peasants leads him into the same kind of conflict with wife and family through which Tolstoy himself was living. It could have been a piece of intimate self-revelation, but the clumsiness of the execution makes it only too possible to imagine what a pair of Tolstoy's home-made boots looked like, and he gave up with one act still to go.*

Amidst the dross, however, he wrote three plays which, in Russia at any rate, have taken their place in the repertoire as classics. The most surprising of them is perhaps the last of the three, *The Living Corpse*, which he wrote in 1900, just after *Resurrection*, when he was seventy-two. The striking thing about it is its moral generosity. Indeed, when it appeared, posthumously, some critics found it 'anti-Tolstoyan'; some even doubted its authenticity. Its hero, Protasov, finding that his wife is in love with another man, takes to drink and low life with the Gypsies. He refuses to involve himself with the lies necessary to give his wife a divorce, but disappears from her life and conscience by faking his suicide. She is then allowed to settle down perfectly happily in a bigamous marriage with her rather stuffy admirer (who, incidentally, is called Karenin), and Protasov is allowed to enjoy a sincere and high-minded love-affair with a Gypsy girl. His wife, he says, 'never had the power to creep into his soul, like Masha . . . There was no sparkle . . . there was no play in our life.' When the possibility of divorce is being considered, and the upright Karenin is asked how he

* My gibe is misplaced. Long after I wrote this piece I saw, displayed in Tolstoy's town house in Moscow, a pair of high boots he had made. I don't know what they were like to wear, but to look at they were as well-made as a well-made play.

can contemplate it, given his belief in the inviolability of marriage, he replies: 'Are we really all so infallible that we cannot diverge in our convictions, when life is so complicated?' When life is so complicated! As in *Anna Karenina*, the rigid moral intention slackens, and Tolstoy becomes absorbed in the richness of what is, instead of in the simplicity of what ought to be. But once again (or so it seems to me) the execution is inadequate to the material. The play is stiff and schematic, and the flesh hangs thin upon the bone.

The two best plays are undoubtedly *The Power of Darkness* and *The Fruits of Enlightenment*. They to some extent form a complementary pair – both about the condition of the peasants, and both started in the same exercise book in the same ink, almost certainly about the same time, in 1886. The late eighties were a difficult time in the Tolstoy household. His two great masterpieces of fiction had been written, and his immense energies were free to be unleashed upon an unworthy world direct. He had undergone his celebrated conversion to Christianity, or at any rate to his own reading of it, which, eschewing all metaphysical and liturgical aspects of the faith, left him free to concentrate upon the most socially disruptive and generally uncomfortable of Christ's ethical teachings. His disciple Chertkov, the high priest of the new priestless sect, was busy solidifying Tolstoy's ideas into a rigid canon, to which he would sometimes recall even the master himself. And Tolstoy had become hugely famous. He might refuse to wash, he might insist upon making boots for his servants and working alongside the peasants in the fields, but Yasnaya Polyana was more and more like the court of some mediaeval monarch. 'It is most curious to see Lev among his Tolstoyans,' wrote Maxim Gorky, after spending a day at the house. 'He is like a great steeple whose bell is heard throughout the world, and all around him scurry contemptible, cringing little curs who try to bark in turn, casting anxious, jealous glances at each other to see who yapped the best, and who has made the best impression on the master.' The only ones at Yasnaya Polyana who failed to yap to the Tolstoyan tune were his family. His relations with his wife, in particular, were becoming hellish. She was jealous of the influence of his disciples, saddened by the waste of his creative abilities, often simply nauseated by the stench of him, and certainly disgusted by his sexual hypocrisy. These were the years obscenely summed up at the end of the decade in *The Kreutzer Sonata*, with its disgusted condemnation of all sexual relations, including those between husband and wife. And yet he could not keep away from her – she was pregnant with their thirteenth child even while he was planning the book. He wallowed in self-loathing. 'Impenitent old Narcissus,' says Henri Troyat, in his sardonically sympathetic biography, 'eternally preoccupied with himself, he blew on his image in the water for the sheer pleasure of seeing it come back again when the ripples died away.'

This was the background against which the two plays were written. *The Power of Darkness* was the positive result of Tolstoy's involvement in the popular theatre movement; it was intended for 'the people', or 'the great world', as he sometimes called it, and its characters are all peasants. It is a horrifying story, set in the same darkness of the moon as Leskov's novella *A Lady Macbeth of the Mtsensk District* (more familiar in England as Shostakovich's opera *Katerina Ismailovna*) or the Ostrovsky play, *The Storm*, that Janacek used in *Katya Kabanova*. A woman murders her husband with a poison supplied by her lover's mother. The lover marries her, but then turns his attentions upon her stepdaughter, as a result of which the girl becomes pregnant. Urged on by his wife and his mother, he murders the baby at birth so that the girl can be married off, and then, at the wedding, falls on his knees and publicly confesses. It was based (like *Anna Karenina*) on an actual case, and the style is naturalistic (the murder of the baby, slowly crushed to death beneath a board, is as harrowing as anything in Edward Bond). Tolstoy said that he had 'raided his notebooks' to secure the authenticity of the peasant dialogue. When it was finished he assembled forty representative peasants, and his friend Stakhovich, a landowner with a talent for acting, read the play to them. Tolstoy asked them what they thought of it. They couldn't say; they hadn't understood a word of it. The only reaction was from the man who ran the buffet on Tula station, who guffawed intermittently throughout.

The Fruits of Enlightenment also took its rise from an actual incident – a seance (unsuccessful) that Tolstoy had sceptically attended in Moscow at the apartment of Prince Lvov. Then, in the summer of

1886, Tolstoy fell off a cart while he was loading hay for a peasant's widow, hurt his leg, and was forced to retire to bed for a couple of months. To entertain him, the obliging Stakhovich read him plays by Ostrovsky and Gogol. Unlike Shakespeare and Chekhov (when the latter began to emerge as a dramatist over a decade later), these were two playwrights whose work Tolstoy enjoyed – particularly *The Government Inspector* – and he proved to be a more receptive audience for Stakhovich's performance than the peasants; the reading roused him to start work on the idea he had been nursing for a comedy about spiritualists.

After writing an act and a bit, however, he dropped it, and did not return to it until the spring of 1889, during a visit to his friend Prince Urusov. His diary entries record rapid progress but little pleasure in the work ('Set to, wrote the comedy badly . . .' 'Sat down to write. Everything just as bad, though a lot of it . . .' etc.) until 1 April, when there occurred a short-lived but touching change in his feelings familiar to anyone who has attempted to write comedy: 'Wrote Act Four very badly . . . In the evening read the comedy to Urusov, he laughed, and it seemed tolerable.' He thought about the play gloomily on and off throughout the summer. Then in December his daughter Tatyana and the rest of the older children decided to get up some amateur theatricals at Yasnaya Polyana for the Christmas season, and asked Tolstoy for the comedy. He set to work to rewrite it – and continued to rewrite it as the cast – the children, their friends, members of the staff, and various neighbours – rehearsed it. Novikov, the children's tutor, who was playing Yakov, later gave a picture of strenuous family fun: 'A handful of the young people would copy out the parts with rapture in the morning, in the evening there would be rehearsals – and afterwards, almost every day, Tolstoy would collect up the parts again and once more rewrite the play.' This jollity (it need hardly be said) was not reflected in Tolstoy's diary. 27 December: 'The children all went off to Tula to rehearse. Oppressed by the dishonesty of the life surrounding me . . . They are performing my play, and truly I think it is having an effect upon them, and that in the depths of their heart they are all conscience-stricken and as a result bored. I am all the time ashamed of this mindless expense in the midst of destitution . . .

Yesterday there was a rehearsal, a great crowd of people, everyone miserable.' Novikov's praise of the play he found 'distasteful even to recall'. Still, on 30 December 1889, it was performed, though Tolstoy continued gloomily rewriting it into February, and reading it to his friends and disciples ('All vanity,' he notes on 25 January). In all he rewrote it seven or eight times. In April the play was performed, by amateurs of aristocratic birth, at Tsarskoye Syelo, in the presence of the Tsar and Tsarina. A ridiculous situation then arose, entirely characteristic of the absurdly ambiguous relations between the Tsar's government and the unwashed but still noble landowner. The play was first passed by the theatrical censorship, but then banned by the Chief Directorate for Press Affairs. According to the Minister for Internal Affairs, Durnovo, the action was taken 'in view of the rumours in some circles alleging that the author intended in this comedy to mock the nobility'. Durnovo proposed to revoke the ban, on the grounds that there had by this time been a number of amateur productions in various places, followed by detailed accounts in the newspapers, 'from which it has not been found that society saw in it a malicious and offensive lampoon upon the nobility as a whole class'. But the Tsar disagreed, and personally forbade it as 'unsuitable for the stage', though he passed it for amateur production.

And really the Tsar was right; a lampoon upon a whole class was what Tolstoy intended – and not only because of their readiness to believe in table-rapping. One of the effects of all that rewriting was to shift the emphasis of the play away from spiritualism and on to the relationship between landowner and peasants. This is of course one of the unchanging concerns of the later Tolstoy, and it has to be said that his treatment of it in the play is rather grindingly simplistic. These are three very cleaned-up peasants who have come to persuade their lord to sell them the land they work. Two of them are comic characters, one of them is sturdily outspoken – but all of them are very decent chaps, and a lesson in the virtues of the simple life. They make a strange contrast with the rapacious, drunken, murderous crew in *The Power of Darkness*. Or with the peasants who over the years had frustrated so many of Tolstoy's plans for reform at Yasnaya Polyana with their shifty, greedy obstinacy. 'Assembled before the steps', he had once written, in his story of a landowner's day, 'were a woman in bloodstained rags, screaming that her father-in-law had tried to kill her; two brothers who had been quarrelling over the division of their property for two years, glaring at each with loathing; a grizzled, unshaven old house-servant with the shaking hands of a drunkard, whom his son, the gardener, had brought to the master be scolded; a muzhik who had run his wife out of his house because she had not done a stroke of work all spring; the wife in question, sick and sobbing, not uttering a word, sitting there on the grass in front of the steps, holding out her swollen leg wrapped in dirty rags.'

Tolstoy's gibes at the credulity of the educated classes weigh a little heavy at times, too. His robust rejection of spiritualism is somewhat devalued by his apparently no less robust rejection of microbes. The sarcasm about piano-playing that he puts in the the mouth of the cook is disingenuous; Tolstoy was moved to tears by music, and used to play piano duets with his wife. On the other hand, there are no jokes at the expense of ether theory, when it is mentioned by the Professor as essential to explain light. In fact the idea of an ether had already been undercut by the Michelson-Morley experiment of 1887, and was to be consigned by Einstein in 1905 to the world of phlogiston and spirit apparitions. But of course Tolstoy could not know that; in physics and microbiology, at any rate, Christian humility and peasant common sense are no substitute for the educated intelligence he wishes to discredit.

Nevertheless, the play is charged with a real sense of fun, in spite of Tolstoy's disdain for it, as recorded in his diary. And, like all Tolstoy's work when the moralising ceases, it has the breath of life. A number of the characters are directly biographical. The Stout Lady was based on the wife of the poet Fet. Professor Wagner, zoologist and spiritualist, recognised a combination of himself and his late friend the chemist and spiritualist Professor Butlerov in the Professor of the play (Professor Kutlerov, as he was called in the early drafts) and wrote Tolstoy a very hurt letter. A well-known hypnotist called Feldmann brought proceedings against the actor who played Grossmann when the play was performed at the Moscow Arts Theatre. Novikov, the tutor, wrote later: 'In the play there appeared many beautifully observed characteristics of the life of the Tolstoys, the Rayevskys, the Trubetskoys, the Samarins, the Filosofovs and other landowning families of my acquaintance . . . The play was an animated representation of life at that time among the higher nobility, even the surnames of the characters were taken originally from real life . . . These characters were played by the very people, or almost the very people, from whom they had been copied (even the servants – Yasha, Fyodor, the footman, the former cook – worked in the Tolstoys' house).'

In fact the play is a marvellous, perhaps unique, picture of a great house at work, below as well as above stairs. And it is the servants who are the most interesting characters. I suspect that Tanya, the spirited and resourceful chambermaid, played at Yasnaya Polyana by Tolstoy's daughter with the same name, was drawn more from life as lived in *The Marriage of Figaro* and elsewhere (indeed it is rather touching to see how Tolstoy, who in fiction created his own forms, has struggled here, as he ventures into the unfamiliar medium of comic theatre, to bend his material to the conventions of the West European high comedy of the eighteenth century). But the others are originals, and they are put in the dramatically interesting position of divided loyalty. They cannot help identifying with the peasants from the estate, who are their kinsfolk – and yet at the same time they cannot help being almost proud of the profligacy of life in the master's house in town, as they expound it to their wide-eyed country cousins. It would be interesting to know what the staff at Yasnaya Polyana thought of their representations. Did they write hurt letters? Did they sue? Or were they as blank as the peasants in the face of *The Power of Darkness*? Perhaps, at any rate, they managed a few guffaws in the right places.

A Note on the Translation

Sir Arthur Pinero, in his introduction to the first English edition of the play in 1890, remarks that its 'adaptability to stage representation may not be very patent to English readers'. I think this is the view that has generally been taken ever since by those few English producers and directors who have read the earlier translations. I can trace only one previous production in London (at the Arts Theatre, in 1928). I hope that this fresh translation, commissioned by the National Theatre in the teeth of received opinion, will make it possible to glimpse what Russian audiences have managed to see in the play for all these years. It is true, however, that Tolstoy's construction does present real difficulties in making the play workable. I have therefore taken the liberty of changing it, by rearranging some of the material in the second half.

As Tolstoy wrote it, the seance occurs on the same day as Semyon is tested as a medium, and its location is 'a small sitting-room, where the Master's experiments usually take place'. More worryingly, it happens in Act Three. This means that there is apparently no plot left during the first half of Act Four, which is set in the entrance hall as the guests come and go on the Mistress's calling day. It is over halfway through this last act before Grigory and Semyon erupt fighting from the pantry, and hopes revive that there may be a little more story still to come. So I have shifted the seance, which is after all the climax of the play, into Act Four, and made it the Master's way of escaping the rigours of his wife's 'day', the guests at which now arrive in Act Three. I have located the seance in the study because we are now outside the study door throughout Act Three, and there is a chance of maintaining a little anticipation. I have had to add a few lines of my own here and there to make this reorganisation fall into place, but they are not obtrusive, and they do not advance any views at variance with the author's own. Tolstoy himself rewrote the play seven or eight times. I like to believe that if he had written another eight drafts he might have hit upon my scheme of things.

I have made a number of discreet cuts, and have merged Tolstoy's Baroness in Act Two into his Countess in the second half of the play; a modern producer does not have a whole houseful of servants and idle guests at his disposal. I have been ruthless with names. Russian patronymics induce symptoms of hysterical withdrawal in English actors and audiences alike. Few characters in this text have been left with more than one name; several have been stripped of even that. I have expanded a number of allusions (to Wallace and Crookes, for example) to make them comprehensible to a twentieth-century audience, and I have removed the division of the acts into scenes at each entrance and exit, in the French manner, to make the text easier to read. And if I have managed to find a workable convention in English for the peasants' dialogue, I shall be forgiven in heaven for all this and more.

(1979)

Exchange

I saw the original production of *Exchange* in Moscow in 1978, and immediately asked the author's permission to translate it; not something I have been moved to do before or since.

It was at the Theatre on the Taganka, then in its heyday under the direction of Yuri Lyubimov. The first breath of artistic freedom was stirring at the Taganka, and everyone in Moscow knew it. Lyubimov had just opened his spectacular production of *The Master and Margarita*, adapted from Bulgakov's novel at a time when the novel itself was still banned, and a visit to the Taganka was a revelation of the excitement that theatre can be made to arouse. Even as you came out of the Metro station on Taganka Square people would be coming up to you offering to buy your ticket. Outside the theatre itself were crowds, as for a football match or a New York first night, being held back by *druzhinniki*, the volunteer police auxiliaries. What were they doing there, all those people who could never get in to see the show? Just gazing at the good fortune of the people with tickets? Hoping one of us would have a heart attack and let a ticket go fluttering free in the evening breeze?

Tickets were impossible even for *Exchange* itself, an intimate play, austerely presented, which had already been in the repertoire for two years. (I asked around in the interval; no one had bought their tickets from a ticket office. They had all, in classic Soviet style, known someone who knew someone.) It was their own lives that people had come to see, shown as they had never been shown in public before, in all their compromise and muddle, in all their dogged intensity of family

245

feeling. In fact the play remained in the repertoire at the Taganka for another six years, until Lyubimov was deprived of his citizenship in 1984. And when I was in Moscow in 1988, there it was again, twelve years after its opening, swept triumphantly back into the Taganka on the rising tide of *glasnost'*.

Yuri Trifonov, who wrote *Exchange*, was born in 1925, and is increasingly recognised as one of the most outstanding of all the fine Russian writers who have emerged since the Second World War. He was a novelist, not a dramatist, and his only two plays, *Exchange* and *The House on the Embankment*, he adapted from short novels, under the aegis of their director, Lyubimov himself. His novels are widely read inside the Soviet Union, and for a long time now have been translated and published in Western Europe. Britain has been slow to discover them, but in 1985 Abacus issued *The House on the Embankment* and *Another Life* in translations by Michael Glenny (also available in the US as a single volume in the Touchstone imprint, published by Simon and Schuster).

Trifonov was never a dissident, but achieved the difficult feat of remaining a member of the Writers' Union (the only way in which Soviet writers can manage to publish) without losing the respect of his many disbarred and banished colleagues. He had his problems. The Taganka's production in 1980 of *The House on the Embankment*, which portrays among other things the privileges of the Soviet ruling class, was passed by the censors only after intense debate and a number of cuts. Trifonov spent ten years of his life in securing the rehabilitation of his father, an Old Bolshevik who disappeared during the purges, and *Disappearance*, the novel which he was finishing when he died in 1981, is about the shattering effect upon Russian families of first the Purges and then the war.

The world of *Exchange*, and of the other novels of his maturity, is the everyday world of Moscow, of life as it is struggled through by office workers, teachers, people clinging to the coat-tails of literature and the theatre; a world of apparently small hopes and small defeats; a world which is instantly recognisable to me through the lives of my friends in Moscow.

To an English audience one particular aspect of this world may seem rather surprisingly familiar. The confrontation of Viktor's family, with their old-fashioned revolutionary high-mindedness, and his wife's, with their down-to-earth concern for number one, may seem to reflect the clash of style that we associate with differences in class. But, in an essay replying to some of his critics, Trifonov insisted that he was not writing about the *intelligentsia* and the *meshchanstvo* (the approximate Russian equivalents of the professional and lower middle classes). His characters were all 'the simplest and most ordinary people', and he was offering no judgements on them. He would have described them all as members of the *meshchanstvo* if the term had not acquired pejorative overtones, like *petit bourgeois*. He was writing about individuals, he said, not groups, and as a general term to describe them all, Dmitrievs and Lukyanovs alike, he suggested simply 'city-dwellers'.

This concentration upon the unheroic and the ordinary aroused the suspicions of some Soviet critics, who attacked him for *bytovism* – for being too concerned with *byt* (pronounced, roughly, 'bit'). *Byt*, as Trifonov pointed out in another essay, is a word which defies translation. Marcus Wheeler's Oxford Russian–English Dictionary (one of the two best foreign-language dictionaries I have ever come across) offers merely 'way of life; life'. You might wonder how a writer can be too concerned with life, and you might continue to wonder even after you had abandoned the idea of translation, and looked up the definition in the Russian equivalent of the OED: 'the general structure of life; the totality of customs and manners characteristic of any people, particular social group, etc.'

The truth, as Trifonov says in his essay, is that 'there is perhaps no more enigmatic, multi-dimensional, incomprehensible word in the Russian language'. The elucidation by example which he goes on to offer reveals a lot about his work, about Soviet and indeed Russian life, and also about one's own experience of the world. For a start, he says, *byt* 'can be something to do with the workaday and the humdrum, with the everyday domestic round, with toiling over the stove, and down to the laundry, and round the shops. The dry-cleaners, the hairdressers . . .' This, says Trifonov, is one aspect of *byt*. In Russia, of course, activities such as shopping bulk particularly large, and it is no doubt *byt* in this sense that the critics are complaining Trifonov is too concerned with.

The meaning of *byt*, though, goes much wider than this. Family life, says Trifonov, is also *byt*. 'How husbands and wives get on together, and parents and children, and close and distant relations – that, too. And people being born, and old men dying, and illnesses, and weddings – that's also *byt*. And the interrelationships of friends and people at work, love, quarrels, jealousy, envy – all this, too, is *byt*.'

But then, as he says, 'this is what life consists in!'

Trifonov complains that foreign commentators on the debate about his books see *byt* as 'just one more legendary, untranslatable Russian concept . . . some special form of Russian life'. In fact, as his account makes clear, *byt* names an aspect of our own life which is only too familiar. It is life seen as a network of everyday concerns, and from this network, whatever our aspirations, we can none of us escape.

In the other essay quoted above, Trifonov describes *byt* as 'the great ordeal', the moral battlefield of modern urban man. 'It shouldn't be spoken of contemptuously, as if it were the base side of human life, unworthy of literature . . . *Byt* . . . is ordeal by life, in which the morality of today is manifested and tested.

'We are located in a tangled and complex structure of *byt*, at the intersection of a multiplicity of connections, views, friendships, acquaintances, enmities, psychologies and ideologies. Everyone living in a big city feels daily and hourly the effect upon them of the persistent magnetic currents of this structure, which sometimes tear him to pieces. A choice has perpetually to be made, something has to be decided upon, overcome, sacrificed. You're tired? Never mind – you can rest in another place. But in this world *byt* is a war that knows no truce.'

Exchange can be seen in this way as one man's ordeal by *byt*, and this creates certain difficulties for the translator. In the first place the story of the play turns upon an aspect of *byt* in the more straightforwardly material of Trifonov's senses – the particular circumstances of Soviet housing. The text takes these for granted; every Russian in the audience has lived his entire life hedged about by them. The problem for the translator is to make certain basic facts clear to a middle-class Western audience. These are:

- that the minimum permitted living-space per person in the Soviet Union is four square metres (two paces by two paces), and the maximum twelve square metres (three paces by four paces);
- that almost all Soviet housing in the cities is owned by the state, and can only be rented, never bought;
- that the only exceptions to this in the cities are the co-operatives which were introduced in the sixties, through which you can build and purchase your own flat – *if* you can find the people to do it with, and *if* you can raise the forty per cent deposit plus the mortgage repayments;
- that dachas, however, the Russian equivalent of country cottages, can be owned and let and bought and sold;
- that you might have to wait ten or twelve years to be allotted a different flat in town, so your only practical hope of moving is to find someone who for one reason or another is prepared to exchange with you.

But it's not just a question of the mechanism of the plot. The whole ethos of the play depends upon *byt* in the second sense – upon a precise context of place and relationships, of family customs and historical associations. It's hard enough to capture these on the page. But at least when you're reading a translation the unfamiliar syllables are spelled out before your eyes. If you don't know who Vera Zasulich was you can look her up; you can stop long enough over the *saira* that Lena liked so much to guess that it must at any rate be something to eat; you may not know that the Kuznetzky Most, where Lena's uncle sold his Gladstone bags in the old days, was the most elegant shopping street of Tsarist Moscow, but if you've got a moment to reflect you can probably imagine its associations from the context. In the theatre, however, you've got only one chance to catch each passing syllable, and no time at all to think about it.

The sense of place in the play, its evocation of Moscow as a city, presents similar difficulties. This is one of the things that so captured my imagination when I first saw it. Moscow is a city about which I have very mixed feelings, but seen through the eyes of Trifonov's characters it seemed to become both more ordinary and more intensely real. How to convey this, though, to audiences without even a passing acquaintance with the city? Muscovites know the raw high-rises of Nagatino, where Tanya lives, and know the brilliant onion domes of the little cathedral at Kolomenskoye on which the new concrete towers look down. They know why the Agent is trying to allay people's fears of moving to Khimki-Khovrino – it's a vast housing estate rather further out of the centre of Moscow than Viktor's mother's dacha. 'Pavlinovo', the location of the dacha, is a fictitious name. But everyone familiar with Moscow would recognise it as Serebryanny Bor – Silver Pinewood – an island formed by the branching of the Moscow River some twelve kilometres out to the west. It is, as Lena's mother declares, a solid and desirable neighbourhood – the British Embassy has a dacha there – and you can, as Viktor laments, see the white towers of Khimki-Khovrino in the distance across the river. His mother's dacha, incidentally, is based on a real one, which Trifonov showed me, still owned and occupied by members of his family.

Translating the play presents other difficulties, too. Trifonov wrote this version for a particular and highly idiosyncratic production. Lyubimov's style, as anyone knows who saw his London productions of *Crime and Punishment* and *The Possessed*, is oblique and allusive – a comment upon the original which often seems to assume the audience's familiarity with the text. I was certainly very glad I had read the original story before I saw the production of *Exchange* at the Taganka. And even this is difficult to reconstruct from the published text, which was intended for people who knew what they were doing anyway, and contains only the most sparse and cryptic stage-directions. There are some plays, of course, which need few stage-directions. This is not one of them. In his stories Trifonov distances the action by presenting it through fragmented layers of memory, and the theatrical equivalent for this which he and Lyubimov devised involves a similar complexity.

All in all, it seemed to me that the play needed not just translating but a good deal of rethinking to make it workable on a British stage. After I had done a first draft I went back to Moscow and got Trifonov's consent to various changes. In the first place I decided to introduce stage-directions that would suggest a rather different style of production from Lyubimov's. The original staging was austere and abstract. So far as I recall, most of the cast remained on for most of the evening, sitting in a line across the stage in front of a heap of assorted bric-à-brac. I felt that a production outside Russia would have to make the physical locations more tangible. It would have to offer us some suggestion of the dacha in Pavlinovo and the co-operative flat in Nagatino. Above all, it would have to make physically clear why it was so imperative for the Dmitrievs to move, by establishing the reality of life in a space of eighteen square metres.

I also adapted the text to make clear how an exchange of flats worked, and I got Trifonov's permission to restore various sections from the original novel – mostly ones that helped to bring alive the physical reality of Moscow, and fleshed out the lives of his characters. I expanded allusions and simplified details (*saira* became tinned salmon, for instance). When my version was finished, Trifonov had it read by a translator friend in Moscow and approved it.

That was in 1979. Since then the translation has been performed on BBC Radio 3, and by drama students at the Guildhall School in London. It has also been given a rehearsed reading to an audience in Chicago, who were reported to be largely uncomprehending. But getting a professional stage production for it has taken ten whole years. I feel rather uneasy that during this time I have made use of at least one of the techniques I learnt from the play – direct narration interspersed with remembered scenes. I think I first saw this in Peter Nichols's *Forget-Me-Not Lane*, back in 1971. But in translating *Exchange* I had the technique in my own hands, so to speak, and it remained there when I came to write *Benefactors*.

When at last Patrick Sandford announced that he would produce it at the Nuffield Theatre in Southampton I decided to celebrate by writing a fresh draft. Seeing it at the Guildhall and hearing of the incomprehension in Chicago have persuaded me to make the action clearer still. I have divided it into two acts, which has meant a certain rearrangement of events at the end of Act One, and cut some of the minor characters. Since I did the earlier version I have translated five more plays from the Russian (and seen them produced), and in the process have found out a little more about how to do it, which has encouraged me to be rather bolder with the dialogue. I hope all my changes have remained faithful to the spirit of the original. But this time Trifonov is no longer there to consult; he died in 1981.

Whatever the translator does, of course, the play can never have the same familiarity to an English audience that it does to a Russian one. But this has some advantages. It has the effect of showing us our own world at a distance, the too familiar tangle of our own existence made new and unfamiliar by being refracted through someone else's *byt*. Because in the end this is us. In these cramped and gimcrack rooms, in these unfamiliar suburbs, we are watching our own small wars, our own small victories and defeats. The little adjustments of the conscience that Viktor makes are the ones we all make, and the cumulative effects they have on him they will have on us, too. And as we see his life slip through his fingers, never fully grasped or properly understood, we for a moment catch a brief hold upon our own.

(1990)

La Belle Vivette

Zola, looking back on what he regarded as the moral swamp of the Second Empire from the healthier highlands of the Third Republic that succeeded it at the end of the 1860s, traces the history of the decade with magisterial dismissal through the career of a prostitute. Nana, in the magnificent novel which bears her name, goes from call-girl to actress to serious *cocotte*, back down to common streetwalker, up again to the ranks of the grandest *grandes cocottes* of all, and on to salutary disfigurement and early death. She symbolises the corruption that runs through the society of the Second Empire, as Zola sees it, from the depths of the gutter to the supposed heights of the old Catholic aristocracy. She both satisfies and embodies its taste for pleasure and ostentation. Her profligate indolence is sustained by the huge new vulgar entrepreneurial energies of the age, by the adrenalin surges of money from its reckless speculation and gambling. This tale of galloping depravity Zola places against a musical background, which provides the novel with a kind of theme-song. And the music he chooses is Offenbach's *La Belle Hélène*.

He doesn't mention the composer by name, and the opera itself is fictionalised, but the circumstances identify it clearly enough. The story begins on the first night of *La Blonde Vénus*, at the Théâtre des Variétés, where *La Belle Hélène* opened in 1864. Like both *Hélène* and Offenbach's first big success six years earlier, *Orphée aux enfers*, it is a flippant joke at the expense of classical mythology. Zola gives a characteristically vivid and thoroughly researched account of a working theatre of the time, with its elaborate stage machinery and its all-pervading smell of coal-gas from the complex gasoliers that lit the stage with newfound brilliance. This is one of the great pleasures of the book – and he got a lot of his information direct from Halévy, the co-author of *Hélène*.

The theatre makes the perfect starting-point for the story because of its traditional connections with prostitution; the fictitious proprietor of the Variétés insists on referring to it as his brothel. Nana is launched upon society by her appearance in the title role of the new show; out in front, watching the new star, are assembled all the characters who will become her victims. The audience represents a wide social spectrum:

> Paris was there – literary Paris, financial Paris, pleasure-loving
> Paris – a lot of journalists, a few writers, men from the stock
> market, more whores than respectable women; a strikingly
> mixed crowd drawn from all walks of life, spoiled by the same
> vices, with the same fatigue and the same fever written in their
> faces.

The music, to Zola's ears, sounds entirely suitable for Nana's 'working-class voice' – it was 'kazoo music, an echo of the fairground'. And at the dénouement of the novel, the grand ball after the cynical wedding that represents the culmination of Nana's career of corruption, the band plays the 'gutter waltz' from the show that launched her. It goes through the tottering great house like 'a dirty laugh . . . some breath of carnality off the street . . .'

Zola was not alone in his contempt. A subsequent success of Offenbach's, *La Grande-duchesse de Gerolstein*, was actually banned by the Republican government. Whether you share this moral horror or not, Offenbach's music does seem to reflect many of the aspects of the world that had come into being in the eighteen years after 1852, when Louis-Napoléon got himself proclaimed emperor (and then, remarkably, secured democratic ratification of his appointment by a landslide plebiscite).

It was a period of huge, if uneven and unsustained, economic expansion in France, when the new men with the new money set the pace. Cock of the walk now, lamented the Goncourt brothers in their journal, are 'boors and bounders, Lyons silk-weavers turned million-aires, stagedoor stockbrokers'. Haussmann, identified like Offenbach with everything that was later deplored about the age, was tearing down the old Paris and driving the great boulevards through it. He built the sewers and gave the city its first clean water supply, which ended the scourge of cholera. He created a world of luxurious new streets, properly paved and lit by gas. But the cost was terrible. Tenants had no protection, and rents soared from month to month. People displaced by the colossal programme of demolition were forced out, like refugees from a war-zone, to the edges of the city, where they lived, according to the Minister of the Interior's own report, 'deprived of all resource, with neither clothes nor bread . . . in such a state of destitution that they would die of hunger if private charity or public benevolence did not come to their assistance'. Does some faint famil-iar echo of this stir in our own recent past?

Haussmann, incidentally, had a very direct influence upon the theatre. In 1862 he made way for the gigantic new place du Château-d'Eau (now de la République) by pulling down the 'boulevard du Crime' – the boulevard du Temple, the traditional street of theatres. (It had earned its sobriquet because many of them specialised in blood-thirsty melodramas – one actor reckoned that he had been murdered in various ways during the course of his career some twenty-seven thousand times.) Two of the big theatres migrated to the place du Châtelet, where they face each other still like two great beasts – the Châtelet and the Théâtre de la Ville. But the smaller theatres joined a migration westwards. The exquisite little jewel-boxes, the *bonbon-nières bourgeoises*, which remain the home of the boulevard theatre in Paris today, are scattered along the same street, the westward exten-sion of the old 'boulevard du Crime', though it changes its name as it goes, from the boulevard St Denis to the boulevard Montmartre, and on beyond to the boulevard des Italiens. This boulevard system was the line of the old city fortifications. A boulevard originally meant a street established on a demolished *Bollwerk* or bulwark, and the three great rings of theatres in Paris are all built on the line of successive defence systems. For once swords actually have been beaten into ploughshares. And perhaps there was something symbolic about this in the 1860s, because the French army turned out to be something of a ploughshare itself when it was put to the test at the end of the epoch.

Offenbach himself was a real man of the Second Empire. He was of German Jewish descent, like many of the new men – born in 1819 in Cologne, where his father was cantor at the synagogue. (He took his name from his father's birthplace, Offenbach-am-Main, just outside Frankfurt.) His father moved the family to Paris, in the hope of finding a more liberal attitude to Jews, and the son studied the cello at the Conservatoire. He converted to Catholicism as a young man, but retained his Rhineland accent, and used to sign himself 'O. de Cologne'. He was dandified, witty, and obsessively hard-working. He was not only the composer of his shows – he was the entrepreneur who produced them. His life is a story of money as much as of music. He raised it, lost it, made it, lost it again on cards and women. His first backer was Henri de Villemessant, the newspaper proprietor who founded *Le Figaro*, and who had also bankrolled the city's first department store. The boom economics of the period are reflected in the sheer scale of Offenbach's commercial success – particularly of the two Greek pieces. *Orphée* set a new standard of financial achievement in the theatre. 'The great success of a piece these days', said the Goncourts, 'is to create the customer who comes back, i.e. the man who sees *Orphée aux enfers* twenty times.' And with the production of *La Belle Hélène* in 1864, said Saint-Saëns, 'opera-madness and the collapse of good taste began . . . Paris took leave of its senses; everyone's head was turned. The most respectable women tried to outdo each other in singing "*Amour divin, ardente flamme*".'

Since the original formula was such a success, it may seem presumptuous to look askance at it now, and wilfully wrong-headed to modify it for the present production. The librettists, Meilhac and Halévy, plainly knew their business; they wrote the book for several more of Offenbach's pieces, including two more big successes – and went on to provide Bizet with the text of *Carmen*. The old *Hélène* has been frequently revived, and become a great favourite in many parts of the world; a Russian friend of mine told me that it was the show she remembered being performed most regularly of all in the Soviet Union.

But, while the music sounds (to my ears, if not to Zola's) as fresh and delightful as ever, the book seems to me to have mouldered over the years. The lyrics are witty, and use French with a delicious untranslatable crispness that I can only envy. Between the numbers, though, come long dialogue scenes. This combination is the traditional form of the *opéra comique*, which is an early version of musical comedy rather than of opera proper. But the dialogue scenes in *Hélène* are leaden, and are heavily cut in most modern productions. They cannot be excised completely, though, because the plot, such as it is, depends upon them. Their inanition comes in part from a lack of dramatic movement in the overall story: Paris and Helen are destined for each other by the gods – they duly fulfil their destiny. It's true that fate needs a little human assistance, and is also an amusing excuse for human inclination. But there is little room left for struggle, conflict, uncertainty – all the elements that are normally required to bring even the least serious story to life.

One of the things that gave the writing colour at the time was the familiarity of its reference. The intolerable riddles competition in Act One, for example, and the game of goose in Act Two, would perhaps have been more amusing to an audience who knew that they were a respectfully irreverent reference to the Emperor and Empress's taste for party games. Some texture must also have derived from the audience's familiarity with the detail of the original myths. Presumably everyone still knows the outlines of the story of Helen and her abduction by Paris. But how many people in an average audience these days would understand Helen's line, which became a catch-phrase at the time, 'Oh, Father, look on your child with a favourable beak'? It must by now have slipped many people's recollection that she was the offspring of the union between Leda and the Swan. Or that the Leucadia to which Orestes urges despatching spoilsport husbands was the island where disappointed lovers traditionally threw themselves into the sea? More damaging even than our fading knowledge of the classical world is our fading respect for it. In the middle of the nineteenth century Offenbach's flippancy had a certain piquancy, even the power to shock. One of the leading critics of the day attacked *Hélène* as a 'sacrilege, a desecration of antiquity'. Zola describes *La Blonde Vénus* as 'Olympus dragged into the mud, a whole religion, a whole poetry jeered at . . . A fever of irreverence seized the literate audience of the first performances; legend was trampled underfoot, the ancient images broken.'

It's difficult now to feel much trace of this excitement; irreverence, particularly towards the classics, has become routine. Alexander Faris, Offenbach's biographer, identifies the tone of the two operettas as what in England is called high camp, and places it in the same tradition as Restoration comedy. I take his point, but can't help feeling that at times the height of the camp wilts discouragingly low. You wouldn't be particularly surprised if Agamemnon turned to the audience and said, 'Titter ye not.' Once again, though, it seems to me that there is a divergence between the words and the music, which is highly theatrical and frequently parodic, but not really camp in any sense. It is vigorous, often erotic, and always melodically downright.

The question of reference is fundamental not only to the texture of the piece, but to its whole structure. The original audience must have seen their own world as a kind of foreground to the action. The very facetiousness of the piece was a reference in itself, to the cocky cynicism of the times. Now this foreground has vanished into the scene-dock of history, and all *we* see is the thinly painted backcloth.

So I've shifted the setting from classical Sparta to Second Empire Paris, which is what (it seems to me) the music itself cries out for in every bar. My story runs parallel to the original one, but I've tried to tell it so far as possible through the music itself, with the minimum of dialogue. To this end I have reprised various numbers, sometimes directly, sometimes with variations in the lyric, and I have imported a couple of numbers from earlier works – the Bellini parody from *Ba-ta-clan*, the Meyerbeer from *Croquefer*. I have also exchanged the power of the gods and destiny for the efforts of the human will and the laws of the market. With nineteenth-century Paris instead of ancient Greece painted on the backcloth, however sketchily, perhaps we can supply a foreground from our own experience.

I also had another objective in mind. Even if this is not the music of the fairground, as Zola suggested, neither is it the music of La Scala or the Palais Garnier. *Hélène* was not presented at the state-subsidised

Opéra-Comique, the official home of the genre. It was done commercially, with private venture capital, in a small commercial house. It is boulevard theatre in the most literal sense – done on the boulevard and for the 'boulevard' – the disparate but homogeneous world that took its pleasures there. Siegfried Kracauer, in his book *Offenbach and the Paris of His Time*, says that at the Variétés everyone knew each other, and that 'there existed between the men about town and the actresses such an intimacy that the stage and the auditorium formed a single whole. As a result of this intimacy the audience had no hesitation in speaking out or freely exchanging witticims; an actress catching a remark on the wing that reached her from the front row of the pit would break off in the middle of a speech and burst into peals of laughter. In fact the only point of playing the part as she saw it was as a way of achieving ends completely alien to her profession. The entire audience was magnetised by the flux emanating from this perpetual interaction . . .' The whole atmosphere was remote from the respectful rituals of the modern opera-house, and I have tried to find a way of suggesting this intimacy between audience and performers.

The enterprise in which my characters are engaged is not party games, but the creation of an operetta – and one not entirely unlike *Hélène* itself. It is of course an entirely fictitious version of the event – but there are good precedents for this, and not only in Zola. Meilhac and Halévy's original was a fictitious account of the classical stories, and is particularly unfair to Menelaus, who in the *Iliad* emerges not as the traditionally feeble cuckold that they have made him into, but as one of the Greeks' most ferocious and feared warriors. (It's sometimes forgotten, too, that as a result of the ten-year-long war with Troy he succeeded in regaining Helen; in the *Odyssey* Telemachus finds them both back in Sparta some nine years after the war has ended, living together in apparent contentment.) But then the classical stories themselves were fictionalisations of the oral myths, which were themselves – well – fictions. Whether, in the green depths of this infinity of mirrors, some real prince ever did abduct some real queen, no one knows. My version does have at least some distant affinities with verifiable history. Offenbach did not, like M. Berger, appear in his own work, but the original Helen, Hortense Schneider, bore some slight resemblance to Vivette. Zola's version of her, the Nana who couldn't sing audibly, and who simply swayed back and forth in time to the music in a revealing dress, is a gross libel. Schneider was a trained and experienced singer, who had a long and successful career in comic opera. But, like many actresses at the time, she did lead a colourful private life; she was the intermittently faithful mistress of one of the most famous of the *viveurs*, the duc de Gramont-Caderousse, who was working hard to die of dissipation before he was killed by his consumption. She had many other lovers, too, before, during, and after, among them possibly the Prince of Wales, though all she claimed about him was that he used to walk her dogs in the passage des Panoramas, at the back of the Variétés, while she was on. In *Hélène*, when she sang her number asking Venus what pleasure the goddess could find in making women's virtue *cascader*, the young bloods in the audience would call out 'Cascade, Hortense!' Like Vivette she was always giving up the stage – she was busy giving it up when Offenbach first tried to persuade her to sing Helen. Her furniture had already been packed up for removal back to Bordeaux, her home town, when he shouted his proposal through the letter-box of her locked front door. Fortunately a piano remained in the empty house, on which he played over the music to her – though finally persuading her also involved the offer of a lot more money. Like Vivette, too, she once refused at the last minute to appear on the first night of a new work (*La Grande-duchesse de Gerolstein*, because the censor had forbidden her to wear a prop royal order) and only relented when she heard the overture start.

Vivette's ignorance of the legend of Helen and Paris may seem farfetched (or disingenuous), but no more so than that of the *cocotte* who was famously said to have refused to meet a friend because she was reading the current best-seller, Renan's *La Vie de Jésus*, and was desperate to find out how the story ended. Nor is the supposed competition from Wagner quite as preposterous as it seems – according to Faris, critics saw them as rivals, and championed them against each other. Offenbach wrote a parody of Wagner, and Wagner never forgave him. The year before *Hélène*, a production of *Tristan* in Vienna was cancelled in favour of a new piece by Offenbach. All the same, in later life Wagner said that Offenbach 'writes like the divine Mozart'. Rossini, too, called him 'our little Mozart of the Champs-Elysées'. Both were being a little over-generous, perhaps, but a life of Mozart was Offenbach's bedside book on all his travels, and Wagner and Rossini plainly have a better ear for the music than Zola did.

I've compressed the time-scale of the decade. But in 1870 the Paris crowds did shout for war with Prussia – they're out on the streets at the end of Zola's novel, as Nana lies dying in a hotel bedroom, sup-purating with smallpox. The pretext for the war was almost as artifi-cial as the one in my version, and the man at the centre of the crisis was the same. Within two months Paris was besieged – and Gambetta, the new young Minister of War, escaped to join other members of the government at Tours by precisely the same novel means of transport as my heroes. But by that time the Emperor himself had been captured at Sedan and the Second Empire had collapsed – which really is the end of our story.

Meilhac and Halévy were right about the two Ajaxes – in the *Iliad* Great and Little Ajax are close fighting companions, even though their having the same name is entirely coincidental. It was irresistible to transform them into the Goncourt brothers, who were writing their journal all through these years in such close collaboration that no one knows who wrote what. My representation of them is as unfair as Meilhac and Halévy's was of Menelaus, or Zola's of Schneider. They did hang around theatres, though, trying to get their plays put on, and they left a marvellous description of the backstage world as they glimpsed it from the director's box at the Opéra – evidently upstage of the curtain – one night in 1862. Perhaps I could make some slight amends by letting them have the last word and quoting it here; though whether it's Edmond or Jules writing is as mysterious as ever:

> While I make conversation, I have my eyes on the wings facing me. Holding on to a wooden upright, lit by the Argand lamp she is standing by, is la Mercier – very blonde, and very weighed down with gilt baubles and paste – radiant in a reddish light that brings out the smooth whiteness of her skin under the glit-ter of fake jewels. With one cheek and one shoulder kissed and flamed by the brilliance of the lamp, she is modelled like the girl

with the chicken in Rembrandt's *Night Watch*. Then, behind the luminous figure of the dancer, a marvellous background of shadows and glimmerings, of darkness pricked by highlights, half-revealing, in smoky, dusty remotenesses, fantastic silhouettes of old women in battered hats, with bonnet-straps made of handkerchiefs around the lower parts of their faces, then overhead, on the walkways, like passengers dangling their legs through the rails of a ship, bodies – heads – overalls – of stagehands waiting attentively in monkey poses . . .

The curtain falls, the rocks go down into the depths of the understage, the clouds go up into the flies, the blue heavens climb back behind the sky-pieces, the doors and windows are taken down and depart piece by piece into the wings, and bit by bit the bare core of the theatre appears. It is as if one were seeing all life's illusions departing one by one. Like these clouds, like this backcloth – so too do the horizons of our youth, our hopes, all our land of dreams, gradually take wing into the skies. Like these rocks our great and lofty passions one by one sink and founder!

And these stagehands I see from my box on the stage, hurrying soundlessly in and out, bit by bit removing all these beautiful clouds and skies and landscapes, rolling up canvases and carpets – don't they represent the years, each one of which bears off in its arms some fine scene from our life, some peak it attained, some goblet made of wood, gilded wood, but which seemed gold to us?

And as I sat there lost in all this, my thoughts drifting, still looking at the completely bare and empty theatre, a voice from below called out: 'Inform those gentlemen in the stage-box.'

The opera had evidently ended. But why do operas end?

(1995)

Index